worksheets allow you to factor in the wide array of variables that affect your financial decision-making and performance. You will also learn to use simple but effective monitoring systems to ensure ongoing progress and the achievement of your own financial goals.

Whether your income is $20,000 or $200,000, being financially fit is crucial to all aspects of your life and the lives of your family members. *Personal Economics* is your most competent guide to attaining the financial health and well-being you have always desired.

PERSONAL ECONOMICS

PERSONAL ECONOMICS

Robert A. Kennedy
Timothy J. Watts

Probus Publishing Company
Chicago, Illinois 60606

This publication is designed to provide accurate and authoritative information in regard to the subject matter covered. It is sold with the understanding that the publisher is not engaged in rendering legal, accounting, or other professional service. If legal advice or other expert assistance is required, the services of a competent professional person should be sought.

FROM A DECLARATION OF PRINCIPLES JOINTLY ADOPTED BY A COMMITTEE OF THE AMERICAN BAR ASSOCIATION AND A COMMITTEE OF PUBLISHERS.

Library of Congress Cataloging in Publication Data
Watts, Timothy J.
  Personal economics.

  Includes index.
  1. Finance, Personal. I. Kennedy, Robert A.
II. Title.
HG179.W35   1985   332.024   84–24909
ISBN 0-917-253-08-6

Library of Congress Catalog Card No. 84–24909

Printed in the United States of America

1 2 3 4 5 6 7 8 9 0

Typeset in Century Schoolbook with Eras Demibold Display by
Publications Development Company of Texas, Crockett, Texas

PREFACE

There is truth in the old axiom: "it's not how much money you make that counts most, rather it's how well you manage the money you do make." And, we might add, "who you deal with."

Through use of our well developed system, you can act as your own coordinator and decision maker and learn to get the most for your money. We will present a step-by-step method for personal financial planning, and upon completion of this process, you will be well on your way to increasing your standard of living and reducing financial pressures in these complex economic times.

After many years of successfully providing financial planning services to individuals and corporations, we decided to investigate why so many people in need of better financial management do not have it.

Common concerns expressed to us by people with respect to financial matters include:

- "I don't have enough money to plan."
- "I never have time."
- "I'm not organized and I don't know where to begin."
- "I don't know who can really help me and who can't, and who has my best interest in mind."
- "I don't know what additional information I need to make better financial decisions."

- "The economy and financial markets are too difficult to understand."

Foremost among our conclusions is the simple fact that no book on the market fully or adequately addresses consumer needs for financial planning; particularly in a way that consumers can learn to organize and manage their personal finances. We are practicing financial counselors and investment managers, with backgrounds in accounting and economics, and have broad and extensive business experience. In essence, we consider ourselves educators and information brokers. In this book, we will share our knowledge so that you the reader can "self-manage" and make better financial decisions in the future.

This book will provide you with a working format for understanding and organizing personal finances, information vital to decision making, outside sources of help, and a maintenance system designed to assure successful on-going monitoring and achievement of financial goals.

Our approach covers the financial planning process we use professionally and takes the format of worksheets for building a financial management system combined with technical knowledge necessary for decision making. Also, because the economy is the base of our society, personalizing economics is a prerequisite to effective financial planning. We will present ideas for absorbing and using economic input in personal financial management.

We act as architects so to speak in that we are future oriented and develop short range and long range action plans. Integration of tax planning, cash flow management, investment planning, insurance needs, retirement planning, estate planning, and other related areas is as important for effective management as are decisions made in each area.

This publication is for busy people, who:

- want to build financial security;
- want to overcome financial frustrations;
- want to maximize use of financial resources;
- want to help sorting through financial complexities;
- want trustable sources of financial products, services, and information;
- want an independent and convenient method of money management and decision making;

- want better methods for accumulating savings; and
- want flexibility in their lives.

We give special thanks to our spouses, our agents of Heinle & Heinle Enterprises, and to author Robert C. Wilson—all for their support and generous assistance in helping us to help people enjoy better lives.

A SPECIAL NOTE ON CHANGES

As this book goes to printing, many proposals are being considered for further changes in federal tax laws; including tax simplification and various forms of flat-type taxation. Yet, many people have not had time to fully absorb the extensive changes included in the Tax Reform Act of 1984.

The frequency of tax law changes makes it more important than ever to carefully manage your personal finances.

We have included in the text the major features of the Tax Reform Act of 1984 as they impact personal planning. We have also made planning suggestions which we expect to be consistent with future directions of taxation, the economy, investment markets, and the financial services industry. There will, though, be many changes which cannot be anticipated.

Learning more about personal finances and taking a more active role in managing your own finances will greatly increase the likelihood that you will profitably respond to new circumstances.

This book is intended to be a guide which you can use in preparation for making your financial decisions. You should also seek the assistance of qualified professionals as appropriate; particularly in regards to matters involving legal and investment advice.

Robert A. Kennedy

Timothy J. Watts

Contents

Preface   v

Chapter 1   **Why the Frustration?**   1

Chapter 2   **The Personal Financial Process**   5
The Planning Process   6

Chapter 3   **Surveying Personal Goals and
Financial Objectives**   10

Chapter 4   **Gathering the Necessary Information**   17
Analysis of Schedules   18

Chapter 5   **Developing Financial Profiles
and Observations**   54
Funding for Retirement for Family and Security   60
Sources   60
Needs   62
Retirement Funding Conclusions   63
Sources   63
Needs   66
Estate Funding Conclusions   66
Sources   67
Needs   70
Disability Funding Conclusions   70

Chapter 6   **Economic Concepts and Strategies**   74

Chapter 7   **Managing Risk**   80

Chapter 8   **Directing Cash Flow**   89
Budgeting   90

Cash and Cash Accounts   100
Using Debt   102
Major Expenses and Expense Reduction   106
Income Sources   117
Important Cash Management Questions   120

Chapter 9   **Purchasing Insurance**   **124**
Insurance Myths   126
Insurance Protection   127
Coordinating Insurance Purchases   140
Insurance Records   141

Chapter 10   **Understanding Income Taxation**   **142**
Tax Rates   144
Gross Taxable Income   151
Adjustments to Gross Income   155
Itemized Deductions   157
Exemptions   160
Tax Credits   160
Tax Payment Requirements   161
Amended Returns and Tax Audits   166

Chapter 11   **Reducing Income Taxes**   **169**
Tax Shelters   170
Qualified Retirement Plans   173
Personal Investing   176
Income Shifting   178
Other Tax Savings Opportunities   180
Some Income Tax Do's   182
Some Income Tax Don'ts   183
Tax Shelter Returns   184
Conclusion   189

Chapter 12   **Selecting Investments**   **190**
Blending the Planning Areas   191
Investment Strategies Success   192
Investment Placement   193
Investment Principles   198
Investment Theories   200
Pooled Investments   202
Investment Misconceptions   206
General Investment Thoughts   207

Chapter 13   **Developing and Refining an Investment Portfolio**   **211**
Analyzing Your Current Position   212

Sample Portfolio 214
Company Stock 223
High Risk/High Return 224
Making Investment Decisions 226
Monitoring Investments 227

Chapter 14   Estimating Estate Taxes   **239**
Federal and State Taxation 240
Assets Subject to Tax 243
Administrative Costs 243
Marital Deduction 245
Charitable Requests 245
Gross Federal Tax 245
State Tax Credit 245
Unified Tax Credit 245
Net State Tax 247

Chapter 15   Providing an Estate   **249**
Deciding on an Approach 250
Gifting 252
Estate Documents 255
Estate Document Provisions 258
Executors and Guardians 269
Business Ownership 271
Miscellaneous Thoughts 272

Chapter 16   Blending the Planning Areas   **277**
Employee Benefits 278
Implementation 279
Knowing the Impacts 279
Implementation Sources 280
Some General Planning Tips 283
Phasing into Monitoring 284

Chapter 17   Monitoring Your Financial Plan   **293**
The Planning Areas 297
Filing and Record Keeping 300
Common Signs of Financial Security 305
Publications 306

Index   **309**

1

WHY THE FRUSTRATION

"Life is the acceptance of responsibilities or their evasion; it is a business of meeting obligations or avoiding them. To every man the choice is continually being offered and by the manner of his choosing you may fairly measure him."

Ben Ames Williams

Money management is frustrating. Investment and financial markets seem increasingly confusing. New investment opportunities continually arise, the insurance-brokerage-banking industries undergo massive restructuring, tax laws frequently change, and economic conditions are volatile. At the same time, traditional financial methods and benchmarks do not necessarily apply to current life styles.

We find many reasons for money management frustrations. One predominant source of frustration is the lack of knowing where to begin addressing personal financial matters. This book addresses that frustration, giving you the tools you need to organize your personal financial affairs.

Another major source of frustration is the multitude of financial choices (many of which are far different from the past) and the often conflicting advice associated with these alternatives. Information from advisors, managers, books, articles, etc., is very fragmented and difficult for busy people to assess and pull together. In this book, we provide you with a framework for sorting through such complex information and for making sound financial decisions in line with your financial and nonfinancial goals.

The huge influx of so-called *financial planners* is compounding personal frustrations. *Financial planner* has become a buzz-word to professionals in the financial industry. Insurance agents, stockbrokers, tax shelter salesmen, bankers and others refer to themselves as financial planners. Many of these representatives lack objectivity in rendering advice because of their interest in selling commissioned financial products or having people use services offered by the organization with which they are affiliated.

Last year a young widow with three children came to see us, on the advice of her attorney, for a "second opinion." She had received approximately $500,000 in securities, insurance proceeds, and other assets, following her husband's death. A broker she had been using wanted her to place the entire $500,000 in a single annuity. Can you imagine? Besides her and the children's needs in the future and protection against future economic conditions, the broker had not accurately informed her of the risk of such a purchase. He assured her it was a safe investment. Annuities can be and have been defaulted on. In some circumstances, a limited portion of funds might be properly placed in carefully selected annuities, but certainly not an entire portfolio in a single annuity. Needless to say, the recommended annuity carried a large commission for the broker.

There has been a large and alarming increase in the number of people becoming licensed to sell financial products. Very often these people are not trained in money management, they are trained in sales. Just think of the increase in solicitous calls and mail to your home, and the huge number of "free seminars."

Salesmen use several tactics in pushing financial products, including:

- disturb the prospect,
- paint the benefits, and
- appeal to greed.

There are numerous and frequent examples of inappropriate, and unfortunate, product pushing. This happens because everyone has financial needs.

- Are there financial problems and difficulties you should be prepared for?
- Are there benefits to financial products and action steps?
- Is it possible for you to achieve financial security?

The answer to all three questions is yes. The problem, however, in dealing with salesmen is that too often your needs and interests are not put first; making commissions is. Also of concern is the fact that we are now seeing many disguised forms of commission.

We are not necessarily opposed to commissions, nor are we attempting to attack professionals with high integrity who make a living selling financial products. We are opposed to financial product pushing. We favor avoiding middlemen when possible and appropriate, and we perceive financial planning from a whole rather than limited-part basis.

Investment products and financial services are necessary for achievement of goals, but your needs should be carefully matched with quality products and services. Don't expect to find everything you need in one spot, and don't expect a commissioned salesman to direct you somewhere else for a better deal. *Buy* and use order takers—don't be *Sold*. Financial "supermarkets" and others who seek *customer control* are not the answer to financial security goals.

We don't want you to be one of the people about whom the unscrupulous tax shelter salesmen says "I know how to work this guy." We have even heard product salesmen say "who cares whether or not the customer needs it, I need some cash and I have to meet my sales quota." Don't become a statistic in another bad deal.

We have helped many clients reorganize their lives after tax shelters they invested in were disallowed by the IRS. Frequently, all the invested money was lost and it took years to pay back taxes and penalties.

We will teach you how to take control of your finances, bypass middlemen, make effective use of professionals and financial services, avoid financial entrapments, and finance your lifestyle choices.

To feel personal economic uncertainty and frustration is not at all unusual, however, you need not accept this as indicative that there is nothing you can do—the uncertainty and frustration can be overcome. You will feel very good about your financial circumstances when you follow through with our system.

This is a time to be optimistic. Investment markets are improving and the economy is becoming more stable. We have recently seen only the beginning of a new emphasis on business enterprises and the values of capitalism. This changing spirit is presenting more opportunities than ever for those with a business outlook and a willingness to restructure their approach to money management.

Successful wealth accumulators are able to adopt business principles to management of their personal finances. They:

- think strategically;
- use cost efficiency techniques;
- think in terms of profits and losses, tax savings, and managing cash flow;
- protect against risk and maintain flexibility;
- seek and maximize opportunities;
- develop reliable and trustable sources of information; and
- use financial analysis and recognize the value of good record keeping.

Whether you are self-employed, an employee, or both, incorporate business thinking into management of your personal finances. Many high level executives take a perspective that they are really their own enterprise. They may be an employee of a particular corporation, but unlike most employees, they view themselves as being independent. They are not reluctant to negotiate employment deals which best meet their personal needs, change employers, market and finance themselves, and prepare for future contingencies.

Business survival is dependent on finding and successfully marketing goods and services, establishing multiple sources of income, effectively managing personal and nonpersonal aspects of an enterprise, and maintaining a willingness to continually evaluate conditions and make changes as necessary. Personal financial success is dependent on similar factors. Sources of income, active and passive, must be optimized, while efficiently managing financial needs, setting goals, and making changes as needed or in response to new opportunities.

2

THE PERSONAL FINANCIAL PLANNING PROCESS

> "Every great man exhibits the talent of organization or construction, whether it be a poem, a philosophical system, a policy, or a strategy. And without method there is no organization nor construction."
>
> *Bulwer*

Our system for personal financial management provides you with a framework for achieving financial independence. Goal setting, personal financial planning, and economics are directly related in the overall structuring of money management.

The benefits of employing our process are numerous and include:

- organization and understanding of finances;
- minimization of financial pressures;
- achievement of personal and family goals;
- cash flow management;
- asset protection and planning;
- lower taxes and appropriate investment selection; and
- increased net worth and financial security.

With organization, knowledge, action, and a future orientation, you can overcome frustration and properly plan for a secure economic future. This book will enable you to understand what your current financial position is and the causes for the position, know the consequences of continuation on the same course, evaluate strengths and weaknesses, recognize needed changes, become aware of more effective alternatives, plan change, and develop strategies for bringing that change about.

Some basic guidelines for planning are:

- Your observations and goals should be written and recorded.
- Every effort should be made to keep the whole process in mind and avoid excessive detail.
- Objectives and strategies should be realistic.
- Planning should be monitored and periodically reviewed.

Each individual should evaluate and understand his or her perspective on wealth. What is financial security for you? Some high salaried people feel they do not have security while some relatively low salaried people have a strong sense of economic security. Personal economic security must be *self-defined.*

Risk is a prime factor in investing and building wealth. Can you tolerate high risk for potentially high return? Risk and reward are directly correlated, but high risk does not necessarily mean high reward. Once comfort is established with respect to risk acceptance and tolerance, perspective can be given to a plan for achieving financial security. The most important prerequisite, however, is self-discipline. The capacity for making choices, formulating a plan, and taking the necessary action to implement the plan.

Financial planning is the study and organization of your various financial matters with the intention of improving each area of finances while simultaneously integrating all areas for optimal balance and structuring. Since you are unique, choices must be made in the context of specific financial and nonfinancial goals. Planning requires a process—a flow of activities (Figure 2–1).

THE PLANNING PROCESS

Surveying Personal Goals and Financial Objectives

Attainment of goals does necessitate trade-offs. Before these can effectively be made, a comprehensive list of choices must be developed. Financial as well as nonfinancial goals should be stated—re-

FIGURE 2-1   THE PLANNING PROCESS

Surveying Personal Goals and Financial Objectives
↓
Gathering the Necessary Information
↓
Developing Financial Profiles and Observations
↓
Determining Strategies
↓
Evaluating Alternatives and Making Decisions
↓
Implementing Decisions
↓
Reviewing and Monitoring

---

alizing that many nonfinancial goals are based on financial resources. Objectives, or financial targets, can then be set so
achievement of desires can occur.

Gathering the Necessary Information

The next step in the financial planning process is to assemble all
relevant financial information and source documents. The process
flows from organization and statement of the current financial
position. Information must be put together in a form from which
interpretation can be made.

Developing Financial Profiles and Observations

The required information, summarized in usable form, is analyzed
to provide a comprehensive understanding of weaknesses and
strengths and areas needing improvements or change. After determining strengths and weaknesses in the current financial position,
and identifying possible goals and objectives, choices are made with
respect to what shall be achieved and a realistic time framework for
achievement.

Determining Strategies

An overall game plan must be set-up, with flexibility incorporated, in the form of an action plan. Integration of all financial planning areas is of extreme importance. Resources must be allocated first towards objectives with high priority and then to other objectives.

Evaluating Alternatives and Making Decisions

There are often many courses of action for pursuing objectives. Optimal money management is based on the concept of cost efficiency and effectiveness. Sorting through the many options, with knowledge and useful methods, will enable you to make the best decisions. Successful financial planning and improvement of financial position is not a random process, but rather a disciplined approach with definite aim.

Implementing Decisions

The best of plans becomes useless without action. Decisions must be implemented. Scheduling activities on both a time basis and order basis will provide guidelines for carrying out the selected tactics.

Reviewing and Monitoring

We must be certain that implementation occurs, yet the financial planning process does not end here. We live in an ever-changing world. You need to continually reevaluate your financial position and objectives, and utilize new information in adapting to changes both with yourself and with external factors which you cannot control.

Chapter 3 covers surveying personal goals and financial objectives; Chapter 4 presents methods for gathering the necessary information; Chapter 5 covers developing financial profiles and observations; Chapter 6 discusses economics as applied to individuals and households; Chapter 7 gives an overview of risk management; and the remaining chapters examine the balance of the planning process.

For optimal planning, maintain the following rules:

- Understand your goals and the financial objectives necessary to achieve the goals—realizing that adjustments may be necessary and priorities reassigned.
- Know your financial position and changes which can be expected.
- Record financial changes with frequent updating and monitor the progress towards financial objectives.
- Continually evaluate strengths and weaknesses.
- Stay current with economic conditions and other outside forces which may affect your finances.
- Selectively use source materials and professional advisors which can efficiently and objectively keep you abreast of changes in the financial industry.
- Continue to learn about new and more sophisticated planning strategies and alternatives, keeping in mind the trade-offs which must be made.
- Monitor your overall financial plan regularly, realizing how each financial area impacts the others.

3

SURVEYING PERSONAL GOALS AND FINANCIAL OBJECTIVES

"Make the most of today. Translate your good intentions into actual deeds. Know that you can do what ought to be done. Improve your plans. Keep a definite goal of achievement constantly in view. Realize that work well and worthily done makes life truly worth living."

Grenville Kleiser

Commitment to improved financial management requires a determination of realistic goals and a strategy or game plan for carrying out actions. Goals may involve nonfinancial as well as financial matters, may be short-term or long-term, and *do* necessitate the development of capacity for adapting to change.

Just as economic activity is central to any society, money management or personal economics is at the core of your life style. We distinguish between the terms goals and objectives by using goals to refer to financial and nonfinancial desires and objectives as financial targets for achieving goals. Future financial objectives must be set in line with goals such as career changes, personal growth, education, children, etc. Goals and objectives in turn must be prioritized and allocation of financial resources established.

Achievement of goals and objectives means trade-offs because you are not capable of realizing an infinite number of goals and objectives. To seek one alternative means to forego another. Evaluation is needed to weigh the benefits of accomplishing a goal or objective against what must be given up in terms of other goals or objectives.

Our premise in this book (derived from our experiences in working with clients) is that financial security, or the satisfaction of a desired standard of living, is commonly the most important financial goal (Figure 3–1). To properly view standard of living, it must be broken down into its simplest components. How much money is needed to purchase a home, raise the desired number of children, travel, pay for education, and so forth? Once these factors are clearly stated, you can proceed to make trade-offs. All goals must be realistic. To function without objectives is to function blindly, with minimal chance of arriving where you would like to be—automatic or free direction is not available.

Ask yourself what lifestyle you desire now; five years from now; and ten years from now. Summarize *in writing* your desires and incorporate a future orientation with a strategic plan. Your goals

FIGURE 3–1

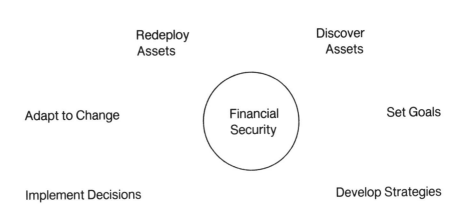

and desires are unique and can be achieved if you learn how to go about it.

As stated, we consider financial security to be foremost among all financial goals. In conjunction with financial security, we categorize financial objectives as follows:

1. *Cash Flow Management*
   Establishing adequate current and future income for necessary and discretionary expenditures while maintaining organization and cash flow control.

2. *Insurance Protection*
   Efficiently and properly insuring insurable risks.

3. *Income Tax Planning*
   Reducing and deferring current and future income tax liabilities in line with all financial needs.

4. *Investment Planning*
   Placing current and future investable dollars on the basis of matching goals, needs, and available investment media.

5. *Estate Planning*
   Structuring estate asset dispositions for compliance with laws, preferences for asset distributions, family security and estate tax, and expense reduction.

While financial security may be the most important financial goal, we also have many other financial and nonfinancial goals. Goals are personal and are best set by you or your family. Write down potential goals, and review the list several times, giving careful evaluation to each. Make sure that goals are realistic and in line with personal needs and capabilities. To assist you in this process we have enclosed the following checklist which may be helpful in compiling your list. Select the goals that apply to you and add goals which have not been included.

The next step is to separate goals into short-term, intermediate, and long-term periods with achievable target dates. Short-term goals should involve a time framework of less than one year, intermediate goals should be categorized in terms of one to seven years, and long-term goals seven years and beyond. Use the Form 3–1 to organize your goals.

Upon completion and selection of target dates, goals need to be prioritized in order of importance. An overall plan can then be developed.

POTENTIAL GOALS   APPLIES (YES/NO)

Change careers

Have a family

Return to school

Start a business

Retire

Develop hobbies

Travel

Relocate

Purchase a home

Get married (divorced)

Contribute to charities

Improve health

Educate children

Others

FORM 3-1 TARGET DATES

Goals	Less than 1 Year	1 Year to 7 Years	7 Years & Beyond

Chapters 4 and 5 will explain how to gather necessary information and perform financial analysis so that specific strategies can be set-up, in conjunction with financial objectives, to achieve desired goals.

Goals and financial objectives are merged by breaking down the goals in terms of the five main financial objective categories. Simply ask each of the following questions for each goal and respond accordingly.

1. Will the goal require cash?
2. Is any type of insurance available for protection as related to the goal?
3. Will pursuit of the goal impact income taxation?
4. Does the goal involve putting assets to work through investing?
5. Does the goal have features or characteristics that will have importance after death?

Complete Form 3–2 by checking appropriate financial objective areas which apply to each goal.

FORM 3-2 GOALS AND FINANCIAL OBJECTIVES

Goals	Cash Flow Management	Insurance Protection	Income Taxation	Investment Planning	Estate Planning

4

GATHERING THE NECESSARY INFORMATION

"Before you organize you ought to analyze and see what the elements of the business are."

Gerard Swope

An initial step in the planning process is to assemble all necessary source documents so that appropriate information can be properly organized and recorded. The importance of this step cannot be over-emphasized. It will serve as a base from which current and future decisions will be made.

The following list is a guide to be used in gathering the necessary documents and information you will need to begin your plan. Source documents include:

- tax returns for the past three years;
- all personal insurance policies (life, disability, auto, etc., including recent premium statements);
- employee benefit booklets, plan statements;
- pension/profit sharing/stock plans/bonus statement, etc.;
- copies of trust documents, wills;
- special stock purchase or buy-sell agreements;
- any special contract or payment obligations, personal or business;

- business balance sheets;
- brokerage account statements; and
- documents describing current and potential inheritances.

In addition, gather any source documents with background information that would be helpful in arriving at the following:

- names and address of advisors;
- listings of assets, liabilities, investments, etc.;
- cost basis of investments;
- listing of income sources (1099s, dividend checks, gifts, etc.); and
- a description of personal expenses, check register, budgets, etc.

Once you have assembled the aforementioned material, you will be ready to record the information.

At the end of the chapter, you are provided sample schedules. Make copies of the schedules and follow the step-by-step guide included on each work schedule. Complete the schedules in the exact order they are presented.

Schedules 1 through 5 are building blocks toward the construction of the main summaries. If you are unable to arrive at precise values for certain items, your best informed estimate will be sufficient. We recommend rounding numbers to the nearest one hundred to facilitate additions.

The main summary schedules are:

- General Information and Personal Data
- Life Insurance Summary
- Net Worth Summary
- Investment Composition
- Death Estate
- Cash Flow Analysis
- Tax Return Analysis

While the recording of information may appear at first to be burdensome, the process will move fluidly and rapidly if you have gathered your sources of information prior to beginning.

ANALYSIS OF THE SCHEDULES

Now that the information has been recorded on the appropriate financial schedules, you should analyze the information for purposes of reaching conclusions and making observations about your situations.

We have provided the following list of sample questions and thoughts that will serve as a guide for you while reviewing each schedule. We suggest that you write down your observations as you go.

General Information and Personal Data

- Are records kept in safe, convenient, consolidated files?
- Is there need to contact, add, or replace any advisor?
- Who in your family knows the whereabouts of important information in case of emergency or catastrophe?
- Have your will(s) and or trust(s) been reviewed and updated recently?
- How are assets distributed to heirs in the event of death?
- Are personal representatives, trustees, etc., still appropriate for your circumstances?

Life Insurance Summary

- Are all policies on a current basis and in force?
- Do beneficiaries of life policies (personal and group) need to be reviewed?
- Have policies been reviewed recently for purposes of updating to modern type contracts that take advantage of favorable mortality, interest, and expense factors?
- Is price per thousand of coverage competitive with modern products?
- Are large sums of cash built-up in cash value accounts, dividend accumulations or paid-up additions?
- How are premiums being paid?

Net Worth Summary

- Is there one asset or liability that stands out as an inordinately large percentage of the whole?
- Do Personal Property Liabilities (except residence mortgage) plus Investment Liabilities exceed Cash & Equivalents plus Discretionary Investments? By how much?
- Should any assets be sold or traded?

- If you are married, is the ownership of your Net Worth weighted heavily in one registration, i.e., His—Hers—Joint?
- Is there a significant amount of leverage employed at this time (i.e., a high percentage of Total Liabilities to Total Assets)?
- Is most everything you own tied up in your business and home?
- If you have an idea of what your Net Worth was in the past, when you compare it to today, are you satisfied with the rate of growth?
- If your Net Worth larger or smaller than you anticipated?

Investment Composition

- Which are you more heavily invested in at present—assets with growth potential or those with no growth potential? Does the result appear appropriate given your age, goals, etc.?
- Is there a large amount invested in one type of investment media, (e.g., Stocks, Tangibles, etc.)?
- In reviewing and summarizing the liquidity column, are you more or less liquid than you would prefer?
- Are there depleting assets (e.g., notes receivable, gold stocks, energy partnerships)? If so, what about reinvestment to maintain your asset base?
- Given your particular circumstances, do you appear adequately diversified?

Death Estate

- If you are married, does one estate far outweigh the other in size? If so, why?
- Are there potential inheritances that would substantially alter your death estate(s)?
- Does insurance in the estate appear adequate?
- Of the total Death Estate, what portion is available to invest for purposes of providing income to beneficiaries?

Cash Flow Analysis

- Of prime importance to us all—does cash inflow exceed outflow? Does inflow depend heavily on one source?
- Are there immediate opportunities for initiating investment

strategies with excess cash flow? If so, where are these funds going now?

- Is the level of debt manageable? Are any loans bearing excessive interest cost? If so, can they be paid off?
- Will investment of cash surpluses be necessary to offset future negative cash flows? When and how much?
- Are any major increases or decreases expected in sources and uses of funds?
- Is current investment income needed? Should it be reinvested?
- Should expenditures be reviewed for possible reductions?

Tax Return Analysis

- What tax bracket do you find yourself in?
- Is the vast majority of your investment income currently being taxed? If so, what techniques can be employed to reduce this liability?
- What level of tax shelter, if any, is needed?
- Are qualified retirement plans being utilized?
- Can withholding and estimated payments be changed to your advantage?
- Are there any planning opportunities regarding the timing of gains and losses on the sale of assets?
- Can deductions be prepaid before year end?

If you are typical of the vast majority of individuals that we counsel, you have just completed, for the first time ever, an overview of your entire financial picture.

The job does not end here, though. You should now be well prepared to enter the analysis phase of the process. Chapter 5 utilizes the various schedules to compute important ratios which will serve as a basis for evaluation.

GENERAL INFORMATION

Family Record: (From Personal Records)   Date: _____
Name   Date of Birth   Social Security Number

_____   _____   _____
_____   _____   _____

Children

_____   _____   _____
_____   _____   _____
_____   _____   _____
_____   _____   _____
_____   _____   _____

Residence Address _____   Business Address _____
Street _____   Street _____
City, State, Zip _____   City, State, Zip _____

_____   _____

Phone (   ) _____   Phone (   ) _____

Advisors (From Personal Records)

Attorney: Accountant:
Name _____   Name _____
Firm _____   Firm _____
Address _____   Address _____

_____   _____

Phone (   ) _____   Phone (   ) _____

Broker/Investment Advisor: Insurance Advisor:
Name _____   Name _____
Firm _____   Firm _____
Address _____   Address _____

_____   _____

Phone (   ) _____   Phone (   ) _____

GENERAL INFORMATION (Continued)

Miscellaneous Important Information (From Personal Papers)

Date:_____

Safe Deposit Box
        Bank _____

        Location/Branch _____

        Address _____

        _____

        Box # or key _____

        Persons authorized for entry _____

        _____

Location of Important Papers (From Personal Papers)

Wills _____   Insurance policies _____

Securities _____   Deeds _____

Birth certificates _____   Valuable papers _____

_____   _____

_____   _____

Information about Wills and Trusts (From Documents)

	His	Hers
Date of execution of Will		
Date of execution of Trust		
Date of execution of Amendments		
Personal representative (Executor)		
Initial Trustee		
Successor Trustee		
Guardian for children or dependents		

SCHEDULE 1   CASH AND EQUIVALENTS

I.   Cash & Equivalents

Checking Accts	Bank	Acct #	Owner	Balance	Estimated Annual Income
	____	____	____	____	____
	____	____	____	____	____
	____	____ ①____		____	____ ②____
	____	____	____	____	____
Total				$_____	$_____

Regular Savings	Bank	Acct #	Owner	Balance	Estimated Annual Income
	____	____	____	____	____
	____	____	____	____	____
	____	____ ①____		____	____ ③____
	____	____	____	____	____
Total				$_____	$_____

Money Market Funds (Regular or tax exempt)	Bank/ Fund	Acct #	Owner	Balance	Estimated Annual Income
	____	____	____	____	____
	____	____	____	____	____
	____	____ ①____		____	____ ④____
	____	____	____	____	____
Total				$_____	$_____

Other-CDS Comm'l Paper Certificates, etc.	Description	Acct #	Owner	Balance	Estimated Annual Income
	____	____ ①____		____	____ ⑤____
	____	____	____	____	____
Total				$_____	$_____
Total Cash & Equivalents				$__⑥__	$__⑦__

Schedule 1 *(continued)*

	Summary		
	By Ownership	Cash Flow	Income Tax
His	_____	Total Income_____	Total Income_____
Hers	_____⑧_____	Less:	Less:
Joint	_____	Accounts Reinvested_____	Tax Exempt_____
Total	$_____	Net $__⑨__	Net $__⑩__

Notes:
1. Information can be obtained from bank statements, passbooks, certificates, etc.
2. Certain checking accounts are interest bearing. Interest will vary each month, however, an estimate of income can be arrived at by multiplying the interest rate times the average daily balance (if relatively consistent).
3. Multiply passbook savings rates times beginning of the year balance.
4. Rates will vary daily, monthly, etc., however, an estimate can be used by applying current rate times balance.
5. Rates are usually fixed for a period certain.
6. Summarize by ownership and post to summary below.
7. Post to cash flow and income tax summaries below.
8. Figures should be posted to the Net Worth Summary (Cash & Equivalents).
9. Post to Cash Flow Analysis (Investment Income-Cash & Equivalents Annual).
10. Post to Tax Return Analysis (Income From Investments).

SCHEDULE 2A STOCK MARKET INVESTMENTS

II. Individual Stocks

Company Name	Date Acquired	Owner	# of Shares	Cost Basis Per Share	Cost Basis	Market Value Per Share	Market Value	Gain (Loss)	Annual Dividend Per Share	Annual Dividends
			①				②			
								④	⑤	⑥
Total							$			$

II. Mutual Funds—Stock

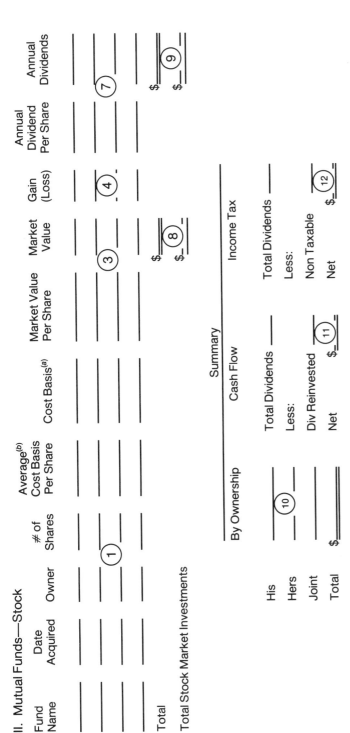

Fund Name	Date Acquired	Owner	# of Shares	Average Cost Basis Per Share[b]	Cost Basis[a]	Market Value Per Share	Market Value	Gain (Loss)	Annual Dividend Per Share	Annual Dividends
			(1)				(3)	(4)		(7)
Total							$ (8)			$ (9)

Total Stock Market Investments

Summary

By Ownership	Cash Flow	Income Tax
His	Total Dividends	Total Dividends
Hers (10)	Less:	Less:
Joint	Div Reinvested	Non Taxable
Total $	Net $ (11)	Net $ (12)

Notes:

a. If you are reinvesting distributions increase cost basis by adding all taxable distributions to original purchase cost.
b. Divide cost basis in (a) above by # of shares currently held to arrive at average cost per share.
1. From personal records, brokerage statements, confirmations, certificates, etc.
2. Listed in paper daily under appropriate exchange, NYSE, AMER, OTC. Use close price.
3. Listed separately under mutual fund heading in paper. Post Net Asset Value or sell price.
4. Difference between Market Value and Cost Basis.
5. Usually quoted immediately to the right of stock in paper as annual rate per share.
6. Extension of number of shares multiplied times annual dividend per share.
7. Dividends are often reinvested in additional shares of the fund. Available by contacting fund and/or advisor, or use estimate.
8. Summarize by ownership and post to summary below.
9. Post to cash-flow and income tax summaries below.
10. Figures should be posted to the Net Worth Summary (Stock Market Inv.).
11. Post Net to Cash Flow Analysis (Dividends Annual).
12. Post Net to Tax Return Analysis (Income from Investments).

SCHEDULE 2B CORPORATE BOND MARKET INVESTMENTS

II. Individual Bonds–Corporate

Name	Maturity Date	Owner	Units	Cost Basis Per Unit	Cost Basis	Market Value Per Unit	Market Value	Gain (Loss)	Stated Yield on Face Value	Annual Yield
			(1)				(2)	(4)	(5)	(7)
Total							$			$

II. Unit Trusts–Corporate

Name	Series #	Owner	Units	Cost Basis Per Unit	Cost Basis	Market Value Per Unit	Market Value	Gain (Loss)	Stated Yield on Units	Annual Yield
			(1)				(2)	(4)	(5)	(7)
Total							$			$

II. Mutual Funds–Bond

Fund Name	Date Acquired	Owner	Shares	Average(b) Cost Basis Per Share	Cost Basis(a)	Market Value Per Share	Market Value	Gain (Loss)	Annual Distribution Per Share	Annual Distributions
			(1)				(3)	(4)	(6)	
Total							$			$
							(8)			(9)

Total Corporate Bond Market Investments

Summary

By Ownership	Cash Flow	Income Tax
	Total Distributions _____	Total Distributions _____
His		
Hers ⑩		
Joint		
Total $	Less:	Less:
	Div Reinvested _____	Non Taxable _____
	Net $ ⑪	Net $ ⑫

Notes:

a. If you are reinvesting distributions increase cost basis by adding all taxable distributions to original purchase cost.
b. Divide cost basis in (a) above by # of shares currently held to arrive at average cost per share.
1. From personal records, brokerage statements, confirmations, certificates, etc.
2. Individual bond prices are usually available in the Wall Street Journal. Brokerage firms can obtain price information on both individual bonds and unit trusts.
3. Listed separately under mutual fund heading in paper. Post Net Asset Value or sell price.
4. Difference between Market Value and Cost Basis.
5. Individual bond yield rates are usually quoted immediately to the right of the bond in Wall Street Journal as annual coupon rate.
6. Distributions are often reinvested in additional shares of the fund and will vary from time to time. Available by contacting fund or advisor or use estimate.
7. Extension of coupon rate times face value of bonds/units.
8. Summarize by ownership and post to summary below.
9. Post to Cash Flow and Income Tax summaries below.
10. Figure should be posted to the Net Worth Summary (Corporate Bond Market Inv.).
11. Post Net to Cash Flow Analysis (Interest Annual).
12. Post Net to Tax Return Analysis (Income From Investments).

SCHEDULE 2C GOVERNMENT OBLIGATIONS

II. U.S. Government Bonds, T-Bills, Notes, and Municipals

Name	Maturity Date	Owner	Units	Cost Basis Per Unit	Cost Basis	Market Value Per Unit	Market Value	Gain (Loss)	Stated Yield on Face Value	Annual Yield
			①				②	④		⑤
Total							$			$

II. Unit Trusts—U.S. and Municipal

Name	Series #	Owner	Units	Cost Basis Per Unit	Cost Basis	Market Value Per Unit	Market Value	Gain (Loss)	Stated Yield on Units	Annual Yield
			①				②	④	⑤	⑦
Total							$			$

II. Mutual Funds–U.S. and Municipal

Fund Name	Date Acquired	Owner	Shares	Cost Basis Per Share	Cost Basis	Market Value Per Share	Market Value	Gain (Loss)	Annual Dividend Per Share	Annual Dividends
			①				③	④	⑥	
Total							$	$		$
Total Government Obligations							$ ⑧			$ ⑨

Summary

By Ownership	Cash Flow		Income Tax	
	Total Distributions ____		Total Distributions ____	
His	Less:		Less:	
Hers ⑩	Div Reinvested ____		Non Taxable ____	
Joint				
Total $ ____	Net $ ____ ⑪		Net $ ____ ⑫	

Notes:

1. From personal records, brokerage statements, confirmations, certificates, etc.
2. Treasury Issues bid and asked quotations are usually available in the Wall Street Journal. Brokerage firms can obtain price information on both individual bonds and unit trust.
3. Listed separately under mutual fund heading in paper. Post Net Asset Value or sell price.
4. Difference between Market Value and Cost Basis.
5. Yield rates are generally available form National Banks, brokerage firms, Wall Street Journal, etc.
6. Distributions are often reinvested in additional shares of the fund and will vary from time to time. Available by contacting fund or advisor or use estimate.
7. Extension of coupon rate times face value of bonds/units.
8. Summarize by ownership and post to summary below.
9. Post to Cash Flow and Income Tax summaries below.
10. Figure should be posted to the Net Worth Summary (Government Obligations).
11. Post Net to Cash Flow Analysis (Interest Annual).
12. Post Net to Tax Return Analysis (Income From Investments).

SCHEDULE 2D   INDIVIDUAL INVESTMENT REAL ESTATE

II. Raw Land (Acreage, Lots, etc.)

Description	Owner	Date Acquired	Cost (Tax Basis)	Fair Market Value	Remaining Loan/Contract Balance	Annual Income	Estimated Annual Cash Expenses
	①						
				③	①	④	⑤
Total				$ ⑥	$ ⑧	$ ⑦	

II. Improved-Non-Residence (Commercial Buildings, Apartments, etc.)

Description	Owner	Date Acquired	Cost (Tax Basis)	Fair Market Value	Remaining Loan/Contract Balance	Annual Income	Estimated Annual Cash Expenses
	①		②	③	①	④	⑤
Total				$ ⑥	$ ⑧	$ ⑦	

Summary

By Ownership	Cash Flow	Income Tax
His _____	Gross Income _____ (10)	Gross Income _____
Hers _____	Less:	Less:
Joint ___(9)___	Cash Expenses ____ (11)	Cash Expenses[a] _____
		Depreciation _____
Total $_____	Net $_____	Net $___ (12) ___

Notes:
1. From personal records.
2. Tax basis on depreciable property is purchase cost less accumulated depreciation. Your tax return generally can provide the required information.
3. Market Value is usually an estimate in as much the true cash value can only be determined by an arms-length sales transaction. For purposes of the exercise your own estimate, an appraisal, or a recent sale of like kind property can be used as a guideline.
4. Generally, unless farmed or leased no income is produced on raw land. Commercial Real Estate on the other hand should have gross rents posted in this column.
5. Include all cash expenses, i.e., taxes, insurance, interest payments, maintenance, etc. These figures are generally summarized and can be found in your tax return.
6. Summarize by ownership and post to summary below.
7. Post to cash flow and income tax summaries below.
8. Post to Investment Liabilities Net Worth Summary.
9. Figure should be posted to Net Worth Summary (Individual Investment Real Estate).
10. Post to Cash Flow Analysis (Investment Real Estate Annual).
11. Post to Cash Flow Analysis (Investment ExpenseAnnual).
12. Post to Tax Return Analysis (Income from Investment).
[a]Do not include principal payments on debt.

SCHEDULE 2E   LIMITED PARTNERSHIPS

II. Energy-Limited Partnerships

Description	Owner	Date Acquired	Cost (Tax Basis)	Fair Market Value	Remaining Notes Loans, etc.	Annual Income/ Expense	Taxable Income (Loss)
		①	②	③	④	⑤	⑥
Total				$ ⑦	$ ⑧	$ ⑤	$ ⑥

II. Real Estate-Limited Partnerships

Description	Owner	Date Acquired	Cost (Tax Basis)	Fair Market Value	Remaining Notes Loans, etc.	Annual Income/ Expense	Taxable Income (Loss)
		①	②	③	④	⑤	⑥
Total				$ ⑦	$ ⑧	$ ⑤	$ ⑥

II. Other-Limited Partnership

Description	Owner	Date Acquired	Cost (Tax Basis)	Fair Market Value	Remaining Notes Loans, etc.	Annual Income Expense	Taxible Income (Loss)
		(1)	(2)	(3)	(4)	(5)	(6)
Total				$ (7)	$ (8)	$ (5)	$ (6)

Summary

By Ownership	Cash Flow	Income Tax
His ___	Gross Income ___ (10)	Taxable Income ___
Hers ___	Less:	Less:
Joint ___ (9)	Cash Expenses ___ (10)	Tax Losses ___
Total $___	Net $___	Net $___ (11)

Notes:
1. From personal records, prospectus, partnership agreement, etc.
2. The tax basis will change with each contribution of capital or write-off of loss against the basis. The latest K-1 partnership return or the general partner can provide this information.
3. The market value of a partnership is generally not an easy figure to obtain since the partnership is usually still in some phase of operation. The general partner could be consulted for an opinion of current market value. Also some partnerships have pre-arranged discount buy back provisions that can be used to arrive at market value.
4. Post remaining payments, obligations and assessments if any. These are usually scheduled in the prospectus.
5. Post estimated cash flow from investment for the year to summaries below.
6. Anticipated tax losses can be obtained from the prospectus, general partner, or advisor. Summarize and post to summary below.
8. Summarize and post to Investment Liabilities on Net Worth Summary.
9. Figures should be posted to Net Worth Summary (Limited Partnership).
10. Post to Cash Flow Analysis (Investment Income); also Post to Cash Flow Analysis (Investment Expense).
11. Post to Tax Return Analysis (Income from Investment).

SCHEDULE 2F   TANGIBLES/MISCELLANEOUS INVESTMENTS

Tangibles-Investments

Description	Owner	Date Acquired	Cost (Tax Basis)	Fair Market Value	Estimated Annual Income	Annual Expenses
		①		②	③	
Total				$ ④	$	$ ⑤

Miscellaneous-Investments

Description	Owner	Date Acquired	Cost (Tax Basis)	Fair Market Value	Estimated Annual Income	Annual Expenses
⑥						
Total				$ ⑦	$ ⑦	$ ⑦

Summary

By Ownership		Cash Flow		Income Tax	
His		Gross Income		Gross Income	
Hers	⑧	Less:		Less:	
Joint		Cash Expenses		Cash Expenses	
				Depreciation	
Total	$	Net	$ ⑨	Net	$ ⑩

Schedule 2F *(continued)*

Notes:
1. From personal records-include only those tangible items that are held for purposes of investment. Examples would include coin, stamp, antique and art collections, etc. If items are owned for more personal reasons e.g., family heirlooms include in personal & household effects in Miscellaneous Assets section.
2. Insured or appraised value is usually the best available measure of fair market.
3. Tangibles seldom produce income unless actively traded.
4. Summarize by owner and forward to Net Worth Summary (Tangibles).
5. Include insurance, storage, and other costs attributable to the holding of this investment and post to cash flow summary below.
6. Include any other investment that may not fit appropriately in other schedules.
7. Summarize and post below.
8. Figures should be posted to Net Worth Summary (Miscellaneous Investment Assets).
9. Post to Cash Flow Analysis (Investment Other).
10. Post to Tax Return Analysis Schedule (Income/(Loss) from Investment).

SCHEDULE 3   RESIDENCE/BUSINESS INTEREST/RETIREMENT–SAVINGS PLANS–IRAs

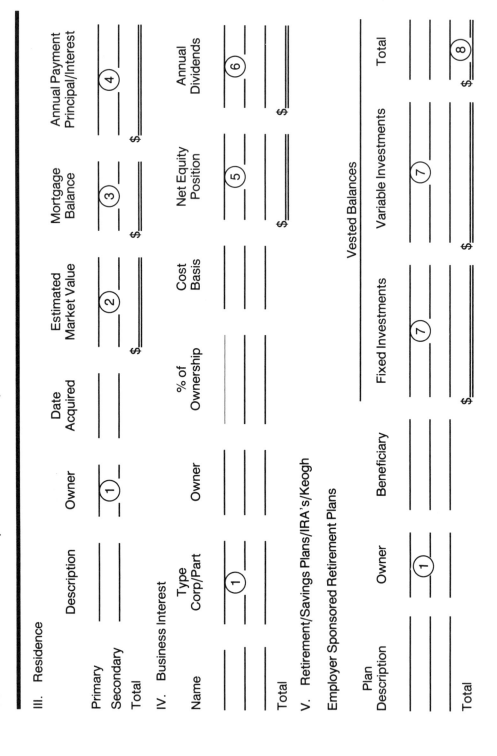

III. Residence

	Description	Owner	Date Acquired	Estimated Market Value	Mortgage Balance	Annual Payment Principal/Interest
Primary						
Secondary		①		②	③	④
Total				$	$	$

IV. Business Interest

Name	Type Corp/Part	Owner	% of Ownership	Cost Basis	Net Equity Position	Annual Dividends
	①				⑤	⑥
Total					$	$

V. Retirement/Savings Plans/IRA's/Keogh

Employer Sponsored Retirement Plans

				Vested Balances		
Plan Description	Owner	Beneficiary		Fixed Investments	Variable Investments	Total
	①			⑦	⑦	⑧
Total				$	$	$

Employer Sponsored Savings, Thrift Stock, Etc.

Plan Description	Owner	Beneficiary	Fixed Investments	Market Value Variable Investment	Total
	①				
Total			$ ⑦	⑦	$ ⑧

Individual Retirement Programs (IRAs) (Rollovers)

Plan Description	Owner	Beneficiary	Fixed Investments	Market Value Variable Investment	Total
	①				
Total			$ ①	①	$ ⑧

Notes:

1. Obtain from personal records.
2. Market value can be obtained from either your own estimate, appraisal, or average based on recent sales of similar homes in your area. Forward to Net Worth Summary (Assets Residence).
3. Lending institutions usually provide annually a detailed summary of the previous years balance. Forward to Net Worth Summary-Personal Property Liabilities (Mortgage-Residence).
4. Forward total payment to Cash Flow Analysis.
5. Net Equity can be arrived at by multiplying your percent ownership times the total Stockholders Equity figure in the balance sheet. Forward to Net Worth Summary (Assets Business Interest).
6. Dividends are seldom paid in private closely held businesses but if they are an estimate is sufficient. Forward to Cash Flow (Dividends Annual) and Income Tax (Income from Investment).
7. Obtain from personal records. Statements are provided by your employer annually summarizing benefits. If you are unclear as to your vested balance contact your personnel department. Be sure to include voluntary contributions if any.
8. Summarize by owner and forward to Net Worth Summary (Assets, Retirement, Savings, IRAs).

SCHEDULE 4 MISCELLANEOUS ASSETS

VI. Personal Effects

Description	Owner ①	Basis	Market Value ②

Total $ ___

VI. Household Goods

Description	Owner ①	Basis	Market Value ②

Total $ ___

VI. Notes Receivable

Description	Owner	Annual Payment		Interest Rate	Remaining Balance
		Principal	Interest ①		

Total $ ___ $ ___ $ ___ ③

VI. Automobiles

Description	Owner (1)	Basis	Estimated Market Value
Total			$ _____ (4)

VI. Miscellaneous Other

Description	Owner (1)	Basis	Estimated Market Value
Total			$ _____ (5)

Notes:
1. Obtain from personal records.
2. Estimate value of personal effects and household goods at liquidating or market value and not replacement cost. Because this can be a cumbersome task, an acceptable approach is to segregate valuables with more known values, e.g. diamonds, furs, then lump the balance at an auction sale value. Summarize by owner and post to Net Worth Summary—Miscellaneous Assets, Personal and Household Effects.
3. Summarize by owner and post to Net Worth Summary Miscellaneous Assets—Notes Receivable.
4. Summarize by owner and post to Net Worth Summary Miscellaneous Assets—Automobiles.
5. Summarize by owner and post to Net Worth Summary Miscellaneous Assets—Miscellaneous.

SCHEDULE 5   LIABILITIES

VII   Personal Property Liabilities

Installment Debt

| Lender | Owner | Annual Payment | | | Remaining |
		Principal	Interest	Total	Balance
		①			
Total		$_____	$_____	$__⑤__	$__②__

Notes Payable

| Lender | Owner | Annual Payment | | | Remaining |
		Principal	Interest	Total	Balance
		①			
Total		$_____	$_____	$__⑤__	$__③__

Schedule 5 *(continued)*

Miscellaneous Liabilities

| Lender | Owner | Annual Payment | | | Remaining |
		Principal	Interest	Total	Balance
___	___	___	___	___	___
___	___	_(1)_	___	___	___
___	___		___	___	___
___	___	___	___	___	___
Total		$___	$___	$_(5)_	$_(4)_

Notes:
1. Obtain from personal records.
2. Summarize by owner and post to Net Worth Summary Personal Property Liabilities-Installment Debt.
3. Summarize by owner and post to Net Worth Summary Personal Property Liabilities-Notes Payable.
4. Summarize by owner and post to Net Worth Summary Personal Property Liabilities-Miscellaneous Liabilities.
5. Post payments to cash flow analysis cash outflow-debt service.

LIFE INSURANCE SUMMARY

Company	Policy #	Issue Date	Type	Benefit			Benefit	Values				Costs			
				Face Amount	Owner	Benef.	Pd Up Adds	Accum Divs	+ Cash Value	− Loans	= Net Cash Value	Gross Annual Prem	− Divs Applied To Prem	+ Interest on Loans	= Net Payment
His Personal		①		②				⑦	⑧	⑦			⑦		
						④									
Group	③														
Totals				⑤			⑨		⑩	⑪					⑬

Hers

Personal

Group

Totals ⑥ ⑫ ⑩ ⑪ ⑬

Notes:

1. Generally this information is found on the face of the policy. It is sufficient to describe type of policy in general, e.g., whole life, term. Include term riders in face amount column.

2. Beneficiary and ownership designations are most often found in the application itself. If changes have been made since issued separate attachments will have been made.

3. Can be obtained from Group Certificates.

4. Generally on enrollment cards or subsequent change form. Personnel Department should have copies available.

5. Total should be forwarded to Death Estate Summary-His.

6. Total should be forwarded to Death Estate Summary-Hers.

7. Information can be obtained from most recent premium notice. If unavailable or policy is a paid-up policy a status report can be obtained from the insurance company.

8. Usually this figure must be calculated by multiplying the number of thousands of face amount times the appropriate rate per thousand under your issue age and year on the table of values page. Sometimes a separate cash value print out is provided which requires no calculation.

9. Total should be forwarded to Death Estate Summary-His.

10. Total accumulated dividends and cash values should be added together and forwarded to Net Worth Summary-Insurance Cash Value.

11. Total loans should be forwarded to Net Worth Summary-Misc. Liabilities.

12. Total should be forwarded to Death Estate Summary-Hers.

13. Gross premium less dividends applied to premium plus interest cost should be forwarded to the Cash Flow Analysis.

NET WORTH SUMMARY

Assets

Description	His	Hers	Joint	Total	%of Total
I. Cash & Equivalents	$_____	(Schedule 1)		_____	_____
II. Discretionary Investments					
Stock Market Inv.	_____	(Schedule 2A)		_____	_____
Corporate Bond Mkt Inv	_____	(Schedule 2B)		_____	_____
Gov't Obligations	_____	(Schedule 2C)		_____	_____
Indl Inv Real Estate	_____	(Schedule 2D)		_____	_____
Limited Partnerships					
Energy	_____	(Schedule 2E)		_____	_____
Real Estate	_____	(Schedule 2E)		_____	_____
Other	_____	(Schedule 2E)		_____	_____
Tangibles	_____	(Schedule 2F)		_____	_____
Insurance Cash Values	_____	(Life Ins.Summary)		_____	_____
Misc Investment Assets	_____	(Schedule 2F)		_____	_____
Total	$_____		_____	_____	_____
III. Residence				① _____	③ _____
Primary	_____	(Schedule 3)		_____	_____
Secondary	_____	(Schedule 3)		_____	_____
Total	$_____	(Schedule 3)		_____	_____
IV. Business Interest	$_____	(Schedule 3)		_____	_____
V. Retirement, Savings					
Plans, IRAs	$_____	(Schedule 3)		_____	_____
VI. Misc. Assets Personal & Household					
Effects	_____	(Schedule 4)		_____	_____
Notes Receivable	_____	(Schedule 4)		_____	_____
Automobiles	_____	(Schedule 4)		_____	_____
Misc.	_____	(Sehedule 4)		_____	_____
Total Miscellaneous	$_____	(Schedule 4)		_____	_____
Total Assets	$_____	① _____		② _____	100%

NET WORTH SUMMARY *(continued)*

Liabilities & Net Worth

Description	His	Hers	Joint	Total	% of Total
VII. Personal Property Liabilities					
Mortgage-Residence					
Primary Residence	_____	_____ (Schedule 3)	_____	_____	_____
Secondary Residence	_____	_____ (Schedule 3)		_____	_____
Total	$ _____	_____	_____		
Installment Debt	_____	_____ (Schedule 5)	①_____	④_____	
Notes Payable	_____	_____ (Schedule 5)	_____		
Miscellaneous Liabilities	_____	(Schedule 5 and Life Ins.Summary)	_____		
Total	$ _____	_____	_____	_____	
VIII. Investment Liabilities					
Individual Inv Real Estate	_____	_____ (Schedule 2D)	_____	_____	
Limited Partnerships	_____	_____ (Schedule 2E)	_____	_____	
Total	$ _____	_____	_____	_____	_____
Total Liabilities	$ _____	_____	_____	_____	100%
Net Worth					
(Assets minus liabilities)	$ _____	_____ ⑤ _____	_____	_____	
Total Liabilities & Net Worth	$ _____	_____ ⑥ _____	_____	_____	

Notes:
1. Total each line horizontally and vertically.
2. Cross-check total to verify additions.
3. Divide each line item by total assets to arrive at what percent each is of the total assets.
4. Divide each line item by total liabilities to arrive at what percent each is of the total liabilities.
5. Net worth is arrived at by subtracting Total Liabilities from Total Assets.
6. Add Total Liabililties and Net Worth. These figures should be exactly the same as the Total Assets by line. If they are not you have made an error and should recheck. If they agree you have probably completed your first ever Balance Sheet - Congratulations.

I'LL BET YOU'RE WORTH MORE THAN YOU THOUGHT!
ON TO THE NEXT SCHEDULE

INVESTMENT COMPOSITION

Balance Fixed Type Investments: (No Growth Potential)	Amount	Liquidity	Diversification % of Total
Checking & Regular Savings	Schedule 1	Total	_____
Money, Mkt, CDS, Cert, etc.	Schedule 1	Total	_____
Bonds, Unit Trusts, Funds, etc.	Schedule 2B	Partial	_____
Gov't obligations	Schedule 2C	Partial	_____
Fixed Portion of	①		④
Retirement Plans	Schedule 3	None	_____
Savings Plans	Schedule 3	Limited	_____
IRAs	Schedule 3	None	_____
Cash Value Life Ins	Life Ins. Summary	Total	_____
Notes Receivable	Schedule 4	Limited	_____
Other Fixed Invest	Schedule 2F		_____
Total Fixed Investment	$___②___		============
Variable Type Investments: (Growth Potential)			
Stocks	Schedule 2A	Partial	_____
Mutual Funds-Stock	Schedule 2A	Partial	_____
Individual Invest			
Real Estate	Schedule 2D	Limited	_____
Limited Partnerships	Schedule 2E	None	_____
Variable Portion of	①		④
Retirement Plans	Schedule 3	None	_____
Savings Plans	Schedule 3	Limited	_____
IRAs		None	
Tangibles	Schedule 2F	Limited	_____
Other Variable Investments	Schedule 2F		
Total Variable Investments	$___②___		============
Total Investments	$___③___		100%

Notes:
1. Figures can be obtained from each respective schedule as indicated.
2. Summarize by category.
3. This total should represent the amount of discretionary investment dollars currently at work.
4. Divide each line item to arrive at what percent each is of the total investment.
Investments with debt should be included net of any such debt.

DEATH ESTATE

His Estate

Net Worth-His Name $___①___

+
50% of Net Joint Assets $___②___

+
Life Insurance Net Death Benefits-His $___③___

+
Other-Miscellaneous-His $___④___

                                                       $_____

Her Estate

Net Worth-Her Name $___①___

+
50 % of Net Joint Assets $___②___

+
Life Insurance Net Death Benefits-Hers $___③___

+
Other-Miscellaneous-Hers $___④___

                                                       $_____

Notes:
1. Figures can be obtained from Net Worth-His/Her section of the Net Worth Summary.
2. Include 50% of the Net Worth-Joint figure from the Net Worth Summary.
3. Figures can be obtained from Life Insurance Summary. Calculate as follows:

	His	Hers
Face Amount Total His/Hers (Life Ins Summary)	$_____	$_____
Plus:		
Paid-up additions His/Hers (Life Ins Summary)	$_____	$_____
Total	$_____	$_____
Less:		
Net Cash Value His/Hers* (Life Ins Summary)	$_____	$_____
Net Death Benefits	$_____	$_____

4. Items that are not included in your net worth or insurance at present but should be noted for purposes of evaluating estate available at death for example: retirement plan death benefits, present value of survivor benefit plans, trust interest, etc.

*Insurance cash value and loans have already been accounted for in net worth.

CASH FLOW ANALYSIS

Cash Inflow	Annual	Monthly
Net Employment Income-His	$_____①_____	$_____
Hers	_____	_____
Investment Income		
Cash & Equivalents (Sch 1)	_____	_____
Dividends (Sch 2A)	_____	_____
Interest (Sch 2B, C)	_____	_____
Inv. Real Estate (Sch 2D)	_____	_____
LTD Partnerships (Sch 2E)	__②___	_____
Other (Sch 2F)	_____	_____
Retirement Income	_____	_____
Social Security Benefits	_____	_____
Gifts	_____	_____
Other	_____	_____
Total Cash Inflow	$_____	$_____

Cash Outflow	Annual ③	Monthly
Basic Living Expenses:		
Housing (Mort. or Rent)(Sch 3)	_____	_____
Property Taxes	_____	_____
House Maint.	_____	_____
Food	_____	_____
Transportation (Fuel & Maint.)	_____	_____
Utilities	_____	_____
Clothing	_____	_____
Personal Care	_____	_____
Medical–Uninsured	_____	_____
Education	_____	_____
Insurance Coverage:		
Life (Life Ins. Summary Net Pymt)	_____	_____
Auto & Homeowners	_____	_____
Disability	_____	_____
Hospitalization	_____	_____
Other	_____	_____

CASH FLOW ANALYSIS *(continued)*

Debt Service:
  Auto Loans (Sch 5) _____ _____
  Installment Loans (Sch 5) _____ _____
  Personal Loans (Sch 5) _____ _____
  Brokerage margin accts _____ _____
Investments Expenses:
  Cash Expenses from Ind Inv Real
    Estate (Sch 2D) _____ _____
  Notes, Loans from Partnerships
    (Sch 2E) _____ _____
  Miscellaneous (Sch 2F) _____ _____
Misc Expense Items:
  Child Support and Alimony _____ _____
  Support of Other Dependents _____ _____
  Charitable Constrislions _____ _____
  Travel & Vacations _____ _____
  Entertainment _____ _____
  Estimated Income Tax Payments _____ _____

Total Cash Outflow $_____ $_____

Gross Margin-Surplus (Deficit) $___④___ $_____

Notes:
1. Net employment income is your actual take-home pay. It is net of all deductions-Federal, State, Local, FICA and miscellaneous payroll deductions.
2. Obtain from various schedules as indicated. Be sure not to include reinvested amounts, remember this is Cash Flow.
3. Obtain from the various schedules indicated, personal records, or estimate to the best of your ability. Significant non-recurring items should be either eliminated or adjusted to reflect more normal circumstances.
4. Subtract Cash Outflow from Cash Inflow and record surplus deficit.

Memo Items

Description	Annual	Monthly
Total Payroll Deductions	$_____	$_____
Payroll Savings	_____	_____
Dividend Reinvestments	_____	_____

TAX RETURN ANALYSIS

Description	Last year 19__	This year 19__
Income:		
Income from occupation	$_____ ①	$_____
Income from investment	_____	_____
_____	_____	_____
_____	_____	_____
_____	_____	_____
_____	_____ ②	_____ ③
_____	_____	_____
_____	_____	_____
_____	_____	_____
_____	_____	_____ ④
Other Income (Pension Annuities, Royalties, Trust)		
Total Income	$_____	$_____
Adjustments to Income:		
IRA, Keogh	_____	_____
Other	_____	_____
Adjusted Gross Income (AGI)	_____	_____
Itemized Deductions:		
Medical & Dental	_____	_____
Taxes	_____	_____
Interest	_____	_____
Contributions	_____	_____
Casualty	_____ ⑤	_____ ⑥
Misc.	_____	_____
Total Itemized Deductions	_____	_____
Less: Zero Bracket	(_____)	(_____ ⑦)

	Actual	Estimated
Net Deductions	_____	_____
Personal Exemptions	_____	___(8)___
Taxable Income (TI)	$_____	$_____

Taxes:	Actual	Estimated
Federal	_____	_____
State	_____	_____
Local	_____	_____
Total	$_____	$_____

Notes:
1. Summarize total gross employment income (Salaries, Bonuses, Self Employment, etc.). Last years can be obtained from your latest tax return and this years estimated.
2. Last years investment income can be best summarized from last years tax return. Only include taxable items, e.g., taxable portion of dividends, interest, capital gains, etc.
3. This years investment income can be summarized from various schedules.
4. Include other taxable investment income not summarized on schedules above, e.g., estimated *taxable* portion of capital gains.
5. From last years tax return.
6. Estimate to the best of your ability using previous years as guidelines.
7. Zero-bracket amounts: $3,540 for married filing joint; $2,390 for single and head of household; or $1,770 for married filing separately.
8. Number of personal exemptions times $1,040.

Summary of This Years Position

	Federal	State	City
Estimated Tax Payable	$_____	$_____	$_____
Less: Tax Credits	(_____)	(_____)	(_____)
Witholding	(_____)	(_____)	(_____)
Estimated payments	(_____)	(_____)	(_____)
Balance due (Refund)	$_____	$_____	$_____

DEVELOPING FINANCIAL PROFILES AND OBSERVATIONS

"If we command our wealth, we shall be rich and free; if our wealth commands us, we are poor indeed."

Burke

Financial information must be analyzed following summarizations. Observations can then be made regarding the selected goals and the referencing of goals to the various financial objective areas.

A number of analytic approaches exist. We prefer utilizing a series of ratios. The following guidelines are not appropriate for everyone. We include these for purposes of establishing a basis for comparison. Each person should set targets based on personal goals which are to be achieved, an awareness of risk comfort levels, general financial knowledge, and state of life.

Refer back to schedules developed in Chapter 4 to obtain numbers to calculate the following financial profiles and make observations based on the results.

From the Net Worth Summary:

$$\text{Relative Indebtedness} = \frac{\text{Total Liabilities}}{\text{Total Assets}}$$

TABLE 5-1 FINANCIAL RATIOS

	Suggested Guidelines	Current Profile
Total liabilities/total assets	30% or less	
Liquid assets/total assets	25% or more	
Savings/cash income	10% or more	
Income tax/cash income	25% or less	
Total investments/net worth	depends*	
Fixed investments/total investments	depends*	
Variable investments/total investments	depends*	
Retirement funding/retirement needs	100%	
Estate funding/estate needs	100%	
Disability funding/disability needs	100%	

*Many factors need to be considered in determining a proper mix of investments. These include: goals, risk tolerance, income, taxes, wealth, life style, and personal circumstances.

A base guideline for debt level is a total amount of debts equaling about 30 percent of total assets. Debt levels above 50 percent to 75 percent of assets indicates a need for development of a plan for reducing debt. Debt levels below 30 percent suggest that opportunities may be available for employing the principal of leverage (that is, borrowing money and making returns in excess of interest costs).

Excessive Debt

- Seek reductions in living expenses through regular budgeting and monitoring of cash outflows.
- Pursue tax reductions which can free-up dollars to be used for debt payments.
- Consider alternatives for debt refinancing and consolidation.

Extremely Low Debt

- Consider making major purchases such as residence and automobiles with debt financing and avoid tying up cash in assets which do not produce investment returns.

- Consider using investment debt in the form of commitment to investments where cash flow and tax savings will be sufficient to finance debt payments.
- Utilize a personal line of credit for short-term, emergency type financing rather than liquidating investments.

$$\text{Total Liquidity} = \frac{\text{Total Liquid Assets}}{\text{Total Assets}}$$

The figures for liquid assets can be obtained from the Investment Composition Schedule—include total and partial liquid items under both Fixed and Variable Investments. Liquid assets are holdings which can be converted to cash with relative ease (i.e., within 0 to 4 weeks). Examples include savings accounts, stocks, and life insurance cash values. Most partnerships, qualified retirement plans, and similar investments should not be considered liquid.

A general target for most individuals and families is about 25 percent. Significantly less than 25 percent suggests that problems could be incurred in the event income falls, expensive emergencies arise, or a death occurs (upon which estate taxes may be due). Liquidity in excess of 60 percent may mean good investment opportunities are being missed or investments are not being built up sufficiently.

Insufficient Liquidity

- Consider asset repositioning which will add flexibility and liquidity to the investment portfolio.
- Increase savings and improve cash control techniques.
- Establish a personal line of credit to draw upon for emergencies.

Excessive Liquidity

- Analyze investment returns carefully to be certain funds are not being held where returns are unnecessarily low.
- Investigate retirement plan use for investing and reducing taxes.
- Become familiar with investments offering high returns (with low liquidity) such as real estate, small business ventures, and partnerships.

From the Cash Flow Analysis:

$$\text{Current Savings Rate} = \frac{\text{Savings}}{\text{Cash Income}}$$

$$= \frac{(\text{Annual Surplus} + \text{Payroll Savings} + \text{Dividend Reinvestments})}{(\text{Total Cash Inflow} + \text{Total Payroll Deductions})}$$

This ratio must be analyzed very carefully. If you participate in payroll deduction plans with your employer, include the deductions (such as government bonds, thrift plan contributions, stock purchases, or retirement plan contributions) as savings. Whether or not you participate in payroll deductions, use *gross* salary or wages (before taxes) rather than net employment income when determining cash income.

The savings ratio should be at least 10 percent of gross cash income. For individuals with well established careers and few major financial expenditures (such as college education costs), the savings rate should be significantly higher.

Low Savings Ratio

- Analyze all expenditures carefully in the process of preparing a formal budgeting structure to identify expenses which could be reduced.
- Shop wiser (i.e., become familiar with timing for bargains).
- Review taxes and tax savings techniques to free up cash for savings.
- Review insurance expenditures for possible replacement with new lower cost insurance.
- Implement improved cash flow control methods to carefully monitor the flow of dollars.
- Seek "forced" savings techniques including possible payroll deductions or monthly payments to investment accounts.

From the Tax Return Analysis:

$$\text{Average Tax Rate} = \frac{\text{Total Income Tax}}{\text{Cash Income}}$$

Total of federal income taxes divided by the sum of *gross* employment income and other income sources. A good guideline is 25 percent of gross income paid out for taxes. Generally, the lower the better, however, we do not encourage excessive use of formal tax shelters—cost to benefit of such tax sheltering is often not justified.

Excessive Income Tax

- Determine your *marginal* federal tax rate from the federal income tax rate schedules to evaluate whether or not investments offering tax free returns such as tax-free money markets or municipal bonds would offer you a better *net* investment return than taxable investments.
- Review use of qualified retirement plans including Individual Retirement Accounts, Keogh Plans, and Pension and Profit Sharing Plans which offer current tax deductions and tax deferred earnings.
- Evaluate your need for current taxable investment income and consider investments which are tax-oriented because of growth (and later long-term capital gain tax treatment), tax write-offs, and tax sheltered cash flow.
- Become very familiar with the types of expenses which are tax deductible, including legitimate business expenses and investment related expenses.
- Analyze carefully the timing flows of income and expenses for optimal tax planning.
- Review employer programs, if available, such as voluntary pension contributions, participation in deferred compensation programs, qualified thrift plans, or "cafeteria" plans providing tax-free reimbursement of certain expenditures.
- If self employed, utilize available tax planning techniques including consideration for incorporation.

From the Investment Composition Statement:

$$\text{Investment Accumulation} = \frac{\text{Total Investments}}{\text{Net Worth}}$$

This ratio depends greatly upon financial opportunities, circumstances, and the extent to which savings have been accumulated. The larger the percentage of net worth is composed of investments, the better. Home ownership, personal effects, and other non-investment assets may be desirable but do not actively build wealth. We suggest that this ratio be increased each year so that by retirement, investments represent at least two-thirds of net worth.

$$\text{No Growth Investments} = \frac{\text{Fixed Investments}}{\text{Total Investments}}$$

Three major reasons for holding investments which do not offer growth are: (1) high returns available during periods of unusually high interest rates; (2) safety and quick accessibility to funds; and (3) a need for regular fixed monthly income from investments for living expenditures.

Individuals not in need of investment income for monthly expenses should not hold more than 25 percent to 30 percent of investments offering only fixed investment return. Approximately 5 percent of investments in very liquid form such as savings accounts or money market fund is adequate for most people to hold for emergencies which may arise.

For individuals in need of regular investment income, such as retirees, the ratio of fixed investment to total investment can reasonably be expanded to 50 percent to 70 percent. Growth will still be needed to overcome inflation.

$$\text{Growth Investments} = \frac{\text{Variable Investments}}{\text{Total Investments}}$$

In addition to protecting investments against inflation and retaining purchasing power of investment funds, growth should be sought to make additional money or economic return in order to build wealth. Growth categorization of investments covers a wide area and distinctions must be made between seeking sound, stable growth investments versus outright speculation—with varying degrees of risk associated with the two extremes and the areas in between. Speculation should be undertaken with only a small portion of investable dollars and only by those individuals possessing high risk tolerance.

Diversification = The Mix of Investments

The complexities and unpredictability of today's investment markets necessitate a broad based approach to investing for optimal results. Funds should not be limited in placement to just a few investment media nor a few investment vehicles within a particular medium. For example, we encourage investors to avoid relatively large holdings of an individual security in favor of a wide number of security holdings, if affordable, or use of mutual funds which pool many investors funds and purchase many securities. An investor should not be fully invested in one medium such as common stocks.

FUNDING FOR RETIREMENT AND FAMILY SECURITY

An efficient method of evaluating financial security for retirement, disability, or death is the use of models based on present value calculations. Future dollars are reported in terms of today's dollars to facilitate understanding and planning. Results show whether or not future savings and/or additional insurance protection are needed.

Assumptions must be made regarding investment returns on investable funds and future inflation rates. The following models assume 8 percent investment return and 8 percent annual average inflation. For several reasons, these assumptions are very conservative. Your actual needs may be somewhat lower than calculated results. The models include the assumption that you will continue to be affected by inflation throughout the remainder of your life. In fact, some people are less affected in later years. Higher investment returns and lower inflation rates will increase calculated surpluses and decrease calculated deficits. Different rates may be used, however, expanded financial tables will be needed and can be obtained through many sources, including most public libraries.

Also, the models are designed for use by a married couple, but are readily adaptable to single individuals by ignoring questions and steps applying to a spouse.

SOURCES

- Pension income—estimate annual pension income for each husband and wife.

  (a) If pension incomes are tied to cost-of-living indices (will rise with inflation), multiply each annual pension amount by the number of years of expected life following retirement (life expectancy minus retirement age).

  (b) If pension incomes are not tied to cost-of-living indices (will not rise with inflation), find the appropriate factors from Column A in Table 5–2 and multiply each annual pension amount by the appropriate factor.

FORM 5-1   RETIREMENT FUNDING

Sources:

Present value of pension income $_____

Present value of Social Security benefits*   _____

Investments available for income generation   _____

Total $_____

Needs:

Present value of husband's and wife's
   combined income needs $_____

Present value of surviving spouse's
income needs after first spouse's death   _____

Total $_____

Surplus: (Deficit) $_____

Plus:

Present value of life insurance on the life of the
   spouse with the shortest life expectancy $_____

Net Surplus: (Deficit) $_____

Calculations for Retirement Funding

Husband's age _____ Life expectancy _____

   Retirement age_____

Wife's age _____ Life expectancy _____

   Retirement age _____

Gross annual income needed for both husband
   and wife during retirement $_____

Gross annual income needed for the surviving
   spouse following the death of the spouse with
   the shortest life expectancy $_____

Note: See Life Expectancies Table 5-3.
*Optional for your analysis; generally we prefer not to count on Social Security for planning purposes.

(c) If one pension income is tied to cost-of-living indices and the other is not follow steps (a) and (b).

(d) Add results for the husband's pension and the wife's pension and enter on the Retirement Funding Schedule.

- Social Security—estimate annual benefits; maximum benefits for individuals collecting at age 65 are now about $10,000 per year with another 50 percent payable to a qualifying spouse for total annual benefits of $15,000; individuals expecting to collect at age 62 should use $8,000 and $12,000; surviving spouse benefits approximate 100 percent of benefits payable to a individual or $10,000 and $8,000 depending upon the age at which benefits commence.

(a) Determine the number of years only one spouse will collect benefits while both are living and multiply this number times the annual amount of benefit.

(b) Determine the number of years both spouses will collect benefits and multiply this number times the combined annual amount of benefit.

(c) Determine the number of years only one spouse will collect benefits following the death of the other spouse and multiply this number times the annual amount of benefit.

(d) Add the results of steps (a), (b), and (c) and enter on the Retirement Funding Schedule.

- Investments available for income generation—refer to the Net Worth Summary and find the amount of total investments; subtract from this figure any investment debt; enter the difference on the Retirement Funding Schedule.

NEEDS

- Combined income needs—multiply the gross amount of annual income needed while both spouses are expected to be alive during retirement, times the number of years they will both be living, and enter the result on the Retirement Funding Schedule.
- Surviving spouse's income needs—multiply the gross amount of annual income needed for the surviving spouse following the death of the first spouse, times the number of years the surviving spouse is expected to outlive the other spouse, and enter the result on the Retirement Funding Schedule.

Surplus (Deficit): Subtract total needs from total sources.

Plus: Present value of life insurance—from the Life Insurance Summary find the total death benefit of coverages on the spouse with the shortest life expectancy; multiply this total times the appropriate factor from Column B in Table 5–2 and enter the result.

Net Surplus (Deficit): Add the present value of life insurance to the surplus (deficit).

RETIREMENT FUNDING CONCLUSIONS

A net surplus indicates that adequate financial resources are available for the desired standard of living in retirement. If life insurance is in force, some may be unnecessary. Emphasis should be given to proper investment positioning now and changes for retirement.

A net deficit means additional savings and/or life insurance on the spouse with the shorter life expectancy is needed. Also, attention must be given to proper positioning of investment funds.

The process of retirement funding analysis should be repeated annually to evaluate progress and improvements in building financial security.

ESTATE FUNDING

The estate funding analysis can be used to determine financial requirements following the death of the spouse now providing the major portion of family income, repeated again reversing spousal death, or for single individuals wishing to provide support for others.

SOURCES

- Pension Income—estimate annual pension income, if any, payable to the surviving spouse upon the death of the first spouse; and annual pension income for the surviving spouse at retirement.

  (a) If pension incomes are tied to cost-of-living indices (will rise with inflation), multiply each annual pension amount by the number of years it is expected to be received.

  (b) If pension incomes are not tied to cost-of-living indices (will not rise with inflation), find the appropriate factors from Column A in Table 5–2 and multiply each annual pension amount by the appropriate factor.

FORM 5-2 ESTATE FUNDING

Sources:

Present value of pension income $_____

Present value of Social Security benefits* _____

Present value of surviving spouse's employment
   income _____

Investments available for income generation _____

Life insurance available for income generation _____

Total $_____

Needs:

Estate expenses and taxes $_____

Present value of surviving spouse's income
   needs following first spouse's death _____

Present value of children's education costs and
   other income needs _____

Total $_____

Net Surplus: (Deficit) $_____

Calculations for Estate Funding

Surviving spouse's age _____ Life expectancy _____

Retirement age _____

Gross annual income needed for the surviving
   spouse following the death of the first spouse $_____

Note: See Life Expectancies Table 5-3.
*Optional for your analysis; generally we prefer not to count on Social Security for
planning purposes.

(c) If one pension income is tied to cost-of-living and the other is not follow steps (a) and (b).

(d) Add results for the decedent's pension payable to the surviving spouse and the surviving spouse's pension and enter on the Estate Funding Schedule.

- Social Security—estimate annual benefits, if any, payable to the surviving spouse upon the death of the first spouse; and annual benefits for the surviving spouse at retirement. Maximum benefits for a widow or widower with dependent children are now about $15,000 per year payable until the youngest child is 16; for each two dollars the widow or widower earns from employment in excess of $5,400, Social Security benefits are reduced by one dollar. Maximum benefits for retirees at age 65 are now about $10,000; for retirees at age 62, $8,000.

  (a) Determine the number of years a widow or widower with dependent children will collect benefits and multiply this number times the annual benefit amount.

  (b) Determine the number of years the surviving spouse will collect benefits upon retirement and multiply this number times the annual amount of benefit.

  (c) Add the results of steps (a) and (b) and enter on the Estate Funding Schedule.

- Surviving Spouse's employment income—estimate annual salary or wages.

  (a) If employment income is expected to increase with inflation, multiply the annual income by the number of years it is expected to be received.

  (b) If employment income is expected to be constant and not increase with inflation, find the appropriate factor from Column A in Table 5–2 and multiply the annual income by the factor.

  (c) Enter the result from either step (a) or (b) on the Estate Funding Schedule.

- Investments available for income generation—refer to the Net Worth Summary and find the amount of total investments, subtract from this figure any investment debt; enter the difference on the Estate Funding Schedule.

- Life insurance available for income generation—refer to the Life Insurance Summary and total death benefits payable on the life of the spouse for which death is being assumed, include employer group life insurance and any lump sum death benefit payable by the employer and enter the total on the Estate Funding Schedule.

NEEDS

- Estate expenses and taxes—estimate amounts due upon death— a good guideline to use is 3 percent of net worth, if more precise figures are desired refer to Chapter 14; add to the amount any debts (excluding investment debts) that you wish paid upon the death of the spouse for which death is being assumed; and enter the total on the Estate Funding Schedule.
- Surviving Spouse's income needs—multiply the gross amount of annual income needed for the surviving spouse following the death of the first spouse, times the number of years the surviving spouse is expected to live, and enter the result on the Estate Funding Schedule.
- Children's education costs and other income needs—estimate annual education costs for each child (average college costs in the United States now approximately $5,500 per year); and estimate additional annual costs for each child.

  (a) For each child, multiply the expected annual education costs times the number of years the costs will be incurred; add the results for each child to arrive at total educational costs.

  (b) For each child, multiply the expected annual costs (other than education) times the number of years the costs will be incurred; add the results for each child to arrive at a total.

  (c) Add the results of steps (a) and (b) and enter on the Estate Funding Schedule.

NET SURPLUS (DEFICIT): Subtract total needs from total sources.

ESTATE FUNDING CONCLUSIONS

A net surplus indicates that adequate financial resources are available to provide for family security in the event of death. If life insurance is in force, some may be unnecessary. Emphasis should be given to estate planning so that assets will be managed and distributed in accordance with personal desires and estate taxes and costs will be minimized.

A net deficit means consideration should be given to increasing life insurance protection on the life of the spouse for which death is being assumed. Also, attention needs to be given to building additional investment funds.

The process of estate funding analysis should be repeated annually to assure financial security for the family and dependents.

DISABILITY FUNDING

The disability funding analysis can be used for determining financial requirements following the disability of the spouse now providing the major portion of the family income, repeated again reversing spousal disability, or for single individuals. The analysis can also be repeated several times based on assumed duration of disability and can be integrated with retirement funding analysis and estate funding analysis in assuming permanent disability.

SOURCES

- Pension income—estimate pension income, if any payable to a disabled spouse by his or her employer pension plan.

    (a) If the disability pension income is tied to cost-of-living indices (will rise with inflation), multiply the annual amount by the number of years of assumed disability.

    (b) If the disability pension income is not tied to cost-of-living indices (will not rise with inflation), find the appropriate factor from Column A in Table 5–2 and multiply the annual amount by the factor.

    (c) Enter the result from either Step (a) or (b) on the Disability Funding Schedule.

Note: In determining the number of years for which payments will be made, do not count the required waiting period (i.e., most plans require extended disability before commencement of benefits).

- Social Security—estimate annual benefits payable to the disabled spouse; maximum benefits for disabled individuals now approximate $10,000 per year and are payable after five consecutive months of disability and only if the disability is expected to last at least one year.

    (a) Multiply the estimated annual benefit times the number of years of assumed disability (do not count the required five month waiting period).

FORM 5-3   DISABILITY FUNDING

Sources:

Present value of pension income $\qquad$ \$_____

Present value of Social Security benefits* _____

Present value of spouse's employment income \$_____

Present value of disability insurance _____

Investments available for income generation _____

Total \$_____

Needs:

Present value of household income needs \$_____

Present value of children's education costs
   and other income needs _____

Total \$_____

Net Surplus: (Deficit) \$_____

Calculations for Disability Funding

Number of years for which disability is to be
   assumed in the analysis _____

Gross annual household income needed \$_____

---

*Optional for your analysis; generally we prefer not to count on Social Security for planning purposes.

(b) Enter the result on the Disability Funding Schedule.

- Spouse's employment income—estimate annual salary or wages.

  (a) If employment income is expected to increase with inflation, multiply the annual income by the number of years of assumed disability.

  (b) If employment income is expected to be constant and not increase with inflation, find the appropriate factor from Column A in Table 5–2 and multiply the annual income by the factor.

  (c) Enter the result on the Disability Funding Schedule.

- Disability Insurance—total annual disability insurance—making sure to distinguish between payments from short-term coverage and long-term coverage, if applicable, and possible various waiting periods and lengths of payments—and note whether or not payments are offset by Social Security and whether or not payments are tied to cost-of-living indices. If payments are offset by Social Security, reduce reported amounts accordingly.
- With several different policies, it may be helpful to follow steps (a) and (b) below for each policy and then add the results.

  (a) If disability insurance benefits are expected to increase with inflation, multiply the annual payment by the number of years of assumed disability (or the number of years insurance is payable if less)—do not count required waiting periods.

  (b) If disability insurance benefits are constant and will not increase with inflation, find the appropriate factor from Column A in Table 5–2 and multiply the annual payment by the factor (in selecting the number of years on the factor table, keep in mind the number of years of assumed disability and the number of years for which insurance is payable—use the lesser of the two)—do not count required waiting periods.

  (c) Enter the result on the Disability Funding Schedule.

- Investments available for income generation—refer to the Net Worth Summary and find the amount of total investments; subtract from this figure any investment debt; enter the difference on the Disability Funding Schedule.

NEEDS

- Household income needs—multiply the gross amount of annual income needed times the number of years of assumed disability, and enter the result on the Disability Funding Schedule.
- Children's education costs and other income needs—estimate annual education costs for each child (average college costs in the United States now approximately $5,500 per year); and estimate additional annual costs for each child.

    (a) For each child, multiply the expected annual education costs times the number of years the costs will be incurred during the period of assumed disability; add the results for each child to arrive at total educational costs.

    (b) For each child, multiply the expected annual costs (other than education) times the number of years the costs will be incurred during the period of assumed disability; add the results for each child to arrive at a total.

    (c) Add the results of steps (a) and (b) and enter on the Disability Funding Schedule.

Net Surplus (Deficit): Subtract total needs from total sources.

**DISABILITY
FUNDING
CONCLUSIONS**

A net surplus indicates that sufficient financial resources are available to provide for family security in the event of a disability. Disability insurance should be reviewed to determine if all current protection is needed. Emphasis should be given to preparation and instruction for asset management if a severe disability should occur.

A net deficit means consideration should be given to increasing disability insurance protection on the spouse for which disability is being assumed, or for both spouses if appropriate. Also, attention needs to be given to building additional investment funds.

The process of disability funding analysis should be repeated annually to assure financial security for the family and dependents.

TABLE 5-2 PRESENT VALUE FACTORS (8% DISCOUNT)

Years[1]	A Equal Annual Payments	B Lump Sum Payment
1	.9259	.9259
2	1.7833	.8573
3	2.5771	.7938
4	3.3121	.7350
5	3.9927	.6806
6	4.6229	.6302
7	5.2064	.5835
8	5.7466	.5403
9	6.2469	.5002
10	6.7101	.4632
11	7.1390	.4289
12	7.5361	.3971
13	7.9038	.3677
14	8.2442	.3405
15	8.5595	.3152
16	8.8514	.2919
17	9.1216	.2703
18	9.3719	.2502
19	9.6036	.2317
20	9.8181	.2145
21	10.0169	.1987
22	10.2007	.1839
23	10.3711	.1703
24	10.5288	.1577
25	10.6748	.1460
30	11.2578	.0994
35	11.6546	.0676
40	11.9246	.0460
45	12.1084	.0313
50	12.2335	.0213

[1]Years for which annual payments will be received or years until lump sum payments will be received.

Personal Economics

TABLE 5-3 LIFE EXPECTANCIES[1]

	All Races				All Races		
Age	Both Sexes	Male	Female	Age	Both Sexes	Male	Female
0	73.7	70.0	77.5	43	33.9	30.9	36.9
				44	33.0	30.0	36.0
1	73.7	70.0	77.4	45	32.1	29.1	35.0
2	72.7	69.0	76.4	46	31.3	28.2	34.1
3	71.8	68.1	75.5	47	30.4	27.4	33.2
4	70.8	67.1	74.5	48	29.5	26.5	32.3
5	69.8	66.1	73.5	49	28.7	25.7	31.4
6	68.9	65.2	72.6	50	27.8	24.9	30.6
7	67.9	64.2	71.6	51	27.0	24.1	29.7
8	66.9	63.2	70.6	52	26.1	23.3	28.8
9	65.9	62.2	69.6	53	25.3	22.5	28.0
10	64.9	61.3	68.6	54	24.5	21.7	27.1
11	64.0	60.3	67.6	55	23.7	21.0	26.3
12	63.0	59.3	66.6	56	22.9	20.2	25.4
13	62.0	58.3	65.7	57	22.2	19.5	24.6
14	61.0	57.3	64.7	58	21.4	18.8	23.8
15	60.0	56.4	63.7	59	20.6	18.0	23.0
16	59.1	55.4	62.7	60	19.9	17.4	22.2
17	58.1	54.5	61.8	61	19.2	16.7	21.4
18	57.2	53.6	60.8	62	18.5	16.0	20.6
19	56.3	52.7	59.8	63	17.8	15.4	19.8
20	55.3	51.8	58.9	64	17.1	14.7	19.1
21	54.4	50.9	57.9	65	16.4	14.1	18.3
22	53.5	50.0	56.9	66	15.7	13.5	17.6
23	52.5	49.1	56.0	67	15.1	12.9	16.9
24	51.6	48.2	55.0	68	14.4	12.3	16.1
25	50.7	47.3	54.0	69	13.8	11.8	15.4
26	49.7	46.4	53.1	70	13.2	11.3	14.8
27	48.8	45.4	52.1	71	12.6	10.7	14.1
28	47.9	44.5	51.1	72	12.0	10.2	13.4
29	46.9	43.6	50.2	73	11.5	9.7	12.8
30	46.0	42.7	49.2	74	10.9	9.3	12.1
31	45.1	41.8	48.2	75	10.4	8.8	11.5
32	44.1	40.9	47.3	76	9.9	8.4	10.9
33	43.2	39.9	46.3	77	9.3	7.9	10.3
34	42.2	39.0	45.4	78	8.9	7.5	9.7
35	41.3	38.1	44.4	79	8.4	7.1	9.2
36	40.4	37.2	43.5	80	7.9	6.7	8.6

TABLE 5-3 (*continued*)

37	39.4	36.3	42.5	81	7.5	6.3	8.1
38	38.5	35.3	41.6	82	7.0	6.0	7.6
39	37.6	34.4	40.6	83	6.6	5.7	7.2
40	36.7	33.5	39.7	84	6.2	5.3	6.8
41	35.7	32.6	38.7	85	5.9	5.0	6.4
42	34.8	31.7	37.8				

[1]From the Department of Health and Human Services, Public Health Service, annual report, *Vital Statistics of the United States,* for the year 1980.

6

ECONOMIC CONCEPTS AND STRATEGIES

"There is deep intuitive wisdom in this American tolerance of economic variety and in our refusal to commit ourselves to any one social and economic system. It is recognition of the fact that life and truth are too varied and complex to be confined within the pattern of any single deliberately planned economic system."

Dr. Arthur E. Morgan

The United States economic system has become increasingly more complex and difficult to predict. However, general economic management techniques and policies are getting better as academicians and policymakers gain more understanding of economic functioning. We do not forecast, nor feel it necessary to prepare for, an economic collapse—recessions, yes; complete collapse, no.

The United States economy will continue to be among the most stable in the world and will play a very dominant role in the world-wide economy. Greater economic interdependence between countries is developing; and because of the closer ties between economies, watching foreign economies will be more important— both for the impact on the United States economy and for investment opportunities.

More investment opportunities will also develop in the United States, especially locally as the federal government reduces deficits, continues to lift business restrictions, and shifts decision making and programs to local governments and businesses. For social and economic reasons, the rapid expansion of new business enterprises will continue along with redevelopment of established companies and economic areas.

We place great importance on the concept of "personalizing" economics as many opportunities for personal financial gain will exist for those who move in conjunction with economic changes. Future investment opportunities will be different than in the past. You need to screen carefully and spread risk.

The need for you to understand basic economics is higher than ever. Financial markets are undergoing major changes and competition among financial institutions and organizations is fierce. You need to become self-reliant in decision making. We have seen, for example, the decline in some real estate values as a result of overall disinflation. Many households unfortunately were led to view housing as a "sure" investment and expected price increases to match those of the 1970s indefinitely. Individuals who forecast housing price movements correctly were able to sell-off and invest profits.

This suggests the concept of "lead" and "lag" economic variables. Understanding and observing key economic variables and the impact on your household is a prerequisite to successful personal financial planning.

- What does an increase in the money supply mean?
- What new industries are being established?
- How can you benefit from higher interest rates?
- Does a rise in the unemployment rate mean depression?
- Who benefits from disinflation?
- How will more foreclosures affect investments in general?
- What does more contract labor versus hired labor mean?
- Which companies are experiencing rising productivity?
- What will fewer industrial companies and more information companies mean to managing finances?
- When should stocks be bought and sold, bonds, etc.?

Lead variables are economic measurements which tend to move or change before general economic activity. Lag variables are factors which follow major economic changes. For example, interest rates—a major lead variable—generally are predictive of things to come. A substantial increase in rates suggests a forthcoming slow-down in general economic activity. Unemployment is a lag variable, rising after a slowdown in general economic activity. As pointed out previously, the United States economy is very complex and a general movement downward does not necessarily mean an erosion of good investment opportunities. Substantial profits have been made in depressed stock markets. In other words, if you look deeply and have a sense of forthcoming activity, personal benefits can be high.

A basic concept to personal economics is "opportunity cost." This simply means that trade-offs exist. To do one thing, necessarily means giving up another. Therefore, with limited resources you must exercise extreme caution in the decisions you make. You may have difficulty recovering from incorrect decisions. Diversification or spreading out your choices increases the probability of success. Economists are noted in recent years for poor predictions and inaccurate economic analysis. If these professionals cannot accurately predict activity, how then can the average person? They cannot, at least not without a great deal of luck. But you can develop a future orientation and through diversification increase your chances for success.

Let's, for example, look at some economic scenarios as related to inflation, and the impact on decision making.

If more inflation is expected, there will be an increase in the rate at which prices go up:

- Borrow money and employ the principle of leverage, investing at a rate of return in excess of interest cost; the loans can be repaid with cheaper dollars.
- Look for investments in companies that benefit from inflation; for example, food and energy companies.
- Move dollars quickly and keep funds working at all times.
- Look to collectibles such as gold, silver, and antiques for profits.
- Pyramid assets such as real estate.
- Invest in foreign countries with stable currencies.
- Forward buy-purchase goods before prices increase.

Disinflation is expected, with a decrease in the rate prices rise:

- Get out of debt—the relative value of the dollar will increase, making repayment more difficult.
- Seek "real" investments such as stocks and bonds, not tangibles or other investments based on the "greater fool" theory.

- Do not forward buy goods needed for living.
- Look for interest and investment returns which remain somewhat high and "lag" behind general interest rate movements.
- Invest in the U.S. economy.

Deflation is expected, the reverse of inflation; falling prices:

- Stay out of debt, the value of money will increase sharply and income will be difficult to earn.
- Buy gold and precious metals as protection against deep recessionary developments in the economy.
- Maintain very frugal living standards and look for barter opportunities.
- Hold cash and be extremely careful in selection of financial institutions.
- As the economy turns and recession begins to end, look for special opportunities for buying at depressed prices (such as with real estate and business enterprises).

We cannot realistically hope to predict economic activity with extreme accuracy, but we can develop scenarios as above and hedge decisions accordingly. We oppose the concept of placing all investable funds in any one particular investment, rather an investment portfolio, no matter how large or small, should be spread among several alternatives to the extent possible. Table 6–1 lists many major economic variables. Through assimilation of many factors, we are able to blend together possibilities and make appropriate decisions.

Various composite indexes, such as the Index of Leading Economic Indicators, are also regularly published. It is important, though, to review individual economic variable movements. It often takes several months for the composites to clearly show trends, and the composites don't necessarily indicate where the best investment opportunities will be.

The movements in Table 6–1 are all suggestive of more favorable economic developments. Some changes would precede a major upturn, others following one. It is unlikely, though, that all variables would point in the same direction. Nevertheless, we can take a consensus view and develop analysis for money making opportunities. Incorporating economics into financial management enhances goal achievement. In Table 6–2, you will find investment media alternatives and corresponding favorability which can be expected

TABLE 6-1 CHANGE SUGGESTIVE OF ECONOMIC UPTURN

Economic Variable	Type of Variable	Movement
Unemployment rate	lag	down
Wholesale price index	lead	down
Gross national product	lag	up
Consumer confidence level	lead	up
Home foreclosures	lag	down
Consumer debt levels	lead	up
Productivity rate	lead	up
Interest rates	lead	down
Income taxes	lead	down
Money supply	lead	up
Bankruptcy rate	lag	down
New business start ups	lead	up
Common stock prices	lead	up
Business investment spending	lead	up
Consumers durable goods purchases	lead	up
Business inventory levels	lag	down

with an economic upturn. You should reposition investment portfolios, as economic changes develop, to maximize returns, yet protect yourself against unexpected developments by having broad diversification.

In addition to analyzing and responding to general economic trends, investors who self-manage funds on a specific basis (i.e., individual stocks) should have the ability of tracing through general developments to specific sectors and economic units. If you do not possess the knowledge, inclination, or time to trace developments, then professional money managers can be relied upon. In fact, we encourage most individuals to retain professional money managers by investing in no-load mutual funds and other types of "pooled" media. Recognize the general trends and find good professionals with specialized expertise to make particular investment choices for you.

The successful investor of the future must know his or her

investment objectives, must understand general economics, and must either be able to make narrowly focused decisions based on economic activity or find people who can advantageously make such decisions.

TABLE 6-2 ECONOMIC UPTURN—IMPACT ON INVESTMENTS

Investment	Favorableness	Reason
Cash and equivalents	not favored	Lower returns because of lower interest rates—less need for liquidity
Bonds	initially favored	With lower interest rates initially increasing values of outstanding bonds, but falling values as extended economic expansion later forces interest rates up
Hard assets	not favored	Less demand as investors are more secure and confident in economy
Stocks	favored	Increased corporate profits result in higher stock values and dividend payments
Real estate	favored	Increased personal and business incomes increase demand and property values rise—lower financing costs
Business ventures	favored	Greater opportunities with greater demand for goods and services—lower financing costs
Commodities	favored	Increasing prices with business expansion
Equipment leasing	favored	Good opportunities for equipment utilization with higher business activity
Oil and gas	favored	More funding available for development and possible price increases with more demand for natural resources

7

MANAGING RISK

"Contrary to the commonly accepted belief, it is the risk element in our capitalistic system which produces an economy of security. Risk brings out the ingenuity and resourcefulness which insure the success of enough ventures to keep the economy growing and secure."

Robert Rawls

A single woman in her midforties came to see us for financial advice. She was earning about $40,000 per year. She lived very comfortably, traveled often, and occasionally helped support her mother. The company she worked for was in an industry subject to great swings in profitability. Her benefits were good, but job security was tenuous. She had not yet qualified for a pension because she had changed employers several times. Besides minor savings accounts, her only assets were a home and personal property. She was heavily in debt through credit card use, did not budget, and had no real source of emergency funds. She was worried.

Ineffective treatment of risk is the most potentially damaging threat to personal economic well-being. Many individuals view risk management as being relatively straightforward; a matter easily understood and handled. In fact, risk management is a very complex area. Frequently, an individual's or family's risk management is in need of improvement and/or revisions.

Problems associated with poor risk management include:

- no planning of future cash inflow and outflow needs;
- inappropriate amounts, types of coverage, and premium payments for insurance products;
- excessive use of tax shelters;
- poor evaluation of risk/return in investment placements;
- improper investment balance, diversification, and liquidity; and
- insufficient estate planning.

Protecting against losses—managing risk—is a very important part of successful money management. Three main principles of managing risk are:

- to understand exposures to risk and the consequences of loss;
- to develop a method for evaluating your tolerance for risk; and
- to properly balance use of available risk management programs and techniques.

There are three basic approaches to select from when acting on issues of risk:

1. Try to avoid risk altogether or ignore it when it does exist.
2. Accept risk and manage the risk yourself or self-fund your own risk protection.
3. Accept risk and shift the risk to a third party.

To avoid risk altogether is very difficult. Risk is present in many parts of life, financial and nonfinancial. Rather than actually achieving total risk avoidance, people who use the first approach can often succeed in reducing risk. Normally, though, reduced risk means reduced return opportunities. To accept a secure job with a large corporation instead of becoming self-employed, lowers risk associated with regularity of income but can preclude achievement of high income levels. Individuals dependent on investment income for living expenses can, for example, purchase low risk federal government bonds in lieu of corporate bonds, but must accept lower return.

Ignoring risk is most dangerous as preparations and strategies can be established to hedge risk in situations for which outright purchase of risk protection is not available. Budgeting and holding emergency funds is an excellent way to protect against risks associated with temporary job losses or transfers of jobs and career changes. Risks associated with family money management in the event of death or disability to the person who normally manages the family finances can be offset by setting up trusts with designated competent individuals or institutions as trustees.

Risk management approaches (2) and (3), or a combination of the two, are most often the preferred means of handling risk. The systems described in this book are designed to manage risk while you are seeking to attain personal goals and financial objectives.

Proper levels and techniques of risk management depend on personal comfort and goals, availability of risk protection programs, cost/benefit ratios of risk protection, financial security and complexity, and economic conditions.

To properly address risk management, you should view it from an overall, as well as detailed, perspective. It enters all financial planning areas, and there is a close inter-relation of financial planning areas with respect to risk management.

As shown in Figure 7–1, self-insuring means to take precautions in the areas of cash flow planning, income tax planning, investment funds placement, and estate planning. Risk is shifted to a third party with formal insurance protection.

The lack of understanding of risk exposure and management causes many individuals to have a poor grasp on their tolerance for risk. This is unfortunate because many financial decisions require a determination of acceptable risk levels in order to make optimal choices. There is no right or wrong level of risk tolerance. It is a matter of personal comfort and the degree to which financial loss will adversely affect the progress towards financial security. Risk tolerance varies greatly among individuals. Choices that are comforting to some people are not so to other people.

We believe that a comfort zone for risk tolerance exists for everyone and the comfort zone definition should be a basic consideration in most financial decisions. It is the core of risk tolerance which enables you to purchase insurance coverage or make an investment decision, and decide on other important financial matters.

Successful risk management requires matching your financial resources to available risk management techniques so that your comfort levels are met to the extent possible. For example, in-

FIGURE 7–1

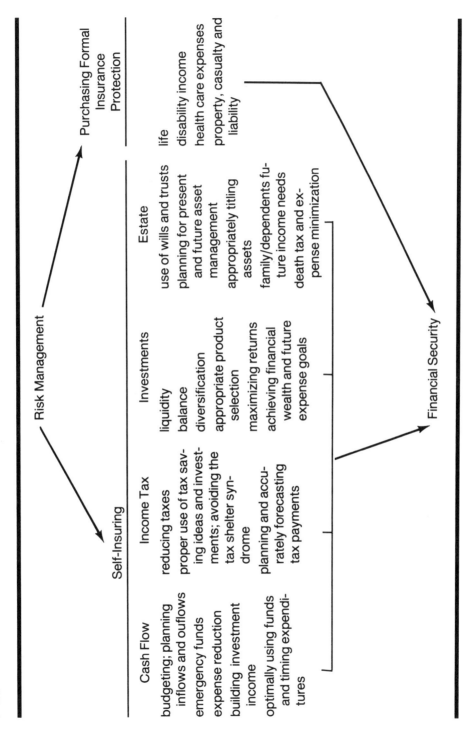

surance coverage may be desired to provide financial and family security but balance must be established between allocating dollars to purchase of coverage versus other expenditure areas, if financial resources are limited. When one of our current clients first came to us, we had him cancel a whole life insurance policy costing $2,000 per year and replace it with about four times the coverage in term insurance for about one-fourth the cost. He is now a very successful professional with several children. But he said that for years he and his wife struggled to pay that insurance premium—even foregoing Christmas presents for their children (the premium was due in December).

Investments should be sought which provide the greatest return for a given level of risk. Often we find investors accepting far greater risk for return levels than necessary to achieve the returns. Improper balance, diversification, and liquidity in investment portfolios prevent goal achievement, or make it much more difficult. Poor investment choices result in unacceptable levels of growth and lack of investment flexibility causes investors to miss good opportunities. Sometimes assets which have the best potential for return have to be liquidated because unexpected or poorly planned expenditures have to be paid and no planned liquidity sources are available.

Investment diversification, balance and liquidity also must be blended in line with portfolio size, savings capacity, security needs and financial objectives. One of our clients who makes an average salary has accumulated a net worth in excess of over $750,000 in ten years through conservative investing. Another client has been making over $100,000 for many years and has a net worth of less than $150,000. He has been through bad movie deals, commodity scams, shady business partners, and other unfortunate events. He has a high propensity for jumping on "the band wagon" to quick riches. Basically, he pays us to keep him out of bad deals. He now knows the value of objective advice.

Reducing taxes is appealing to most individuals. Aggressiveness in seeking tax reduction must be evaluated. The "tax shelter syndrome" is another example of poor risk management. The eagerness to reduce taxes on a current basis produces broad negative ramifications later (especially in cash flow and investment portfolio development).

To build financial security, you must accumulate wealth and

protect against possible adverse events. Expense and tax reduction lead to greater accumulation of savings for investing. Insurance protection needs to be purchased until wealth accumulations are great enough to provide for insurable losses. Successful investing also entails making provisions for asset management and distribution in the event of disability or death. Combinations of risk management techniques and approaches can be developed to meet individual needs.

Identifying individual comfort zones with respect to risk is difficult. However, it is of vital importance to identify them as best as possible and to realize that risk tolerance levels will change over time as financial and nonfinancial conditions change. Figure 7–2 shows four categories of risk takers: pure speculators, aggressive risk takers, moderate risk takers, and extremely conservative risk takers. You may find yourself in one or more categories because risk is present in many financial decisions. You may, for example, be very conservative with cash flow (wanting to protect earned income and be very cautious with outflow), yet be an aggressive investor.

A good method for determining your comfort with risk is to understand your current exposure to risk and identify the areas where you are either comfortable or uncomfortable. Ask yourself the following questions:

- What do you like most about your overall financial situation?
- What do you like least about your overall financial situation?
- Do you feel you have financial security?
- How dependent are you on earned income to meet living expenditures?
- Do you have adequate funds set aside to meet emergencies?
- Are you relying on Social Security benefits to be a major source of income for you (or dependents) in the event of disability, retirement, and/or death?
- Are you "vested" in a qualified retirement plan?
- What plans have you made for increasing your net worth in each of the next several years?
- Do you expect to receive inheritances? If so, are you counting on receipt in planning your financial future?
- Do you feel either overly aggressive or not aggressive enough with respect to income tax planning?
- How much monthly income, on average, do you need to meet all expenditures?

FIGURE 7—2 RISK TAKERS

Theory/Motivation	Cash Flow by	Investing by	Treats or Covers		Estate Plan by
			Taxes by	Insurance by	
Extreme Conservative motivated by fear of loss and uncertainty	Holding large cash reserves, planning expenditures in advance and seldom using debt or leverage	Diversifying within a narrow scope of government obligations, insured investments, and generally conservative holdings	Not utilizing tax code or tax advantaged investments to any great degree for fear of audit	Generally purchasing large amounts of insurance covering most exposures	Implementing base or expanded estate documents optimizing tax and dispositive techniques
Moderate Risk Taker motivated by risk-reward theory	Holding a base of cash reserves for comfort; utilizing occasional debt	Diversifying his/her portfolio utilizing several investment media about half of which is growth oriented	Using some tax techniques as well as pooled tax advantaged investments	Covering most or all exposures with adequate coverage and low deductions	Implementing base documents designed primarily to treat dispositive concerns
Aggressive Risk Taker motivated by nothing ventured/nothing gained theory	Holding modest cash reserve, borrowing for all emergencies and non-recurring large expenses	Concentrating holdings into fewer and more volatile investments with significant capital gain potential	Looking for aggressive tax write-off thru use of tax shelters	Utilizing high deductible- and self-insurance concepts	Implementing base documents to take care of testamentary desires
Pure Speculator motivated by greed, excitement and gamble	Minimizing cash reserves, relying on debt or credit to cover emergency and/or opportunity needs	Typically investing in limited areas with perceived large rewards, searching for the "big hit"	Attempting to eliminate to the greatest extent all or most personal tax thru use of tax shelters and code	Often being uninsured or grossly under insured	Implementing minimal or no plan on the theory that all will take care of self

- Do you spend freely? On what types of things?
- Do you use a cash management system?
- Approximately how much will you pay in income taxes next year?
- When you made your most recent investment, what criteria did you use in making the decision?
- Are your investments diversified?
- Are your investments mainly income oriented? Growth oriented? Or, a combination of both?
- Have you pre-funded major expense commitments such as your children's education costs?
- Is it important that your children or other heirs receive a large estate following the deaths of you and your spouse?
- Who will manage family assets in the event of your disability or death?
- What type of risk taker do friends and relatives consider you to be?
- If you have a spouse, do the two of you usually agree on investment and other important financial decisions?
- What is the most precious personal asset you own? Is it adequately insured?
- Is it easy or difficult for you to make decisions that involve risk?
- Do you usually find yourself looking for guaranteed return type investments?
- Do you act on investment and other types of information tips "given" to you at social functions, the office, etc.?
- Do you have unusual liability exposure because of your life style, business ownership, etc.?
- Are you concerned with tax aspects of investments?
- From whom or where do you get investment information?
- Is the health history of your family good or poor?
- Are you "rated" or uninsurable for disability and life insurance purposes?
- Do you feel adequately insured?
- How much of your various insurance needs are provided for through employer sponsored programs?
- Were you "sold" your last life insurance policy or did you "buy" it (i.e., shop around for the best deal)?
- Do you purchase all your personally owned insurance through the same agent?

- Who determines how much protection you need from various types of insurance?
- Is your insurance agent(s) independent or does he or she represent one company?
- For each insurance policy you own, can you explain why you own the type of policy you purchased?
- Have you checked recently to see if available insurance rates for types of coverage you own have changed?
- When you compare insurance rates, what basis do you use (i.e., cost per thousand, comparing equal terms and coverage, etc.)?

After answering the questions, summarize your concerns and areas of uncomfortableness (adding others you can think of) and make plans to alleviate the concerns. Prioritize your concerns and allocate cash and financial resources first to the most immediate (such as budgeting), then to mid-term concerns (such as college cost funding), and then to long-term concerns (such as retirement planning). Periodically revaluate your risk management programs.

8

DIRECTING CASH FLOW

"Save a part of your income and begin now, for the man with a surplus controls circumstances and the man without a surplus is controlled by circumstances."

Henry H. Buckley

Some of the very best savers are people who are accustomed to living on fluctuating incomes. The ups and downs help prevent overspending and excessive use of higher income for higher living standards. One of our clients is in a very volatile construction business. He has big years and low-income years. The low-income years can lead to investment principal liquidation. This causes him to be more aware than most people about his inflows and outflows of cash. Unlike many people, he tends to put great emphasis on what money is coming in and what action is being taken to bring money in. He allocates time for determining sources of income.

We have set up a system for him whereby income is segregated for current expenses, taxes, future expenses, and long-term savings. Importantly, we have built in flexibility and are helping him establish multiple sources of income. Having multiple sources of income, from employment and investing, increases the likelihood of building wealth and creates more true security.

You must gain control and understanding over amounts of income coming in and amounts going out. Control and understanding can be achieved through use of personalized cash management systems. Once the systems are functioning, fear caused by lack of understanding will be reduced or eliminated and actual cash management will involve less time. Disorganization creates inefficiencies which are translated into wasted time and which in turn translates into lost personal profit.

Directing cash flow into savings and investments is mandatory for achieving financial security and independence. View yourself as a profit center, just as businesses are viewed as profit centers. You sell time and services in the work environment. If you can operate personally at a profitable level, demonstrated through savings, financial objectives can be achieved. We will show you ways to improve your savings.

Asset build-up sufficient for financial independence in today's world requires two forms of savings. First, you need to save on a regular periodic basis, and secondly, you must have a reasonably stable level of expenditures so that sudden large inflows of cash (such as bonuses, inheritances, profitable investments, etc.) can be added to investments. Of course, making good investments is of critical importance.

BUDGETING

Budgeting is often viewed as difficult, tedious, restrictive, and not practical. Several steps can help you overcome a negative outlook on budgeting.

- Change the word budget to overhead and view management of your cash inflows and outflows with a business perspective. Make a profit on your employment and investment efforts.
- Do not try to adhere to traditional budgeting benchmarks; allocate your income in ways which best suit your lifestyle choices.
- Set up a good system of handling income, savings, and expenses, including use of the best available cash accounts.
- Make investments in yourself to increase future income, particularly by pursuing activities you prefer.
- Structure the inflows of your income to increase the probability of savings.
- Seek savings not only in the form of direct cash savings but also through income tax reduction, living expense reduction, time management, and appropriate investment and financial product selection.

- Participate in planned, but flexible, investment programs.
- Realize that it takes many small steps, as well as big steps, to build up sizeable savings; think in terms of various stages, with financial security the long-term goal.

Use the Cash Flow Analysis Worksheet included in Chapter 4 to summarize inflows and outflows.

The budgeting process should begin with a complete review of last year's household and family living expenditures. The figures should then be inflated to determine expenditures for the current year and thereafter. Attention should be given to additional expenditures that might be incurred or past expenditures that are not expected to be forthcoming in the future. In addition to reviewing amounts of expenditures, timing of expenditures should also be carefully reviewed.

Debt payments, income taxes, and targeted savings should also be incorporated into the budgeting. Income taxes should be projected as discussed in Chapter 10 and the difference between withholdings and anticipated balances due (either in April or through quarterly payments), if any, should be included as a budgeted expenditure.

Use forms similar to those shown next to record budgeting and budgeting variance. Importantly, it is necessary to allocate income and expenses on a percentage basis as well, to allow accurate comparison in future years when actual dollar income and expenditures may differ from those of the current year. Improvements in expense allocations are best noted through percentage changes.

It will probably take several months and several adjustments until you are comfortable with your budget and cash flow system. Once you are comfortable, though, you will have less worry about cash flows, more time for other activities, an understanding of where your money goes, and a much greater chance of achieving your financial objectives. Each year new budget figures should be established as your personal finances and circumstances change.

These principles should be remembered in budgeting:

- Set financial objectives and periodically review and monitor the objectives.
- Understand amounts and timing of income inflows and outflows.
- For planning purposes, allocate income and expenses on a monthly (or other periodic) basis even though not received or paid on a monthly basis.

FORM 8-1   PLANNED BUDGET BEGINNING OF THE YEAR

	Planned Annual	Planned Monthly.	Percent
Cash Inflow			
Net Employment–His	$ _____	$ _____	_____ %
Hers	_____	_____	_____
Investment Income			
Cash & Equivalents-(SCH 1)	_____	_____	_____
Dividends/(SCH 2A,3)	_____	_____	_____
Interest (SCH 2B,C, 4)	_____	_____	_____
Inv Real Estate (SCH 2D)	_____	_____	_____
LTD Partnerships (SCH 2E)	_____	_____	_____
Other (SCH 2F)	_____	_____	_____
Retirement Income	_____	_____	_____
Social Security Benefits	_____	_____	_____
Gifts	_____	_____	_____
Other	_____	_____	
Total Cash Inflow	$ _____	$ _____	100 %
Cash Outflow			
Basic Living Expenses:			
Housing (mort or rent) + taxes	$ _____	$ _____	_____ %
House Maintenance	_____	_____	_____
Food	_____	_____	_____
Transportation–Fuel & Maintenance	_____	_____	_____
Utilities	_____	_____	_____
Clothing	_____	_____	_____
Personal Care	_____	_____	_____
Medical–Uninsured	_____	_____	_____
Education	_____	_____	_____
Insurance Coverage:			
Life (Life Ins. Summary)	_____	_____	_____
Auto & Homeowners	_____	_____	_____
Disability	_____	_____	_____
Hospitalization	_____	_____	_____
Other	_____	_____	_____

FORM 8-1 *(continued)*

Debt Service:

  Auto Loans (SCH 5)

  Installment Loans (SCH 5)

  Ins. Loans (Life Ins. Summary)

  Personal Loans (SCH 5)

  Brokerage Margin Accts

Investment Expenses:

  Cash Expenses From Ind Inv
    Real Estate (SCH 2D)

  Notes, Loans From
    Partnerships (SCH 2E)

  Miscellaneous (SCH 2F)

Miscellaneous Expense Items:

  Child Support and Alimony

  Support of Other Dependents

  Charitable Contributions

  Travel & Vacations

  Entertainment

  Other

Income Taxes In Addition
  To Withholdings:

Fixed Savings:

Total Cash Outflow $ _____ $ _____   ___100_ %

Difference Equals Surplus (+)
or Shortage (−) $ __0__ $ __0__

FORM 8-2   MONTHLY BUDGET SHEET

	Planned	Actual	Variance
Cash Inflow			
Net Employment–His	$ _____	$ _____	_____ %
Hers	_____	_____	_____
Investment Income			
Cash & Equivalents	_____	_____	_____
Dividends	_____	_____	_____
Interest	_____	_____	_____
Inv Real Estate	_____	_____	_____
LTD Partnerships	_____	_____	_____
Other	_____	_____	_____
Retirement Income	_____	_____	_____
Social Security Benefits	_____	_____	_____
Gifts	_____	_____	_____
Other	_____	_____	_____
Total Cash Flow	$ _____	$ _____	_____ %
Cash Outflow			
Basic Living Expenses:			
Housing (mort or rent) + taxes	$ _____	$ _____	_____ %
House Maintenance	_____	_____	_____
Food	_____	_____	_____
Transportation–Fuel & Maintenance	_____	_____	_____
Utilities	_____	_____	_____
Clothing	_____	_____	_____
Personal Care	_____	_____	_____
Medical–Uninsured	_____	_____	_____
Education	_____	_____	_____
Insurance Coverage:			
Life	_____	_____	_____
Auto & Homeowners	_____	_____	_____
Disability	_____	_____	_____
Hospitalization	_____	_____	_____
Other	_____	_____	_____

FORM 8-2 (continued)

Debt Service:

   Auto Loans   _____   _____   _____
   Installment Loans   _____   _____   _____
   Ins. Loans   _____   _____   _____
   Personal Loans   _____   _____   _____
   Brokerage Margin Accts   _____   _____   _____

Investment Expenses:

   Cash Expenses From Ind Inv
      Real Estate   _____   _____   _____
   Notes, Loans From
      Partnerships   _____   _____   _____
   Miscellaneous   _____   _____   _____

Miscellaneous Expense Items:

   Child Support and Alimony   _____   _____   _____
   Support of Other Dependents _____   _____   _____
   Charitable Contributions   _____   _____   _____
   Travel & Vacations   _____   _____   _____
   Entertainment   _____   _____   _____
   Other   _____   _____   _____

Income Taxes In Addition
  To Withholdings: _____   _____   _____

Fixed Savings: _____   _____   _____

Total Cash Outflow $ _____ $ _____   _____ %

Difference Equals Surplus (+)
  or Shortage (−) $ __0__ $ _____

FORM 8-3   BUDGET VARIANCE

Month	Cash Inflow Above Expected Amount Reason Amount(+)	Cash Inflow Below Expected Amount Reason (Amount(−)	Cash Outflow Above Expected Amount Reason Amount(−)	Cash Outflow Below Expected Amount Reason Amount(+)	Net Variance To Be Adjusted Amount
January					
February					
March					
April					
May					
June					
July					
August					
September					
October					
November					
December					

FORM 8-4 BUDGET RECONCILIATION/END OF THE YEAR

	Planned Annual	Planned Percent	Actual Annual	Actual Percent	Dollar Variance	Percent Variance
Cash Inflow						
Net Employment–His	$ _____	_____ %	_____	_____ %	$ _____	_____ %
Hers	_____	_____	_____	_____	_____	_____
Investment Income						
Cash & Equivalents	_____	_____	_____	_____	_____	_____
Dividends	_____	_____	_____	_____	_____	_____
Interest	_____	_____	_____	_____	_____	_____
Inv Real Estate	_____	_____	_____	_____	_____	_____
LTD Partnerships	_____	_____	_____	_____	_____	_____
Other	_____	_____	_____	_____	_____	_____
Retirement Income	_____	_____	_____	_____	_____	_____
Social Security Benefits	_____	_____	_____	_____	_____	_____
Gifts	_____	_____	_____	_____	_____	_____
Other	_____	_____	_____	_____	_____	_____
Total Cash Inflow	$ _____	100 %	_____	_____ %	$ _____	_____ %
Cash Outflow						
Basic Living Expenses:						
Housing (mort or rent) + Taxes	$ _____	_____ %	_____	_____ %	$ _____	_____ %
House Maintenance	_____	_____	_____	_____	_____	_____
Food	_____	_____	_____	_____	_____	_____
Transportation–Fuel & Maintenance	_____	_____	_____	_____	_____	_____
Utilities	_____	_____	_____	_____	_____	_____
Clothing	_____	_____	_____	_____	_____	_____
Personal Care	_____	_____	_____	_____	_____	_____
Medical-Uninsured	_____	_____	_____	_____	_____	_____
Education	_____	_____	_____	_____	_____	_____

Insurance Coverage:
- Life
- Auto & Homeowners
- Disability
- Hospitalization
- Other

Debt Service:
- Auto Loans
- Installment Loans
- Ins. Loans
- Personal Loans
- Brokerage Margin Accts

Investment Expenses:
- Cash Expenses From Ind Inv
- Real Estate
- Notes, Loans From
- Partnerships
- Miscellaneous

Miscellaneous Expense Items:
- Child Support and Alimony
- Support of Other Dependents
- Charitable Contributions
- Travel & Vacations
- Entertainment
- Other

Income Taxes In Addition
To Withholdings:

Fixed Savings:

Total Cash Outflow $ _____ $ _____ 100 % $ _____ % $ _____ % _____ %

Difference Equals Surplus (+)
or Shortage (−) $ _____ 0 % $ _____ 0 % $ _____ % _____ %

- Set priorities for expenditures and see that the priorities are maintained, but do not try to account for every dollar spent.
- Maintain good records and keep the records current.

Use the following steps for controlling cash flow:

- Monthly expenditures should be outlined and written down (with a budgeting sheet for each month of the year).
- Total monthly income needed should be determined and a determination should be made of the portions of various income sources that will be needed for expenditures.
- Deposit employment, investment, and other investment checks in your checking account.
- As bills are paid monthly, record the expenditures and "close-out" each monthly budgeting sheet.
- In the process of closing out each month's budgeting sheet, determine excess cash flow amounts and make deposits to a special "control" account. We suggest a regular or tax-free money market fund (depending upon your marginal tax bracket).

FIGURE 8-1   INCOME SOURCES FLOW CHART

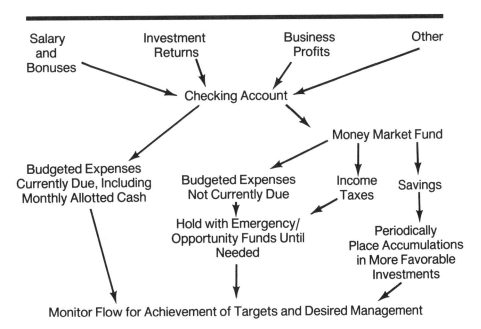

- Because expense timing will vary, amounts may have to be withdrawn from the "control" account and deposited in the checking account if income is insufficient for some months (including large living expenditures and taxes).
- Most variance should be predictable, and the variance should be noted at the time monthly income and expenditures are first outlined and written.
- If you find it more convenient, some major expenses such as education costs or tax payments can be paid directly from the money market fund but should be included in the summarization of total expenses.
- If convenient, automatic bill paying by your bank or financial institution may be appropriate.

A worksheet similar to that at the end of this chapter should be used to monitor the "control" account.

CASH AND CASH ACCOUNTS

Differentiate between expenses to be paid with cash and checks. Once a month, as income checks are being deposited at your bank, receive a portion of the checks in cash sufficient to pay all monthly cash expenses. Store the cash in a safe and convenient place at home with a listing or file system which allocates cash to the expenses. Some individuals, for security, may prefer to maintain only small cash balances. Adjust to your own comfort level. Do avoid, though, repeated bank trips and writing of "cash" checks as this can destroy the budgeting process and cause loss of cash flow control. To facilitate budgeting we encourage payment of the following types of expenses in cash:

- food purchases between major shopping trips;
- gasoline, parking, and other routine transportation expenses;
- spending money for all family members for personal needs;
- entertainment; and
- a small miscellaneous allotment.

Many couples prefer separate checking accounts to a joint checking account. Decide which you prefer and utilize the account(s) for bill paying. Make sure that all expenses are recorded as suggested, and in the event some privacy is desired, simply allocate an unnamed sum to each spouse, each month.

Banks generally offer a broader array of financial services than do savings and loan associations and credit unions, and hence, we favor use of bank checking accounts for bill paying (which will help establish banking relationships in the event loans or other services are needed). Credit union members may also keep a small interest paying share draft account to maintain access to other services such as favorable loan rates.

Carefully evaluate the choice between a free, noninterest checking account and a free, interest-bearing checking account. While free and interest bearing suggest immediate appeal, this is not necessarily the best choice. Most interest bearing checking accounts pay about 5 1/2 percent interest and require minimum balance deposits in low yielding accounts. Loss of investment earnings from better yielding investments (opportunity cost) may outweigh charges which would be incurred monthly on a free, noninterest bearing checking account. Estimate foregone earnings on your best investment alternative if minimum deposits are required and compare this to fees on a noninterest bearing account. Choose the option with the lower cost.

If you establish an interest-bearing account and minimum balance requirements are not maintained, fees will be assessed. Banks are increasingly assessing fees for various services, including in many instances use of automatic tellers. Include evaluation of various fees in comparing banks. Seek to minimize your incurrence of fees.

Additional cash type accounts (i.e., funds which are very liquid) we recommend are money market mutual funds—regular, taxable funds for low and moderate tax bracket taxpayers, and tax-free money market funds for high marginal bracket taxpayers. Banks also offer money market type accounts (which are often insured) with interest in excess of passbook accounts. However, we favor money market funds because:

- Interest rates are usually higher with money market mutual funds.
- Funds are managed by professional money managers.
- There is value for cash control where separateness and different access is involved.
- Funds often can be easily transferred (by phone, etc.) to other types of mutual funds such as growth funds.
- Check writing privileges are available and often unlimited.
- Even though often uninsured, loss of funds is unlikely because of the wide diversification of money market funds.

The money market fund should be used to maintain emergency/opportunity funds (typically 10 percent to 20 percent of annual income requirements), store funds for later expenditures or tax payments, and be a conduit or "control" account for transferring savings to investments. Amounts above emergency/opportunity levels, plus upcoming expenditures and taxes for which money market withdrawals will be needed, should be placed about every four to six months in new investments in line with investment strategies. A proper balance level should be maintained (and replaced when depleted) to meet unexpected expenditures or to participate on short notice in good investment opportunities.

It may be advantageous to establish two money market funds. One for emergency/opportunity funds and later expenditures. The other to be used exclusively for long-term savings.

In selecting a money market fund, become aware of the more progressive funds which offer services such as monthly budgeting summaries, and debit cards.

Banks have had many restrictions lifted and are offering new services at a very rapid rate. Periodically check with your banker about service additions. Two services we like, in particular, are unsecured lines of credit with check writing privileges and discount stock brokerage services.

A personal line of credit should be retained (without cost) so that, if needed, more funds will be available without time delay and investments with favorable returns will not have to be liquidated. If exercised, the credit line should be repaid from cash inflows over the next several months following exercise.

Discount stock brokerage firms offer services, excluding research and specific stock recommendations, at commission rates substantially below rates charged by traditional brokerage firms. If obtained through your bank, transactions (including securities sales, purchases, interest payments and dividend receipts) can automatically flow through your checking account.

USING DEBT

Two closely related principles of successful money management are "leverage" and "using other people's money." Leverage means to borrow money and put the money to work so that investment return exceeds borrowing costs. The value of using other people's money is twofold; you do not tie up your own funds, and you generate a much greater amount of working capital which allows for achievement of objectives either not obtainable or obtainable over a much longer time period if you rely solely on your own capital.

We recommend balanced debt usage. That is, do not under-utilize or over-utilize debt. The proper balance is dependent on your situation and needs, including repayments which fit into your budget without interfering with savings. To go strictly on a cash basis severely limits progress towards financial security. Excessive debt causes "cash drains" and blocks the potential for transferring cash inflow to investments.

Recognizing personal goals and financial objectives, carefully self-determine right and wrong reasons for borrowing and in doing so realize that investment return can come in many forms:

- Borrowed funds placed in investments can generate interest, dividends, tax savings, and capital appreciation.
- Borrowed funds used for direct expenses, or to facilitate general living expenses, can allow an individual to pursue opportunities such as career or business development which will produce higher future earnings.
- Nonfinancial personal goals, such as helping others or changing circumstances or self improvement, can ultimately lead to better self feelings resulting in greater productivity and money earnings.
- Timing expense payments such as insurance premiums, charge account balances, and taxes can result in investment returns from temporary placement of funds in investments until payment must be made.

Try to clearly understand direct investment returns, which are easily measured, and indirect investment returns which are subjective and difficult to measure and decide whether or not return will exceed interest costs. For example:

If $10,000 is borrowed at 12 percent interest for two years and the funds are placed in an investment which produces appreciation (capital gains) of 20 percent per year and you are in the 40 percent marginal tax bracket you will gain $2,256 over two years.

Appreciated Investment Value	$14,400
Less Long-Term Capital Gains Tax	−704
Net On Liquidation	$13,696
Less After Tax Interest Costs	−1,440
Less Principal Repayment	−10,000
Net Gain	$2,256

If you borrow $15,000 for career training at 12 percent interest per year which will result in average annual earnings $10,000 above what you would otherwise make over the next 25 years, take 5 years to repay the money, and are in the 40 percent marginal tax bracket, this would result in a present value gain of $132,000.

Present Value of Additional Earnings (after tax) (assuming 8 percent inflation and 8 percent discount)	$150,000
Less After Tax Interest Costs	−3,000
Less Principal Repayment	−15,000
Net Gain	$132,000

Typically, we find the following types of debt acceptable and appropriate for most individuals:

- home and vacation home mortgage financing;
- automobile purchase;
- short-term emergency type borrowing;
- commitment to investments or tax sheltering where return will exceed debt cost or cash flow and tax savings will be sufficient to finance debt payments or commitments;
- low-cost student loans; and
- financing a business enterprise.

Other forms of debt may or may not be appropriate depending upon personal circumstances. Of course, interest rate levels and cash outflow impacts of debt repayments are important determining factors of debt use. The higher the level of interest the more difficult it is to gain from debt use. Do seek the lowest interest possible and check as many sources of funds as possible.

Debt repayment should not become so burdensome that living standard, savings, or tax payments are jeopardized. In the event of over-extension, debt consolidation and extended repayment may be prudent. Do anticipate the flow of repayment and realize that judgment must be made of the probability that expected future cash inflows will actually be received. Risk acceptance is a personal matter and depends on tolerance and comfort, and consequences of unsuccessful plans should be thought through completely before implementation.

Develop summaries for debt usage which may apply to you and keep these thoughts in mind:

- Understand how debt and repayment works.
- Know the difference between simple interest and compound interest debt.
- Comparison shop debt sources.
- Stay current on interest rate levels and determine when refinancing may be appropriate.
- Stay abreast of the many new sources and forms of debt (check with banks, other financial institutions, financial centers, etc.).
- Continually update your knowledge of investment alternatives and the many forms of investment returns.
- Monitor your progress toward achievement of financial objectives and the role debt might play at different times.
- Make sure to maintain good records of debt use.
- Always know your current debt level.
- Do not purchase "credit life insurance" (decreasing term insurance) because it is usually expensive, instead cover (if needed) death debt repayment with straight term life insurance and include debt amounts in determining your total needs for life insurance.
- Minimize credit card debt and other expensive forms of debt.

TABLE 8-1 AFTER TAX INTEREST RATE ON DEBT

Interest	Marginal Tax Bracket							
Interest Rate (%)	15%	20%	25%	30%	35%	40%	45%	50%
6	5.1	4.8	4.5	4.2	3.9	3.6	3.3	3.0
8	6.8	6.4	6.0	5.6	5.2	4.8	4.4	4.0
10	8.5	8.0	7.5	7.0	6.5	6.0	5.5	5.0
12	10.2	9.6	9.0	8.4	7.8	7.2	6.6	6.0
14	11.9	11.2	10.5	9.8	9.1	8.4	7.7	7.0
16	13.6	12.8	12.0	11.2	10.4	9.6	8.8	8.0
18	15.3	14.4	13.5	12.6	11.7	10.8	9.9	9.0
20	17.0	16.0	15.0	14.0	13.0	12.0	11.0	10.0
22	18.7	17.6	16.5	15.4	14.3	13.2	12.1	11.0
24	20.4	19.2	18.0	16.8	15.6	14.4	13.2	12.0

**MAJOR
EXPENSES AND
EXPENSE
REDUCTION**

Wealth building is a function of income generation and expense management producing savings, which in turn must be successfully invested. Over time, then, reliance on earned income such as salary and bonuses can be shifted to passive income from investments. Effective expense management is a combination of properly planning and choosing expense incurrence, optimally financing major expenses, and the summation impact of many minor expense savings. The cumulative results of what often appears to be minor expense savings can be substantial and build as investments do on a compound basis. Sample practices for reducing expenses include:

• buying the lowest cost insurance protections;
• avoiding commission expenses on placing investment dollars;
• being highly selective in purchasing goods and services and purchasing quality;
• "bartering" where profitable;
• deferring taxes and paying with cheaper dollars in the future;
• timing purchases for sales; and
• coordinating family purchases and knowing exactly what is needed.

Often, too, people fail to perceive the benefits of eliminating indirect expenses; particularly as related to time. Successful people understand time management and view time commitments in terms of income and expense. Inefficiencies can be eliminated by using concise sources of information for decision making. Cash outlays for professional services or materials and publications can result in savings many times over. The outlays should be viewed as

FIGURE 8–2

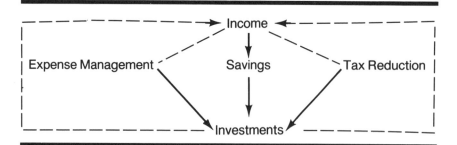

investments which produce future expense savings such as avoidance of poor investment decisions or unnecessary overpayments for taxes or financial products. Time is a very costly commitment today. In this "do-it-yourself" society large expenses can be incurred because of lost work time, where one is most effective. Concentrating on professional expertise and earning money can produce returns far above what it might cost to hire labor or services. Do take control and understand activities in your life but delegate functions where profitable.

Optimal financing of major expenses, which includes getting the best price for a decided purchase, should be viewed with integration of other planning areas. In determining methods for payment and financing of major expenses, investigate the opportunities and/or impacts on cash flow management, income tax planning, investment planning, and insurances and estate planning. Ask yourself:

Cash Flow Management

- How will the expenditure impact your budget?
- What time period is involved or available and how should the expense be planned?
- What sources of debt financing are available and at what cost?

Income Tax Planning

- Do opportunities for "income shifting" for tax reduction exist in financing the expenditures?
- Will liquidation of investments for expenditures trigger income taxation; how much?
- If debt is used, what is the net after tax cost of deductible interest?
- Are tax favorable sources of debt financing available such as your pension plan or profit sharing plan?
- How much in gross income, before taxes, must be earned to finance expenditures?

Investment Planning

- What impact will the expenditure have on your savings flow?
- Should investments be liquidated?

- How will other objectives be affected if investments are liquidated?
- If investments are to be liquidated, what is the proper timing and form of liquidation?
- Is their value in setting up and segregating sources of investment income for certain expenses?
- Are unique investment related sources of debt such as borrowing or brokerage accounts available?
- Which investment media should be sought for different types of funds accumulation, different individuals, and during different economic time periods?

Insurances and Estate Planning

- Can and should future expense contingencies be covered by insurance?

FIGURE 8-3

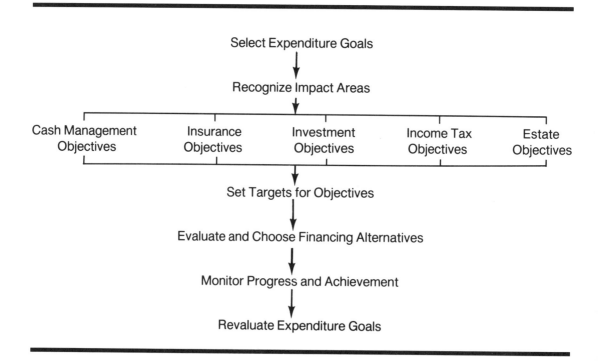

Select Expenditure Goals

Recognize Impact Areas

| Cash Management Objectives | Insurance Objectives | Investment Objectives | Income Tax Objectives | Estate Objectives |

Set Targets for Objectives

Evaluate and Choose Financing Alternatives

Monitor Progress and Achievement

Revaluate Expenditure Goals

- How are contingent money management, expense management, and asset distribution best included in estate documents?
- In the event of death, who will be responsible for future, family expense management?
- Have preparations been made for death expenses and debts?

Upon selection and prioritization of expenditure goals, determine impact areas and set targets for the objectives. Accumulation and allocation of funds will be needed along with timing of expense payouts. Even if funds are already available, the best source of financing must still be determined. Debt financing may be optimal in certain circumstances. Chapters 12 and 13 contain recommendations and planning tools necessary for structuring and achieving financial targets.

Multiple goals are usually sought simultaneously and you must figure dollar application to goals so that priorities can be made and contingencies can be planned. Necessary expenses must be funded before discretionary expenses but many options are available. For example, for both financial and nonfinancial reasons, many people prefer to own a home rather than to rent one. Because of tax write-offs and possible appreciation, people often feel owning is preferable. In fact, owning (particularly during high interest rate periods) is often more expensive, even on a net after tax basis, than renting. Although owning does provide a form of forced savings for many people. While we concur with nonfinancial reasons for home ownership, we do not view home ownership as an investment. Cash outflows can be significant and the market for homes can be volatile. Renting may allow for achievement of other goals not otherwise achievable if a home is purchased.

The example in Figure 8–4 would result in about $1,450 of funds available for application to other goals if a home were rented rather than purchased.

A major expense faced by many families is the cost of educating children. We can analyze possible funding to demonstrate the techniques involved in planning and financing major expenditures. Similar analysis would be applicable to most other goals (such as retirement, travel, career development, home purchase, etc.), with variations depending upon the goals and time allotted to achievement. Assume you have a three-year-old child and you wish to plan college funding. Furthermore, you expect four years of college, which in today's dollars will average $6,000 per year.

FIGURE 8-4   RENT VS BUY

($75,000 home purchase with 20 percent down and 13 percent mortgage – 40 percent tax bracket – or rent for $625 per month)

Annual Rent	$7,500
Renters Insurance	150
Opportunity Cost of Principal (1)	0
	$7,650 (2)
Annual Net after Tax Interest	$4,680
Property Taxes (Net of Income Tax Deduction)	1,500
Homeowners Insurance	375
Opportunity Cost of Principal (1)	1,050
Annual Maintenance and Upkeep	1,500
	$9,105 (2)

(1) Assumes investment return of 15 percent available on alternative investments in contrast to assumed 8 percent housing appreciation, for annual spread of 7 percent.

(2) Excludes impact of principal payments on debt, which could be placed in alternative investments.

Inflate the expenses (let's assume 7 percent per year inflation).

Year	Cost
2000	$ 8,300 ($\frac{1}{2}$ year)
2001	17,700
2002	19,000
2003	20,300
2004	10,800 ($\frac{1}{2}$ year)
Total	$76,100

If you wish to accumulate enough funds by the time the child begins college to finance the costs, the assumed return on investments must be decided. Using tables in Chapter 13 we can figure the following.

	8 Percent Net Annual Investment Return	12 Percent Net Annual Investment Return
Lump sum investment needed today	$24,000	$13,900
Equal annual savings amount	$ 2,800	$ 2,000
Beginning annual savings if savings increase 5 percent per year	$ 1,900	$ 1,400
Beginning annual savings if savings increase 10 percent per year	$ 1,400	$ 1,000

Given the time factors and investment return alternatives, decisions can be made for optimal financing based on personal financial

FORM 8–5 ALLOCATION OF FUNDS/YEAR

Major Goals	1	2	3	4	5	6	7	8	9	10
	$	$	$	$	$	$	$	$	$	$
Total	$	$	$	$	$	$	$	$	$	$

FORM 8-6   ANNUAL REVIEW OF ACCUMULATIONS TO DATE

Major Goals	Amount	Investment Placement
	$	
Total	$	

condition, the importance of other goals, and the impact and/or opportunities of other financial planning areas. For example, "income shifting" alternatives and other tax reduction possibilities are discussed later in this book as related to financing major expenditures. After applying numbers to the goals, review again the questions related to the financial planning and objective areas before deciding upon your strategy.

There is no prescription for allocating funds to personal goals that is appropriate for everyone. Goal setting is a very subjective process, and only you can determine what is and is not a priority. Planning and implementing decisions will put you on a course towards accomplishing the many goals which you desire to achieve.

Periodically measure and monitor your progress and reallocate funds or change strategies as conditions change using Forms 8–5 and 8–6.

Sample Uses of Table 8–2

1. Monthly payment on a loan

    PAYMENT = LOAN × FACTOR

TABLE 8-2   FACTORS FOR DETERMINING MONTHLY PAYMENT OF PRINCIPAL AND INTEREST IF INTEREST IS CHARGED ON THE UNPAID BALANCE

Interest Rate(%)	Years											
	1	2	3	4	5	10	15	20	25	30	35	40
6	.088	.044	.030	.023	.019	.011	.00844	.00716	.006443	.005996	.005702	.005502
8	.090	.045	.031	.024	.020	.012	.00956	.00836	.007718	.007338	.007103	.006953
10	.092	.046	.032	.025	.021	.013	.01075	.00965	.009087	.008776	.008597	.008491
12	.093	.047	.033	.026	.022	.014	.01200	.01101	.010532	.010286	.010156	.010085
14	.095	.048	.034	.027	.023	.015	.01332	.01244	.012038	.011849	.011757	.011711
16	.097	.049	.035	.028	.024	.016	.01469	.01391	.013589	.013448	.013385	.013356
18	.098	.050	.036	.029	.025	.018	.01610	.01543	.015174	.015071	.015029	.015012
20	.100	.051	.037	.030	.026	.019	.01756	.01699	.016785	.016710	.016683	.016673
22	.102	.052	.038	.031	.027	.021	.01906	.01857	.018412	.018360	.018342	.018336
24	.103	.053	.039	.032	.029	.022	.02058	.02017	.020053	.020016	.020005	.020001

2. Amount which can be financed based on given payment level

$$\text{LOAN} = \frac{\text{PAYMENT}}{\text{FACTOR}}$$

3. Period of time it will take to pay off a loan balance

    (a) $\text{FACTOR} = \dfrac{\text{PAYMENT}}{\text{LOAN}}$

    (b) YEARS = FIND INTEREST RATE ROW AND LOOK ACROSS TO FIND FACTOR, THEN YEARS COLUMN HEADING

4. Maximum interest rate which can be afforded for a loan with a given payment level.

    (a) $\text{FACTOR} = \dfrac{\text{PAYMENT}}{\text{LOAN}}$

    (b) INTEREST RATE = FIND YEARS COLUMN AND LOOK DOWN TO FIND FACTOR, THEN INTEREST RATE ROW HEAD- ING

SAVINGS FLOW

The patterns of living expenses, taxes, and savings illustrated in Figure 8–5 are common for many people. Savings should not be negative (cash outflow exceeding cash inflow). Every attempt should be made to save, even if a small monthly amount is actually saved. As income increases, savings should also rise, although increases may be relatively low during high expense years and accelerate thereafter until retirement. The higher savings are and the more rapidly the rate increases, the better. Realize, though, that the Figure 8–5 depicts savings flow and periodically savings accumulations may have to be liquidated to meet major expense goals.

Try to increase your savings flow level and accelerate it over time. To accomplish this, you must understand whether or not you are good at voluntary (or nonforced) savings, and the techniques

FIGURE 8-5   SAVINGS FLOW

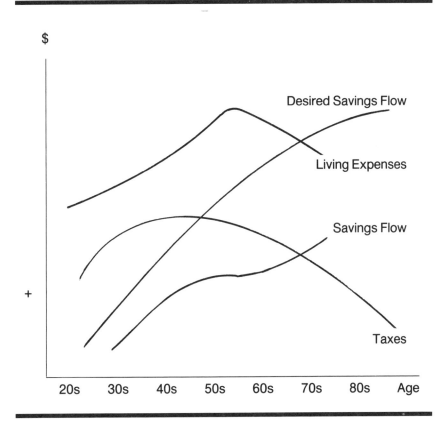

available to you to increase savings and integrate savings with other financial planning areas.

Alter your method of savings to meet your needs and personal characteristics. If you have not previously been a good saver, force yourself to save by writing a check for deposit to a money market fund each month before you pay any bills or spend money on yourself. You will be surprised at the small recognizable effect this will have on your life style.

Create base levels of income and other sources of income. For example, if you are an employee of an organization, do not seek all compensation in the form of regular salary. Request that your employer structure your income as a combination of salary/bonus, salary/commission, or other incentive system. Emphasize cash pay and direct investment compensation (stock options, stock rewards, etc.).

Save part of the base salary income and most of the other employment income. Payroll deductions and commitments to qualified retirement plans and stock purchase arrangements and other appropriate investments can generate "forced savings," especially valuable if you have difficulty saving.

Self-employed individuals have the ability to structure personal income any way they prefer. If you are self-employed, do not draw out most income on a regular basis. Take a base income for living expenses and accumulate balances for later bonus payments, qualified plan contributions, or additional business investing.

Also look for favorable structuring of investment income for additional savings. Dividends and interest payments on many investments can be automatically reinvested so that checks are not personally received.

Seek savings forms which will allow not only for accumulation of funds but will also accomplish multiple objectives such as income tax reduction and investment portfolio development. Examples are:

• Participation in employer sponsored programs which reduce taxes, like deferred compensation plans and qualified thrift plans.
• Making voluntary contributions to programs such as corporate pension plans, which will not provide immediate tax write-offs but will allow for tax deferral and compounded investment earnings.
• Maximizing contributions to company sponsored matching programs, like stock purchase plans that call for contributions from the employer based on employee contributions.
• Special tax deductible and tax deferred annuities for teachers and health care workers.

Payroll deductions and other forms of forced savings may be worthwhile even if available investment options are not exactly what you seek. For example, we find Series E Government Bonds to be an unattractive investment alternative. However, regular purchases can accomplish forced savings and the bonds can be periodically liquidated with proceeds placed in more favorable investments. So, too, can periodic repositioning be applied to other forms of savings/investments (credit union deposits, etc.) to meet investment objectives.

Learn what special rules and opportunities apply to you to increase savings and remember that savings comes in many forms, including:

- direct cash savings;
- income tax reduction;
- expense reduction;
- time management; and
- appropriate investment selection.

Regularly monitor your savings rate and flow of savings and at least annually revaluate the application to and progress towards chosen goals.

INCOME SOURCES

Income may come in several forms. Everyone's situation is unique and, therefore, the budgeting process should include a specialized allocation of income to expenses, savings, and taxes. Increasing savings leads to financial independence and ultimately to reliance on investment or passive income sources.

As mentioned before, temporary expense increases to change personal circumstances or qualifications can lead to higher incomes just as building wealth will result in higher income and standard of living potential.

Sort out current sources of income and clearly understand where the sources flow as well as the relative importance of each of the various sources. Determine the best means of directing sources to budget allocations and know your alternatives for managing income sources; such as:

- structuring timing of sources;
- automatic deposits to bank accounts and investments;
- reinvestment of investment distributions;
- taxation differences for various forms of income receipt;
- use of cash management systems offered by financial institutions; and
- the extent to which you can afford to participate in payroll savings/deduction plans.

Find which sources and flows of income work best for you. This will require some budget adjustments over time.

Plan future sources of income and levels of income you should realistically seek. Continually evaluate options with respect to future income and integrate all your planning needs and objectives. Ask the following types of questions in your evaluation:

- Given two job alternatives, which will produce or lead to more income and satisfaction in the long-run? Do not make your decision solely on the basis of short-term factors.
- Should you seek taxable or tax-free investment income? Make your decision on the basis of net after-tax considerations.
- Do you need management of your income sources? If so, how can the sources best be managed and monitored?
- How long will certain types of income sources be needed?
- How will inflation impact your income needs and sources?
- If you seek fixed income investment sources, will some funds also be placed in growth investments?
- Do you know what dollar accumulation targets are needed to generate desired levels of income?
- If career moves (job changes or business start-ups) are going to be pursued, do you know ahead of time how you will finance yourself?
- Do second jobs really result in more income for you or result in reduced productivity (because of lack of relaxation)?
- Are you aware of the "opportunity cost" of each income decision?

Plan future income needs and make investment decisions based on present value evaluation. Using tables in Chapters 11 and 13, the following two examples demonstrate this technique.

Suppose you are planning retirement 15 years from now and estimate that you will need to have $25,000 of investment income per year in today's dollars and have this income increase by 5 percent per year during retirement. How much must you save in each of the next 15 years to meet your retirement objective if you are expected to live 20 years after retirement?

- $25,000 (with 5 percent annual inflation) will have an equivalent of $52,000 per year income in 15 years.
- $52,000 increasing 5 percent per year during retirement will require a capital accumulation of $805,500 at retirement (assuming liquidation of principal over retirement and investment earnings of 8 percent on the nonliquidated principal balances).

- To accumulate this amount you will need to save:

	8% Annual Net Investment Return	12% Annual Net Investment Return
Equal annual savings	$29,700	$21,500
First year savings with savings increasing 5 percent per year	$20,500	$14,800
First year savings with savings increasing 10 percent per year	$14,900	$11,100

Suppose you are about to retire and you have three alternatives, from which you must decide, for receipt of your pension funds. Your life expectancy is 15 years and your spouse's life expectancy is 20 years.

- $100,000 lump sum immediate distribution after taxes.
- $1,000 per month life annuity (payable for your life only) after taxes.
- $900 per month 50% joint and survivor annuity ($900 per month payable to you during your lifetime and $450 per month payable to your spouse following your death) after taxes.

	Present Value (Discounted 8%)	Present Value (Discounted 12%)
Lump sum	$100,000	$100,000
Life annuity	$102,700	$ 81,700
50 Percent Joint annuity	$ 99,200	$ 77,100

The higher the investment return you feel you could earn if a lump sum distribution were made, the more favorable that option becomes. Realize, that if you were to select a life annuity and die prematurely, the present value of this choice would be significantly less as heirs would receive no additional pay out. If you were to outlive your life expectancy, the present value would be higher as you would collect benefits for a longer period of time. Similar thought, with inclusion for your spouse, applies to the joint and survivor annuity. Therefore, health, family history, life expectancy, and possible investment return must be evaluated in determining which option should be chosen. On balance, in this case, the lump sum distribution may be the best alternative.

Strategic thinking is extremely important in setting up income sources and flexibility should be retained to the extent reasonable and possible. This will allow you more options availability. Use Form 8–7 to help you.

IMPORTANT CASH MANAGEMENT QUESTIONS

- Do you stay current by reading information on cash management?
- Do you know percentages of total cash inflow which are represented by each inflow source?

FORM 8-7   STRATEGIC PLANNING

Income		Income Application			
Source	Amount	Living Expenses	Debt Payments	Income Taxes	Savings
	$	$	$	$	$
Total	$	$	$	$	$

FIGURE 8-6

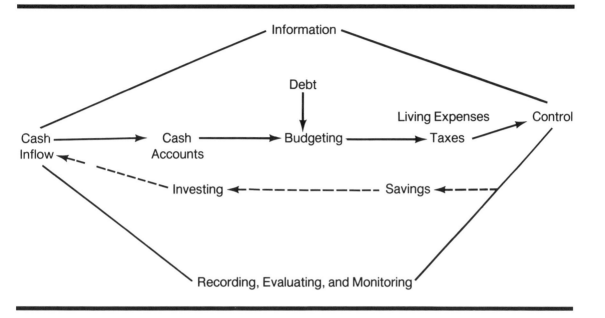

- How will you increase your income in each of the next several years?
- What type of cash accounts are best for you?
- How much actual cash do you spend per month?
- How is income transferred to savings and then to investments?
- How much debt should you use?
- What portion of monthly income goes toward debt repayment?
- How will you reduce income taxes in each of the next several years?
- How should your investment planning be integrated with cash inflow needs?
- Can you account for living expense outflows?
- Is your budgeting process excessively detailed and time consuming?
- What steps do you intend to take to control living expenses and taxes and increase your savings rate?
- Have you designated savings for different financial objectives to achieve goals?

- Is your record keeping such that you can find answers to questions quickly?
- How often do you evaluate your cash management system?
- What steps do you take to monitor cash inflow and outflow?
- How do you decide questions or make choices with respect to cash inflows and cash outflows?

FORM 8-8 MONEY MARKET CONTROL ACCOUNT

| Month | Account Balance | | | Inflows into Money Market Account | | | Outflows from Money Market Account | | |
	Beginning Balance	Ending Balance	Net Change	Salary & Deposits	Investment Liquidations	Account Yield	Investment Purchases	Major Expenses & Taxes	Misc.
January	$	$	$	$	$	$	$	$	$
February									
March									
April									
May									
June									
July									
August									
September									
October									
November									
December									
Total			$	$	$	$	$	$	$

9

PURCHASING INSURANCE

"More people should learn to tell their dollars where to go instead of asking them where they went."

Roger Babson

We have a client who was paying about $9,000 per year for a one million dollar "Adjustable Life" insurance contract. It's quite possible that about $8,000 of the first year's premium went to agent and general agent commissions, with annual residual commissions of about $1,500. That is a lot of money for selling one insurance policy. The client was able to replace the coverage with term insurance for a first year premium of about $1,500. We expect that he will need substantial life insurance coverage for only about five more years as his net worth is increasing each year and his obligations to dependents are decreasing.

The insurance industry has become immensely competitive as financial services have been expanded by many types of institutions. Product names are confusing and agents are hungry for business. True commissions often are not disclosed.

The person who overinsures can be as vulnerable from an inefficient planning point of view as the person who underinsures.

Insurance protection relates closely to the financial areas of cash flow management, investment planning, and estate planning. Excessive premiums because of high-priced policy purchases or over-protection deplete cash flow revenues and inhibit savings ability and net worth growth. Inadequate insurance protection exposes families to large and unnecessary asset losses and greatly jeopardizes family security and future income.

Form 9–1 is a summary designed to help you survey your exposure to insurable risk. The objective of reviewing insurance coverages is to enable you to implement a total insurance program, which fits your comfort levels, maximizes the utility of premium dollars, and minimizes—in a relative sense—economic loss. Remember that financial decisions always have opportunity cost. To purchase more insurance means something else must be given up. Also, risk management areas are interrelated. For example, an individual

FORM 9–1 INSURABLE RISK EXPOSURE SURVEY

		Potential Losses			
		Covered by			
	Life and Health Insurance		Property Insurance		Liability Insurance
Description	Yes/No Coverage	Description	Yes/No Coverage	Description	Yes/No Coverage
Life —Him	————	Home-Owners	————	Auto Liab.	————
Life —Her	————	Renters	————	Homeowners Liability	————
Life —Children	————	Contents	————	Unbrella Liability	————
Disability —Him	————	Scheduled Property	————		
Disability —Her	————	Auto	————		
Hospitalization	————	Aircraft	————		
Major Medical	————	Boat	————		
Dental	————	Flood	————		
Soc. or Gov. Ins.	————	Earthquake	————		

who is inadequately insured may tend to avoid sound growth investments because of fear of investment loss. Whereas, if that individual had adequate insurance protection, prudent investment growth could be sought and progress made towards true financial security. Accepted risks which are inconsistent with risk tolerance (or comfort) levels and/or out of line with financial goals and objectives create problems and poor results.

INSURANCE MYTHS

Insurance is a greatly misunderstood financial product. Policies are complex and confusing and great variation between policies exist. Some of the myths we encounter in working with individuals are listed next.

Myth   My personal insurance from four ordinary life policies of $50,000 plus group insurance of $100,000 should be sufficient to provide my wife and children a life style with which they are accustomed; age 40, earning $50,000 per year, with a small investment portfolio.

Fact   Many people are significantly under-insured; with inflation and increased longevity, capital requirements to support family income needs are very high today; and often financial programs such as pension plans do not pay off in the event of early death.

Myth   I have $100,000 of life insurance protection, all of which is ordinary life.

Fact   You have something less than $100,000 of insurance protection because the cash value portion of the $100,000 increases over time and actual insurance decreases; many people confuse risk and mortality elements with investment characteristics of ordinary life insurance.

Myth   The chances of becoming disabled are extremely low.

Fact   Unfortunately the disability rate is high (and exceeds the death rate before age 65) and disabilities often last an extended period of time.

Myth   Good health insurance coverage is too expensive to purchase individually.

Fact   Comprehensive major medical coverages insuring catastrophic illness are available at reasonable premium prices. (Often individuals who are not covered by employer sponsored plans can obtain policies through various types of groups and associations.)

Myth   My exposure to liability is minimal and I am already covered through my automobile insurance.

Fact   Exposure to liability is high and increasing with time as more law suits are being filed and juries and courts are awarding large settlements; automobile and homeowners liability protections are generally insufficient.

Myth   The best insurance coverage of any type is the most comprehensive.

Fact   It may be prudent to accept high deductibles on certain types of coverage (such as collision on auto policies) to reduce premium expenses and free up dollars for other risk protection alternatives.

INSURANCE PROTECTION

Insurance needs, like most financial needs, are unique to personal situations. Some individuals may need highly specialized insurance. An athlete, for example, may appropriately purchase special "career" insurance. Most people, however, do not need specialized insurance protection and waste money by purchasing it. Duplicating insurance protection or purchasing protection on remote occurrences is also wasteful. Examples of typically unnecessary insurance include: credit life insurance, credit card insurance, accidental death insurance, IRS audit insurance, cancer insurance, and job protection insurance. Sometimes coverages such as rental car insurance may also be unnecessary. To avoid excessive insurance premium expenditures, know your needs for insurance well, and know the exact coverages provided by the policies you purchase. If, for example, you are single and have no dependents, it is unlikely that you need life insurance, but you do need other forms of insurance. The less you spend on insurance, the more you can save and invest for financial security.

Terminate unnecessary insurance coverages. Again, review funding analyses in Chapter 5. If you show surpluses for either disability or estate funding, you may have life or disability insurance policies which you no longer need.

Basic personal insurance coverages which most individuals and families need are:

- life insurance;
- disability income insurance;
- health insurance;

- automobile insurance;
- homeowners insurance; and
- umbrella liability insurance.

Other types of insurance such as worker's compensation insurance or Social Security insurance are provided for by, or in conjunction with, employers and are mandatory according to state/federal laws. FDIC insurance on bank deposits, federal insurance on defined benefit pensions, and insurance protecting securities held by brokerage firms are examples of insurances which are important but not individually purchased. Be careful of new insurance "schemes." Many fraudulent and deceptive types of insurance have been sold to consumers. Make sure you deal with financially solvent companies and reputable agents.

Know the cost/benefit ratios on insurance coverages which you do own and need. Comparison shop insurance to get the best buy for your money and do so at least every few years. Look for special cost discounts, such as nonsmoker rates for life and disability insurance and various fire prevention techniques for homeowners insurance. Purchase new replacement insurance before you cancel old policies to be certain that you are insurable and that no lapses in coverage occur. Be very truthful and understand contestability in policies—a company's right to contest coverage if information provided at purchase time was not accurate. You may not be able to use cheaper insurance in some instances because of insurability problems. For example, too many traffic violations may exclude you from consideration by other good automobile insurance companies or deterioration in your health may make you uninsurable for new health, life, or disability insurance policies. In these instances, retain needed coverage even if it is expensive.

In shopping for various insurance policies, compare both individual purchase rates and available group rates. Some employers sponsor group plans through which employees may purchase additional life, disability, and health insurance—some even offer automobile and homeowners insurance. Professional and other types of organizations also sponsor group insurance policies. Group insurance policies have traditionally provided consumers the lowest cost form of insurance (and often people uninsurable for individual policies can obtain coverage through group policies). Interestingly, though, some individual policy rates are now lower than group rates because of increased competition in the insurance industry.

Insurance is available from many sources, in addition to traditional agents. Some insurance companies are offering "no-load" (no sales commission) policies for consumers who bypass agents and purchase directly from the company. Department stores, grocery stores, credit card companies, brokerage firms, banks, and other financial conglomerates now offer insurance. Check the various sources which are available to you. When purchasing through an agent, select an independent agent representing many companies, not an agent affiliated only with one company.

Accurately segregate financial planning area decisions even with consideration for the interrelations. Do not confuse objectives with integration of areas. For example, some individuals deposit money at credit unions because the credit unions will provide an equal amount of "free" life insurance. This often, in fact, is expensive insurance because of foregone investment return on investment alternatives which provide much better return.

Depending on your level of financial well being, it may be prudent in some instances to not formally insure, or not insure some portions of, insurable risks. "Self-funding," especially in a precautionary nature with money set aside, in lieu of purchasing insurance policies may be more favorable. If a loss does occur you will have to absorb it personally, but factors such as investment return on funds set aside and invested prior to loss and possible tax write-offs may offset losses.

Life Insurance

The major reason for life insurance purchase should be income security for dependents, so that their future expenditures will be met in the event of the provider's death. Individuals, without dependents, rarely need life insurance. Chapter 5 includes an estate funding analysis to determine appropriate insurance amounts. Deficits in estate funding should be made up with additional life insurance protection, until additional assets are accumulated.

The need for life insurance normally decreases as net worth increases and dependents get older.

A secondary reason for life insurance purchase is to assure estate liquidity at death—the availability, without adverse asset sales, of cash to pay death taxes and expenses. With current federal estate tax laws, most estates (especially on the first death of spouses) do not incur federal estate taxes. Proper estate planning reduces estate taxes and expenses. Estates that will incur large federal estate taxes usually have adequate assets to provide estate liquidity. Estate liquidity, in most instances, is no longer a major reason for life insurance purchase. If assets are to be preserved for children and other heirs, then insurance may be desired to pay death expenses.

Families dependent on two incomes should consider life insurance on both income earners (or spouses). Families dependent mainly on one income should consider life insurance only on the life of that income earner. Insurance on the lives of nonincome earning spouses or children is rarely a worthwhile expenditure.

Do not purchase whole life or cash value of any type—ordinary life, endowment, limited pay life, universal life, etc. Two old arguments presented in favor of cash value insurance are "forced savings" and lifetime insurance expenses. If you need "forced savings" more profitable methods are available. Agents and life insurance company representatives sometimes state that over a lifetime, whole life insurance is cheaper than term insurance. Whole life premium rates usually remained fixed while term rates increase with age. Nevertheless, competition in the industry has forced term rates down to a point such that for most people term is in fact cheaper if insurance is kept in force for life (especially when time value of money and investment return alternatives are considered). Furthermore, most people do not need to retain life insurance coverage for their whole life. The need occurs mainly in high financial responsibility years.

People who have either outdated term insurance or whole life policies should keep the insurance in force, if insurance is needed, until cheaper insurance is actually in force. Someone with poor health may have no choice but to keep expensive insurance. If whole life insurance is retained, liquidate any accumulated dividends and borrow all available cash values for more favorable investment placement.

We recommend, with extremely rare exception, that only annual renewable term life insurance be purchased. This will allow much greater coverage during peak need years for each premium dollar spent than available with whole life coverage. The insurance should have a level face value and be noncancellable and guaranteed renewable to age 65. Term insurance issued more than a couple of years ago should be compared, on a cost basis, to new term insurance.

Avoid credit life insurance and other types of decreasing term insurance. If you wish to cover debts with insurance, factor debt amounts into your determination of total life coverage needs.

Generally, it is cheaper to purchase one large policy in contrast to several smaller policies. Insurance companies offer reduced premium rates at various "break points" in coverage amount.

Be careful to understand insurance language and shop on a true comparison basis. Insurance companies offer many types of hybrid products and use various names for policies. Do not purchase these hybrid policies.

We favor "stripped" policies, that is, do not add extra features such as waiver of premium for disability, accidental death coverage, inflation indexing, family protection, and other riders.

Because of differences in ownership form of insurance companies, some policies pay policyholders annual dividends. Subtract the average dividend expected (use reasonable estimates based on the company's past dividend record) from the gross premiums to arrive at net premium. Compare net premium on policies from dividend paying companies to gross premium on policies from companies which do not pay dividends.

Use any dividends payable on policies to reduce premiums or receive the dividends on a cash basis. Do not use the premiums to purchase paid-up additional insurance, nor accumulate the dividends with the insurance company.

Some companies offer "re-entry" options on life and other types of policies. This is frequently favorable. Basically, re-entry rates are premium rates, which are lower than guaranteed rates, and are payable if you are able to pass physical exams or health questionnaires at certain points in the future. If you do not pass a physical, or do not wish to take one, you pay premiums according to the initially guaranteed rate schedule. Re-entry rates are particularly favorable if you anticipate good health in the future. Often a re-entry option is offered along with a guaranteed rate schedule which is higher than guaranteed rates for which no re-entry option is available.

Coordinate insurance planning with estate planning and be certain that policy ownerships and beneficiary designations are made appropriately, and are both periodically reviewed. Settlement is usually best made in lump sum at death and proceeds can be paid to a trust if you desire staggered payouts to beneficiaries. Most insurance companies allow payment over various time periods but these pay-out options are unfavorable from an investment return point of view.

Do not tie or combine life insurance policies with other financial products such as annuities. Annuities, in concept, are the opposite of life insurance in that at some point the contracts begin pay-outs and payments are made while the annuitant(s) lives.

Disability Insurance

Unfortunately disabilities do occur at an alarmingly high rate and often last several years. Therefore, individuals and families need to consider protection of future income. Potential sources of income in the event of disability include Social Security benefits, worker's compensation (if job related), salary continuation, investment income, asset liquidation (which could be very unfavorable), and disability income insurance.

The Social Security regulations have a very strict definition of disability which basically states that benefits are payable only if an

TABLE 9-1   ESTIMATED SAMPLE LIFE INSURANCE RATES

| | Initial Annual Premium per Thousand | | | |
| | Term | | Whole Life | |
Age of Purchase	Male	Female	Male	Female
30	$1.15	$1.10	$12.50	$11.95
35	1.20	1.15	15.25	14.50
40	1.45	1.25	18.85	17.60
45	1.85	1.60	23.55	21.65
50	2.30	2.00	29.75	27.05
55	3.20	2.55	38.00	34.20
60	5.35	3.90	49.10	44.45

individual is unable to perform any gainful employment duties (regardless of occupational training) and the disability is expected (as medically verified) to last at least 12 months. Benefits payable to qualifying individuals begin after five months of continuous disability. Many families find Social Security benefits insufficient to meet needs.

If financial independence has been achieved, disability income protection is not necessary and disability insurance policies should not be purchased. Financial independence does mean income from investments and possible retirement plan(s) benefits are substantial enough to cover family expenditures for life.

Asset depletion can have a severe affect on financial security and even disabilities of short duration can take a long time to recover from financially. Most people have not achieved financial independence and do not possess the financial resources to afford going without disability income insurance protection.

If a family has, and is dependent on, two income earners, both should have disability income protection. As with life insurance, the need for protection should decrease in later years as assets are accumulated and financial commitments are lower. Disability insurance expense does increase with age.

The need for disability insurance is dependent on other sources of income. For example, if you have adequate emergency fund reserves or your employer provides salary continuation for several months, you can purchase disability insurance with a relatively long waiting period before benefits begin to reduce premium cost.

Many employees are covered by employer sponsored (and sometimes employer paid) disability income protection. Supplemental additions may be available to employees at a group rate. If coverage through employer plans is not available, or the coverage is low in amount or payable only for a short term, personal coverage may be needed. We discourage reliance on worker's compensation in planning because disabilities may not be job related.

Benefits received from employer (or business) paid disability insurance is subject to income taxation as received. Personally paid disability insurance results in tax-free benefits if disability occurs (unless premium payments were reimbursed through a qualified reimbursement plan). Owners of closely held corporations have the choice of expensing disability insurance costs through the corporation as a fringe benefit or paying for the insurance personally with after-tax dollars. The time value of money combined with current tax deductions and the uncertainty of disability makes the fringe benefit technique more favorable.

Extreme caution should be exercised in purchasing disability insurance, particularly with respect to the company used, definition of disability, and the conditions set for benefits payment. Costs should be compared to obtain the best price, but quality is important, and only good companies and policies should be considered.

Any policy purchased should be guaranteed renewable and non-cancellable to age 65 for sickness or accident. This means a policy is renewable at the policy holders option (not the company's) and premiums will not change from the initially scheduled levels (sometimes fixed, more often increasing with staggered age categories). If group coverage is being purchased, make sure conversion to individual coverage is guaranteed if the group coverage is terminated. Coverage is available after age 65 but usually not on a guaranteed basis.

Seek one of two definitions of disability:

- Benefits are payable if you are unable to perform the material and substantial duties of your regular occupation for a specified period (usually one to three years), and thereafter, the duties of any occupation for which you are reasonably suited for by education, training, or experience.
- Benefits are payable if your earned income goes down as a result of sickness or accident.

Do not purchase policies which have vague definitions, definitions referring to any occupation, or cover only sickness or accident but not both.

Disability insurance may be difficult to obtain or costly if you have a hazardous occupation. The riskier an occupation is, in terms of possible accidents, the more expensive coverage is. Individuals in high risk occupations should emphasize "self-funding" and maintain higher than normal levels of emergency funds.

Policies often do not cover disabilities attributable to preexisting medical conditions, self-inflicted disabilities, disabilities incurred in war, and other unique types of disability causes. Most forms of sickness or accident disability are covered by good policies.

Insurance companies usually will not sell policies providing benefits which, when combined with other disability benefits (including other insurance, Social Security benefits, etc.), will exceed 60 percent to 70 percent of normal earned income. Policies often carry "offset" clauses reducing payments if limits will be exceeded. Gross salary income, including factors such as pension contributions and deferred compensation, is used in figuring normal earned income. As with other insurances, like automobile and homeowners, there is no point in over-insuring and wasting premium dollars.

Disability policies can and should be obtained which include payments for partial and/or residual disability. An individual may incur only a partial disability and be able to continue working but not at full capacity; or may incur full disability for a while and then be able to return to work only on a limited basis. If a disability occurs, ends, and then recurs within six months, it is usually treated as a continuation of the initial disability for purposes of waiting period determination and the total benefit period may or may not, depending on the policy, be adjusted.

The waiting period is the length of time an individual must be disabled before benefits begin. We usually suggest waiting periods of between 30 and 360 days depending on financial strength, emergency cash reserves, employment benefits, and financial commitments. The longer the waiting period, the lower premium cost.

Policies can be written with monthly benefit payments for short or long time periods. Often benefits are payable in the event of sickness or accident to age 65. Other variations are available including payments for life or for only a few years. The shorter the benefit time period, the lower premium cost. Factors similar to those used in choosing a waiting period should be used in selecting benefit payment period. Special supplemental payments can be added as well; for example, a basic policy amount may be added to in early months until Social Security payments begin.

To protect income against future inflation, we suggest purchasing one of two options with a policy. An inflation indexing rider means that the benefit amount will automatically increase each year if prices in general rise. Alternatively, the right to increase the benefit amount may be included in a policy. Premium cost on additional increments is usually priced according to the age at which time the increased benefit amount is purchased.

In shopping for the best policy buy, do be certain equal comparisons are made and do not mix in other insurance needs such as a combined life and disability policy. Net out dividends from gross premium on participating policies to equally compare the policies with nonparticipating policies.

Medical Insurance

Medical insurance is needed by almost all individuals and families as costs of care are extremely high. Uninsured medical expenses can set families back years. Many employers provide employees with coverage.

Working married couples may have insurance coverage through both employers. Reimbursement on similar expenses will not be possible from both policies. Pick the best policy if it will cover both spouses or use both if different coverages are offered so that all or most medical expenses will be covered.

Self-employed individuals should consider expensing medical insurance premium cost through their business as a fringe benefit to pay premiums with pre-tax dollars.

Some large employers now have self-funded medical insurance plans or participate in Health Maintenance Organizations. Regardless of the source of your coverage (provided by others or paid by yourself), several important factors should be included.

TABLE 9–2   ESTIMATED SAMPLE DISABILITY INSURANCE RATES

| Age | Annual Cost per Hundred Dollars of Monthly Benefit* | | | |
| | Sickness or Accident for 5 Years | | Sickness or Accident to Age 65 | |
	Male	Female	Male	Female
30	$16.90	$27.45	$25.95	$46.75
35	20.95	31.00	33.50	52.50
40	26.20	35.55	42.65	57.95
45	32.95	40.85	52.05	62.45
50	41.50	46.35	60.30	64.60
55	52.25	51.80	66.05	65.40

*Class I Occupations—90–day elimination.

Basic hospital and surgical expenses should be covered. In addition, comprehensive expense clauses should cover other health care services and supplies. Most policies carry limits. Make sure various limits are reasonable and lifetime maximums are high. For example, different surgical procedures may carry various expense limits and comprehensive policies usually have lifetime maximums (which should be at least $250,000, preferably $1,000,000). Annual combined limits on medical expenses may also be included.

Policies have deductibles—the portion the insured pays of expenses before company payments begin—and the deductibles should be in the range of $100 to $500 per year.

Co-insurance clauses, whereby the insured shares with the insurance company in expenses incurred after the deductible amount, are common. 80 percent to the company, 20 percent to the insured, up to $2,500 per year, and 100 percent to the company thereafter, is a reasonable coinsurance arrangement.

Know exactly what your policy covers and does not cover and be sure it meets your families needs. If for example, it is likely that you will need expensive prescription drugs, include this in your coverage. Otherwise you can save premium expense by not including it. If you intend on having children, make sure pregnancy expenses are covered.

Automobile Insurance

Automobile insurance rates vary greatly. Factors causing the variance include state laws, marital status, driving record, previous claims, insurance coverages purchased, value and model of insured automobiles, amount of driving, number of drivers covered by a policy, residence location, length of policy, and deductibles.

With adequate cash reserves, use high deductibles on collision and comprehensive coverages to reduce premium costs.

In addition to protecting your vehicle(s), make sure to carry liability coverage. Coverage should be at least $300,000/$100,000 on damage to persons—the smaller figure representing payment per person, the larger total payment to all persons per incident. Property damage coverage should be at least $25,000.

For business owners, and nonbusiness owners preferring not to tie up cash in automobiles, leasing, with insurance coverage included, may be preferable to owning an automobile and making a direct purchase of insurance. Be certain that insurance obtained through the lease agreement will not be cancelled without notification to you.

Discounts may be given by insurance companies to policyholders insuring more than one car.

Avoid making small claims which may result in insurance premium increases.

Automobiles should be titled in the name of the individual who most frequently uses a particular automobile. This will eliminate unnecessary exposure of personal assets to a high liability or damage claim/suit.

Homeowners Insurance

Frequently, it is both beneficial (because of rates and claims) and convenient to purchase homeowners insurance from the same company carrying your automobile insurance.

There are three basic parts to a homeowners insurance policy: the dwelling, the contents of the dwelling; and personal liability.

Renters should also purchase homeowners type of insurance—actually another variation of property and casualty insurance, referred to as renters insurance. A standard renters policy covers personal property and personal liability.

Seek broad definitions of insurable damages to a dwelling or personal property and coverage to liability exposure. Damages could result from fire, theft, adverse weather conditions, etc. Liability exposure could result from injuries incurred by others on your property, dog bites, children causing damages to neighbors' property, etc.

Liability coverage on either a standard homeowners policy or renters policy should be at least $100,000 and preferably $300,000.

A dwelling and personal property can be covered for either "replacement value" or "depreciated value." The former being more expensive. For example, if you have a four-year-old stereo stolen, depreciated value coverage will be substantially less than replacement value.

Homeowners protection on residence and vacation property should cover physical property for at least 80 percent (and for most people 100 percent) of replacement cost. Some policies are tied to cost-of-living indices and coverage amount automatically increases annually with inflation. These type of policies, as well as nonindexed policies, should be reviewed annually to assure full protection. Get assistance from insurance agents, builders, or appraisers in determining replacement cost of property.

Homeowners policies usually cover personal property for a fixed percent of dwelling coverage such as 50 percent (i.e., if the dwelling is covered for $100,000 personal property coverage limits are $50,000 per incident). Renters policy coverage on personal property increases in cost with the amount of coverage purchased. Policies often exclude particular items. Know exactly what is covered and what is not covered. Purchase additional property "riders" for valuable items which are not covered, either because of total value amounts or nature of the personal property. Separate policies may be needed on assets such as boats and airplanes.

Inventory your personal property and take pictures of particularly valuable items. Place the inventory list and pictures in either a fire-proof safe at home or a safe deposit box at a financial institution. This will facilitate claim procedures and reimbursement for losses.

Personal property coverage usually "follows" the property. That is, items stolen from an automobile (and not covered by automobile insurance) will often be covered by homeowners insurance as will property lost on a vacation trip, etc. There are some special exclusions with which you should become familiar. An important typical exclusion is property held in a safe deposit box at a financial institution. Separate insurance coverage must be purchased for such property.

Do not overinsure nor underinsure. Overinsuring produces no extra payment benefits and is wasteful. Underinsuring definition depends upon your ability to absorb financial loss. If you can afford to lose something, do not insure it unless coverage falls under a standard policy. If personal emergency funds are adequate, or financial resources are low, consider high deductibles on property and casualty insurance policies.

Homeowners policies are often regulated by states, and therefore, coverage is standardized. Do make sure, though, that you are dealing with a reputable company. Standard policies usually also include coverage for "additional living expenses" and other associated costs if you are forced to leave your dwelling because of insurable damage.

Umbrella Liability Insurance

To prevent devastating personal losses in the event of lawsuits for personal liability, people who have accumulated a significant amount of assets should purchase separate liability coverage, usually coverage in the range of $1 million to $2 million is appropriate.

Umbrella liability coverage is inexpensive and supplements liability coverage included in automobile, homeowners, and other types of property insurance.

COORDINATING INSURANCE PURCHASES

Formal insurance protection purchase is appropriate in some forms for most individuals. Health care insurance and property and liability insurance have the widest application. If you have not achieved financial independence, you need disability income insurance and, if you have dependents, life insurance.

Cost efficiency in purchasing insurance is very important as quality coverage can often vary greatly in price. Included in cost efficiency, besides direct premium cost, is the time value of money. Frequently, insurance premiums can be paid annually, semi-annually, quarterly, or monthly. Insurance companies add charges for greater frequency of payment. If you can earn more by retailing your funds longer than it costs in additional charges, a frequent payment method should be selected. Maximizing funds use and minimizing premium payments through purchase of only necessary insurance at reasonable cost increases surplus funds available for investing.

Insurance purchases enable individuals and families to protect future cash flow needs and avoid damaging asset depletion. Risk management also entails proper planning and structuring of cash flow, income taxes, investments and estates. Risk acceptance and management is a subjective process and balance must be met between comfort levels and allocations of financial resources. Each area of financial planning should be addressed and then all areas blended together. With determination of risk management priorities, optimal use of funds can be made.

Business owners must also address a series of risk questions including business structure, management, cost control, and variety of insurable business risks. These questions are outside the realm of personal financial planning but choices made do have very important effects on personal finances. The business and personal planning must be carefully blended to achieve successful results. Business owners also have special personal planning opportunities available to them such as placing and expensing insurance policies through the business and making premium payments with before-tax dollars rather than after-tax dollars.

INSURANCE RECORDS

Insurance policies should be purchased only after careful need evaluation and cost comparison. Employer provided, and other forms of group coverage, should be considered before buying personal insurance policies.

Policies should be stored in a safe and convenient place at home (such as a fire proof box) and be reviewed prior to renewal. If policies are lost, or destroyed, replacement policies can be obtained, sometimes with nominal charge by the issuing insurance company.

Of course, insurance premiums should be included in the budgeting process both with respect to affordability and future planning. Payment of premiums should be planned in accordance with cash management and use of cash control accounts. Payment should be noted on receipts and filed in appropriate cash outflow files. Destroy old policies after new replacement policies are received.

10

UNDERSTANDING INCOME TAXATION

"The hardest thing in the world to understand is income tax."

Albert Einstein

Two years ago, a successful business owner came to us for review of his financial positioning. In reviewing his income tax returns, we discovered that he did not pay any income tax to the federal government for the prior year. It was all legitimate. His net taxable income was zero (actually it computed to a negative amount). He had invested heavily in several formal tax shelters.

You may initially find this appealing, but if you analyze the situation carefully you will realize that a lot of his money has been wasted. Some of the write-offs were actually useless because he had no income to offset with the losses. To save taxes from tax shelters when you are in a high tax bracket can, in some instances, make sense. But to invest in shelters where tax losses are the main investment return component and losses are offsetting low tax rate levels (or no tax rates) does not make sense. By the way, several of his shelter investments have not yet returned any cash or gain to him.

Obviously, many people feel they pay too much in taxes. Surprisingly, its not uncommon for us to find that people often pay too little in taxes (and we are not referring to people who cheat). The main reasons for underpayment are excessive tax sheltering, poor investment selection, and poor planning regarding timing of deductions and income receipt.

We are not in a position to comment on moral obligations individuals should feel toward paying taxes. We are, however, in a position to evaluate tax payments from a financial point of view. Before you attempt to determine a proper level of tax payments for yourself, have a full grasp of income taxation; understand;

- how taxation is calculated for various types of taxes;
- the difference between treatments of income and gains;
- techniques for reducing different types of taxes;
- timing requirements for tax payments;
- the difference between tax deferral and tax elimination;
- true versus phony tax reduction methods;
- the distinctions among and within tax losses, tax deductions, and tax credits; and
- the interrelation of income taxation to other financial planning areas.

Many people spend excessive energy and money, along with emotional discomfort and concern, trying to pursue income tax reduction. A coordinated approach to income tax reduction will eliminate the unnecessary worry and expenditures and allow you to seek the level of taxation you feel appropriate within the guidelines established by the government.

Often tax law is viewed as black or white; i.e., you can or you cannot do something. We believe there are many "gray" areas as demonstrated by the frequent issues of new tax rulings by tax courts. You must determine the degree of aggressiveness you are comfortable with in reducing taxes both with respect to interpretation of tax law and participation in investment and other opportunities, which reduce taxes.

As with all important financial matters, take an overall position of being in charge and making your own decisions, but do seek professional advice as necessary. Tax accountants and tax attorneys should be sought for advice on complex tax issues. Tax-oriented investments should be purchased from product salespeople only after objective evaluation and determination of appropriateness.

It may not be prudent for you to prepare your own tax returns either because of time efficiencies or complexities of your tax situation. Do, though, understand your returns and, if necessary, have the preparer explain the return to you line-by-line. This understanding will enhance future tax and financial planning, and decision making.

In pursuing tax reduction goals recognize that there is a clear difference between tax deferral and tax elimination. Tax elimination, such as from allowable deductions means not paying taxes on some income and realizing the income tax-free. Tax deferral is to postpone tax payments to the future, such as with IRAs. This too has value because taxes will ultimately be paid with cheaper dollars and funds can be placed for investment returns in the interim.

TAX RATES

The United States federal income tax is a progressive tax, which means the more taxable income you have, the higher the rate you pay on additional dollars. The higher rates are applied only to additional dollars, not to all dollars. The rate at which your highest dollars are taxed is referred to as your marginal tax rate. If you divide your total income tax bill by your taxable income, you will calculate your average tax rate. To say someone is in the 50 percent tax bracket does not mean that 50 percent of income goes to taxes, it means simply that some dollars are taxed at a rate of 50 percent.

**FIGURE 10-1   CALCULATING FEDERAL
INCOME TAX**

	Gross Taxable Income
Less:	Adjustments to Gross Income
Equals:	Adjusted Gross Income
Less:	Itemized Deductions
Less:	Personal Exemptions
Equals:	Net Taxable Income
	Gross Federal Income Tax
Less:	Tax Credits
Equals:	Net Federal Income Tax

There is a common misconception that it is not wise to work extra hours for additional compensation because one will actually come out behind in net pay. Net pay reductions or minimal net pay increases from additional compensation are attributable to misuse of withholding tables; i.e., calculating withholding taxes as if that period's compensation is paid regularly throughout the year. Withholding adjustments can be made to correct this problem. Additional compensation or income always pays off in terms of net additional income as U.S. tax rates do not equal or exceed 100 percent.

Know your marginal tax rate for federal income taxes as it is an important factor in making cash, income, and investment decisions. Use your average tax rate to determine whether or not you pay too much in tax. Realize that both rates are based on taxable income which differs from gross income. To emphasize the difference between marginal rates and average rates, suppose a married couple with net federal taxable income of $35,200 files jointly. Refer to Tables 10–1 and 10–2.

On total income of $35,200, the couple's tax liability (1984) will

TABLE 10-1   ANALYSIS OF THE EXAMPLE

	Income	Tax Rate	Tax
First	$ 3,400	0%	$ 0
Next	2,100	11	231
Next	2,100	12	252
Next	4,300	14	602
Next	4,100	16	656
Next	4,200	18	756
Next	4,400	22	968
Next	5,300	25	1,325
Next	5,300	28	1,484
Total	$35,200		$6,274

Marginal Tax Rate = 28%

Average Tax Rate = $\frac{\text{Total Tax}}{\text{Income}}$ = $\frac{6,274}{35,200}$ = 17.8%

TABLE 10-2

Federal Tax Rate Schedule for Married Couples Filing Jointly*

1984

Net Taxable Income	Base Amount +	Marginal Rate	On Excess Over
Less than $3,400	$ 0	0%	$ —
3,400–5,500	0	11	3,400
5,500–7,600	231	12	5,500
7,600–11,900	483	14	7,600
11,900–16,000	1,085	16	11,900
16,000–20,200	1,741	18	16,000
20,200–24,600	2,497	22	20,200
24,600–29,900	3,465	25	24,600
29,900–35,200	4,790	28	29,900
35,200–45,800	6,274	33	35,200
45,800–60,000	9,772	38	45,800
60,000–85,600	15,168	42	60,000
85,600–109,400	25,920	45	85,600
109,400–162,400	36,630	49	109,400
162,400 and above	62,600	50	162,400

Federal Tax Rate Schedule for Married Couples Filing Separately

1984

Net Taxable Income	Base Amount +	Marginal Rate	On Excess Over
Less Than $1,700	$ 0	0%	$ —
1,700–2,750	0	11	1,700
2,750–3,800	115	12	2,750
3,800–5,950	241	14	3,800
5,950–8,000	542	16	5,950
8,000–10,100	870	18	8,000
10,100–12,300	1,248	22	10,100
12,300–14,950	1,732	25	12,300
14,950–17,600	2,395	28	14,950
17,600–22,900	3,137	33	17,600
22,900–30,000	4,886	38	22,900
30,000–42,800	7,584	42	30,000
42,800–54,700	12,960	45	42,800
54,700–81,200	18,315	49	54,700
81,200 and above	31,300	50	81,200

Beginning in 1985, income tax brackets, zero-bracket amounts, and personal exemptions will be indexed with inflation (the rate is 4.1% for 1985).

*A surviving spouse can file a joint return for the year in which the deceased spouse's death occurred.

TABLE 10-2 (continued)

Federal Tax Rate Schedule for Single Individuals
1984

Net Taxable Income	Base Amount	+	Marginal Rate	On Excess Over
Less than $2,300	$ 0		0%	$ —
2,300–3,400	0		11	2,300
3,400–4,400	121		12	3,400
4,400–6,500	241		14	4,400
6,500–8,500	535		15	6,500
8,500–10,800	835		16	8,500
10,800–12,900	1,203		18	10,800
12,900–15,000	1,581		20	12,900
15,000–18,200	2,001		23	15,000
18,200–23,500	2,737		26	18,200
23,500–28,800	4,115		30	23,500
28,800–34,100	5,705		34	28,800
34,100–41,500	7,507		38	34,100
41,500–55,300	10,319		42	41,500
55,300–81,800	16,115		48	55,300
81,800 and above	28,835		50	81,800

Federal Tax Rate Schedule for Head of Household
1984

Net Taxable Income	Base Amount	+	Marginal Rate	On Excess Over
Less than $2,300	$ 0		0%	$ —
2,300–4,400	0		11	2,300
4,400–6,500	231		12	4,400
6,500–8,700	483		14	6,500
8,700–11,800	791		17	8,700
11,800–15,000	1,318		18	11,800
15,000–18,200	1,894		20	15,000
18,200–23,500	2,534		24	18,200
23,500–28,800	3,806		28	23,500
28,800–34,100	5,290		32	28,800
34,100–44,700	6,986		35	34,100
44,700–60,600	10,696		42	44,700
60,600–81,800	17,374		45	60,600
81,800–108,300	26,914		48	81,800
108,300 and above	39,634		50	108,300

Beginning in 1985, income tax brackets, zero-bracket amounts, and personal exemptions will be indexed with inflation (the rate is 4.1% for 1985).

TABLE 10–2 *(concluded)*

Net Taxable Income	Federal Tax Rate Schedule for Estates and Trusts			
	1984			
	Base Amount	+	Marginal Rate	On Excess Over
Less than $1,050	$ 0		11%	$ 0
1,050–2,100	115		12	1,050
2,100–4,250	241		14	2,100
4,250–6,300	542		16	4,250
6,300–8,400	870		18	6,300
8,400–10,600	1,248		22	8,400
10,600–13,250	1,732		25	10,600
13,250–15,900	2,395		28	13,250
15,900–21,200	3,137		33	15,900
21,200–28,300	4,886		38	21,200
28,300–41,100	7,584		42	28,300
41,100–53,000	12,960		45	41,100
53,000–79,500	18,315		49	53,000
79,500 and above	31,300		50	79,500

Beginning in 1985, income tax brackets, zero-bracket amounts, and personal exemptions will be indexed with inflation (the rate is 4.1% for 1985).

be $6,274, or an average 17.8 percent of the income goes for federal income taxes, while the dollars above $29,900 are taxed at a rate of 28 percent.

The federal income tax tables should be used to calculate regular federal income taxation. Use the table which applies to your situation. Married couples have the option of filing jointly or separately. Taxes should be figured both ways and the least costly option should be elected. If incomes of husband and wife are very close, it may be advantageous to file separately. If there is significant difference in spousal earned income it will probably be best to file jointly. However, the optimal method depends on several factors including marginal tax brackets.

If you are unmarried at the end of a tax year and have a qualifying dependent, or you are a qualifying widow(er), you may file as "head of household." Otherwise you must file as single and incur more taxes. A surviving spouse can file a joint return for the year in which the deceased spouse's death occurred.

Special tax rates apply to trusts and estates and you should become familiar with the rates as unique planning opportunities are available through placement of assets in trust and/or special post-mortem elections by executors or heirs.

In addition to regular taxation, you should consider the applicability of three other forms of federal income taxation.

Alternative Minimum Tax   This is an additional tax which you will have to pay if you have a large amount of so-called tax preference items. The tax is payable only if it exceeds your regular income tax, and if so, the difference between AMT and regular tax is payable in addition to your regular tax. The AMT rate is 20 percent of Alternative Minimum Taxable Income that exceeds $30,000 in the case of single taxpayers or $40,000 in the case of married taxpayers filing a joint return ($20,000 for married taxpayers filing separately, and trusts and estates). Preference items include dividend exclusions, accelerated depreciation, depletion, intangible drilling costs, the bargain element on incentive stock options, and long-term capital gains exclusions. Most individuals do not incur the AMT. If you have, or think you may have, large amounts of preference items, consult with a qualified tax planner to reduce or avoid AMT, or plan payment.

Four-Year Income Averaging   This is a substitute tax method to regular income taxation for qualifying taxpayers. A complex formula is used that will result in lower taxation for years in which income is substantially above income of previous years. Current income is averaged with taxable income from each of the previous three years and taxed according to regular tax rate schedules. If your income for the current year (or foreseeable future planning years) is expected to substantially exceed past income, request four year averaging instructions from the IRS for calculation and qualification instructions.

Special 10-Year Forward Averaging   This is a special tax method which applies only to the portion of a year's income attributable to lump sum distributions from certain types of qualified employment related plans (including Keogh, Profit-Sharing, Pensions, Deferred Compensation, Salary Reduction, and Thrift Plans, but excluding Individual Retirement Accounts). The portion of income from the lump sum distribution is taxed separately and as if it is received over 10 years (as a single taxpayer), thus subjecting the income to lower marginal tax rates; although the tax is paid in full for the tax year in which the distribution is received. This taxation can be elected more than once before age 59 1/2, but only once after age 59 1/2. Careful evaluation is needed to time election for this method, particularly if a lump sum distribution is to be made at your discretion. You should be aware of instances where the advantages of this taxation technique could be lost such as if a profit-sharing plan distribution is "rolled-over" to an Individual Retirement Account to avoid current taxation.

FICA or Social Security taxation for mandatory participation (with some exceptions such as certain government workers) in the federal program is applied to both employees and employers. Social Security is a regressive tax because there is a limitation to the amount of earned income subject to tax. A drawback to attempting to reduce Social Security taxes is possible reduction in benefits which will ultimately be received. We discourage planned reliance on Social Security benefits for retirement funding because of program problems and benefit limitations. Some individuals may be comfortable in seeking reductions of current Social Security taxes even though future benefits could be reduced. The tax is applied to gross earned income for employees (net earned profit for self-employed individuals) and deductions allowed in computing federal income tax are not allowable; nor is Social Security tax a deductible expense for federal income tax purposes. Techniques for reduction of Social Security taxes are very limited. With husband and wife business owners, one salary can be set well below the base limit and one above so as to minimize total tax in comparison to both salaries being set at or above the base limit; in other words, seek more disproportion in salary rather than equalization. In some instances, employed family members (such as children) are exempt from Social Security taxation.

State and local income taxes vary greatly, with some states imposing high taxes and others none. Computation methods also differ. For example, some states allow deductions for IRA contributions, others do not; some states allow itemized deductions and exemptions while others impose variations of flat rate taxes. Know how your particular state income taxation works and plan steps for reducing the taxation, including your selection of income sources. If you have options for declaring residency status, consider a state with more favorable taxation.

Some income subject to federal income taxation is not subject to state income taxation and vice versa. Common examples are:

- Interest on federal government notes and bonds is taxed by the federal government but not state and local governments.
- Municipal bond interest, which many states tax if the bonds have been issued by other states, is not subject to federal income taxation.

GROSS TAXABLE INCOME

Federal gross taxable income can be segregated into two main categories, ordinary income and capital gain income. Ordinary income can be active or passive; that is, from employment which is referred to as earned income or from sources such as dividends and interest which are considered to be unearned income. Interest can include "accrued" (earned but not received) income for cash basis taxpayers on bonds purchased at a discount from face value, such as zero-coupon and market-discounted bonds.

Capital gain income is attributable to gain or loss on the purchase and subsequent sale of an asset. For assets purchased before June 23, 1984, short-term capital gains are gains which occur over a period of one year or less; long-term gains over a period of more than one year. For assets purchased after June 22, 1984, short-term capital gains are gains which occur over a period of six months or less; long-term gains over a period of more than six months (the six months is scheduled to revert to one year for assets purchased after December 31, 1987). Short-term capital gains are fully taxable, whereas only 40 percent of long-term capital gains are subject to tax at marginal tax rates (making, for example, an effective long-term capital gain tax rate of 16 percent of all gain for a 40 percent marginal bracket taxpayer).

Negative income or losses are also possible and offset positive income. Ordinary losses can result from ownership in business enterprises or partnership investments. Losses may or may not mean actual cash losses (losses can be so-called "paper losses"). Losses can be reported, even though cash losses are not incurred, because of certain noncash business expenses such as depreciation or depletion.

Short-term capital losses are 100 percent reportable, and long-

Personal Economics

term losses 50 percent reportable, both subject to a combined maximum net reportable capital loss per year of $3,000 in excess of capital gains. Net losses which exceed $3,000 per year can be carried forward and used in future years to offset income.

There is an exception to the short-term loss time limitation and the amount limitation for so-called Section 1244 stock. Most small businesses should elect 1244 treatment because in the event of

TABLE 10–3

Marginal Tax Bracket (%)	Net Long-Term Capital Gain Tax Rate (%)	Net Long-Term Capital Loss Tax Rate (%)
12	4.8	6.0
14	5.6	7.0
16	6.4	8.0
18	7.2	9.0
20	8.0	10.0
22	8.8	11.0
24	9.6	12.0
26	10.4	13.0
28	11.2	14.0
30	12.0	15.0
32	12.8	16.0
34	13.6	17.0
36	14.4	18.0
38	15.2	19.0
40	16.0	20.0
42	16.8	21.0
44	17.6	22.0
46	18.4	23.0
48	19.2	24.0
50	20.0	25.0

Net Short-Term Capital Gains = Total Short-Term Gains – Total Short-Term Losses

Net Long-Term Capital Gains = Total Long-Term Gains – Total Long-Term Losses

Net Reportable Capital Gains = Net Short-Term Capital Gains + Net Long-Term Capital Gains

loss, up to $50,000 ($100,000 on a joint return) per year is deductible in full.

Special postponement of gains on stock sales to Employee Stock Ownership Plans can be made, provided certain reinvestment and other requirements are met.

Special opportunities are also available to delay or avoid tax

TABLE 10–4 POSSIBLE CAPITAL GAIN COMBINATIONS

Net Short-Term Gain	Net Short-Term Loss	Net Long-Term Gain	Net Long-Term Loss	Taxation	Annual $ Limit
Yes	No	No	No	100% taxable in addition to ordinary income	None
No	Yes	No	No	100% offset to ordinary income	3,000
No	No	Yes	No	40% taxable in addition to ordinary income	None
No	No	No	Yes	50% offset to ordinary income	6,000
Yes	No	Yes	No	Short-term—100% taxable/long-term—40% taxable	None
Yes	No	No	Yes	Gain > Loss—100% taxable on net difference/gain < loss—50% offset on net difference	None/6,000
No	Yes	Yes	No	Loss > Gain—100% offset on net difference/loss < gain—40% taxable on net difference	3,000/None
No	Yes	No	Yes	Short-term—100% offset/long-term—50% offset	3,000/6,000 with net combined reportable limit 3,000
No	No	No	No	None	None

payments on gains from the sale of a home (principal residence). Taxation is postponed if a new residence of equal or more value is purchased within 24 months from the date of sale. The cost basis of the new residence is reduced by the amount of gain on the old residence. If gains are not reported in the year of sale, and a new home is not purchased within 24 months, an amended return must be filed with interest due on back taxes. There is, however, a once-in-a-lifetime $125,000 exclusion after age 55 on the sale of a principal residence.

Short-term losses are first applied against short-term gains (if any), then net long-term gains (if any), and then to ordinary income. Long-term losses are applied in order to long-term gains, short-term gains, and ordinary income. Timing realization of capital gains or losses (i.e., asset sales) is very important and should be evaluated several times a year, especially close to year end. For example:

• It is favorable to apply long-term losses (normally 50 percent deductible) against short-term gains to in effect convert the losses to 100 percent deductible.
• It is unfavorable to apply short-term losses against long-term gains because otherwise short-term losses are 100 percent deductible and long-term gains 40 percent taxable; in effect the 60 percent long-term gain exclusion is lost.

Investments or income sources can generate both ordinary income (loss) and capital gain (loss) income. For example, if you own a rental duplex, typically rent income in early years will be more than offset by expenses, especially depreciation, so that a net loss is reported. This loss will reduce other taxable income such as salary or interest income, resulting in income tax savings. The amount of savings will depend on your marginal tax bracket—the higher your bracket, the more valuable the loss is.

To understand the workings of tax loss with tax-free cash flow review the example (Table 10–5) of a real estate investment with assumed 45 percent marginal tax bracket for the investor.

A tax loss (paper loss) is incurred, yet cash flow is positive.

If you decide to sell a property after several years of ownership, the difference between selling price and your cost basis is capital gain or loss. Cost basis of an asset is the price paid plus additional expenditures or investment in the asset less certain allowable

TABLE 10-5 TAX LOSS THROUGH REAL ESTATE INVESTMENT

Rental Income	$14,000
Less Expenses:	
Interest	$ 5,000
Taxes	1,000
Depreciation	6,000
Insurance	750
Utilities	2,500
Maintenance	2,000
Miscellaneous	1,500
Total Expenses	$18,750
Net Taxable Income (Loss)	$(4,750)
Plus: Depreciation	$ 6,000
Less: Debt Principal Payments	1,000
Net Cash Inflow (Outflow)	$ 250
Plus: Tax Savings	2,138
Net Cash Inflow (Outflow) after Tax	$ 2,388

losses or expenses reported such as depreciation. If, for example, you pay $50,000 for a rental property, make no additional investment, and report $10,000 of depreciation prior to sale, your basis at sale is $40,000. It is important to note that, in some instances (such as where accelerated depreciation has been used) a portion of the difference between selling price and cost basis can be subject to ordinary income tax (and not qualify for capital gain taxation). This is known as *recapture*.

ADJUSTMENTS TO GROSS INCOME

Adjustments to gross are direct subtractions from gross income to arrive at adjusted gross income. This is an important figure which affects allowable medical expense deductions, casualty losses, and other factors and may affect your state income taxation.

Categories of adjustment to gross income include:

- job-related moving expenses;
- employment-related business expenses;
- alimony paid;
- deduction for working married couple;
- Keogh contributions; and
- IRA contributions.

The deduction for a working married couple is equal to 10 percent of the lesser of $30,000 or the earned income of the lower earning spouse for a maximum annual deduction of $3,000. This would save, for example, $1,200 for a couple in the 40 percent tax bracket.

Everyone with earned income is now eligible for participation in Individual Retirement Accounts. To allow write-offs for a particular tax year, funding of an IRA must occur by April 15 following the tax year. The earlier contributions are made each tax year the longer earnings can compound on a tax deferred basis. Allowable annual funding is the lesser of $2,000 or the amount of earned income per person. Total funding for a married couple, if only one spouse has earned income, cannot exceed $2,250 per year and not more than $2,000 for one person. Funding two accounts totaling $2,250 will save about $1,100 a year in federal income taxes for a married couple in the 50 percent marginal tax bracket.

Taxpayers can participate in IRAs by establishing their own accounts (s) and/or by making contributions to employer sponsored plans. We generally favor the former. Individuals may utilize many different accounts as desired (provided dollar limits are not exceeded) and accounts may be "rolled-over" to alternate investments. Roll-overs are subject to a 60-day turnover period and a limitation of once per year if funds are distributed to a taxpayer/investor and then reinvested. There is no annual limitation on the number of roll-overs made directly from one trustee to another trustee. As with Keoghs, withdrawals from IRAs must begin by age 70 1/2 and withdrawals before age 59 1/2 are subject to a 10 percent tax penalty (with exceptions in the case of death or permanent disability). Taxes will be incurred upon withdrawal and several planning thoughts should be considered.

- IRA lump sum withdrawal does not qualify for favorable 10-year forward averaging taxation as does Keogh lump sum withdrawal.
- IRA withdrawals do qualify for four-year income averaging and, therefore, large withdrawal may be prudent.
- Required installment withdrawal at age 70 1/2 is based on life expectancy at that time so withdrawal can occur over many years to reduce tax impacts and continue tax-deferred earnings. Each year thereafter, withdrawal amount can be determined on the basis of the individual's current life expectancy.

- Withdrawals can also be made on a joint life expectancy basis (determined by age of the individual with the IRA and the age of his or her designated beneficiary). At least 50 percent must be distributed over the life expectancy of the IRA title holder. Beneficiaries, following the IRA holder's death, can draw benefits in lump sum or spread payments over several years (up to their life expectancy).
- Because of withdrawal requirements, a married couple with a nonworking spouse, might place the greater portion of contributions in the name of the younger spouse to allow for tax-deferred earnings for a greater period of time.

IRAs must be established with qualified trustees or custodians. These include: mutual funds, trust companies, insurance companies, brokerage firms, banks and other thrift institutions. IRAs can be self-directed but, unlike corporate retirement plans and Keoghs, cannot be self-trust.

Multiple retirement plan participation is certainly possible. For example, suppose you work for a corporation and are covered by company contributions to a pension/profit sharing plan. You may also be able to make voluntary contributions to the plan. You can establish and fund an IRA for each tax year. In addition, if you are also self-employed with some type of qualifying side business, you could set up a Keogh Plan.

Of course, participation in retirement plans should, as with most financial opportunities, be evaluated in conjunction with all financial planning needs. Participation should not be based solely on income tax considerations.

ITEMIZED DEDUCTIONS

Itemized Deductions, like Adjustments to Gross Income, reduce Net Taxable Income and, therefore, reduce federal income taxes. The reduction in federal taxes attributable to deductions is dependent on the taxpayer's marginal tax bracket—the higher one's bracket the more impact a deduction has in the form of tax savings. Apply your tax rate to deduction amounts to determine tax savings. We commonly hear people say an expense is going to be written off so why not go ahead with it, as if expense will end up being free or financed by the government.

Table 10–6 shows the net after tax cost of a $100 deductible expenditure for various bracket taxpayers. Similar analyses will

TABLE 10-6 $100 DEDUCTIBLE EXPENDITURE

Marginal Tax Bracket (%)	Tax Savings ($)	Net after Tax Cost ($)
12	12	88
18	18	82
26	26	74
34	34	66
42	42	58
50	50	50

show the tax savings from ordinary losses, net capital losses, or adjustments to gross income because the savings from these items are also dependent on marginal tax bracket.

To itemize deductions on your federal income tax return, single individuals need at least $2,300 of total itemized deductions, married couples filing jointly need $3,400, and married couples filing separately need $1,700 each. These amounts will be $2,390, $3,540, and $1,700, respectively in 1985. Future indexing will increase these amounts. Major categories for itemized deductions are:

1. Medical Expenses—to the extent such expenses exceed 5 percent of adjusted Gross Income.
2. Taxes—certain qualifying tax payments:
   State and local income taxes,
   Real estate property taxes;
   Sales taxes (either per IRS tables or detailed itemization); and
   Other specifically approved taxes such as personal property taxes.
3. Interest Expenses—most types of legal interest payments are deductible, including interest on home mortgages, automobile and major purchase installment interest, credit card interest, etc. Three common exceptions are:
   - Life insurance policy loan interest if at least four of the first seven annual premium payments are not actually made by the owner (that is, cash values are borrowed to make the payments) or if interest is not actually paid (that is, if additional loans are used to pay interest).
   - Investment related interest expenses that exceed $10,000 plus the total amount of taxpayer investment income.

- Interest incurred on debt used to finance the purchase of nontaxable investments, such as municipal bonds.

4. Charitable Contributions—to approved charitable organizations and governmental units subject to the following constraints:

   - 50 percent of adjusted gross income for cash contributions to most qualifying charities (30 percent of adjusted gross income on some).
   - Appreciated property and other property limited to fair market value and depending upon the type of property and donee, several limitations on adjusted gross income none of which exceed 50 percent; unless the property is considered publicly traded securities, an independent appraisal is needed to claim more than $5,000 on a gifted property.
   - Total annual limitation of 50 percent of adjusted gross income; charitable contributions which exceed limitations may be carried forward to future tax years.

5. Casualty and Theft Losses—to the extent total qualifying losses (for which insurance reimbursement is not received), each exceed $100, and then to the extent the total of net losses exceeds 10 percent of Adjusted Gross Income.

6. Miscellaneous Deductions—a wide variety of other deductions are allowed, samples include:

   - Investment related expenses such as advisor fees, account fees, investment publications, or investment computer programs.
   - Job related costs such as union dues, certain educational expenses, or specialized uniforms or equipment.
   - Tax preparation fees or legal fees for investment or income tax advice.
   - Nonreimbursed business related entertainment expenses.

One exception to qualifying amounts and types of itemized deductions is charitable contributions. Taxpayers who do not itemize may deduct up to $75 for 1984, 50 percent of all contributions in 1985, and 100 percent of contributions in 1986 and thereafter.

Deductible expenses are reportable for the tax year in which the expense is incurred and paid. In some instances, payment with a charge card can qualify a deduction for a particular tax year.

EXEMPTIONS   An exemption is also a reduction in taxable income. Each allowable exemption is worth $1,000 for 1984 ($1,040 in 1985) (future indexing will increase this amount). A taxpayer is allowed one exemption for:

- Himself or herself; plus
- A spousal exemption (to be reported either on the joint return or separate return whichever is appropriate); plus
- An exemption for each qualifying dependent (basically anyone with less than $1,000 of taxable income for the tax year, and generally for whom the taxpayer provides more than 50 percent of support); plus
- Additional exemptions for those age 65 or over and/or blind.

Children who are under 19 years of age or are full time students may earn more than $1,000 per year, report their own exemption, and still be claimed by their parents as dependents. Dependency questions for reporting exemptions can be very important in many instances, including divorces or separations, decisions for a married couple filing separately or jointly, and overall financial analysis in determining whether or not to support another individual.

TAX CREDITS   Tax credits can be significantly more valuable than tax losses, deductions, or exemptions because tax credits are direct subtractions from tax liability rather than subtractions from taxable income. Reductions in taxable income reduce taxes at a rate equivalent to a taxpayer's marginal tax rate. Net tax credits reduce taxes on a dollar for dollar basis after calculation of gross tax liability. Major credits are:

- Special credit for the elderly and disabled.
- Foreign tax credit.
- Jobs credit.
- Residential energy credit.
- Partial credit for political contributions.
- Investment credit.
- Credit for child and dependent care expenses.
- Special State issued mortgage credits.

Each credit is based on different types of rules and calculation methods. Learn about the credits which apply to your tax situation. The investment tax credit, for example, is often an important component of tax shelters or business investment. The credit is equal to 10 percent of the value of qualifying equipment and property purchases (25 percent in the case of qualified rehabilitation expenditures, and there are other variations and qualifications on value to which the credit may be applied). There are various ceilings on use of the credit depending upon the type of property, but unused credits can be carried back to previous tax years or carried forward to future tax years.

The credit for child and dependent care expenses frequently applies because of the large number of households with both spouses working outside the home and the many single parents. The credit is based on qualifying employment related expenses and Adjusted Gross Income of the taxpayer(s). The maximum amount of expenses to which the credit can be applied are $2,400 for one dependent and $4,800 for two or more qualifying dependents. Table 10–7 shows maximum tax savings from use of the credit for child and dependent care expenses.

TAX PAYMENT REQUIREMENTS

In general, federal taxpayers must have withheld from compensation checks, investment returns, or paid through quarterly tax payments an amount equal to 80 percent of the current year's liability, or an amount equal to the prior year's tax, during the tax year in order to avoid interest charges and penalties.

Avoid interest charges and penalties but do maximize use of your funds and make tax payments only as necessary. Withholding 100 percent or more of your tax liability during the year provides the federal government an interest-free loan and prevents you from earning investment returns on tax balances which do not have to be paid until April following the tax year.

At the beginning of each year, and several times throughout the year, estimate your federal income tax liability for the coming year. Withholdings are adjusted through the number of exemptions claimed on the Federal Tax Form W–4 which all employees must complete (and variations of the basic form for investors with certain financial institutions and companies under new withholding laws). Periodically you may, through your employer, refile this form. The form is accompanied by a worksheet which will help you determine the filing status to select and the number of exemptions to claim. Increasing exemptions reduces withholding tax. If you claim more than 14 exemptions, your employer is required by law to

Personal Economics

TABLE 10-7

Adjusted Gross Income	Credit Rate	Maximum Tax Savings Schedule	
		One Dependent	Two or More Dependents
Less than $10,000	30%	$720	$1,440
10,000 to 12,000	29%	696	1,392
12,000 to 14,000	28%	672	1,344
14,000 to 16,000	27%	648	1,296
16,000 to 18,000	26%	624	1,248
18,000 to 20,000	25%	600	1,200
20,000 to 22,000	24%	576	1,152
22,000 to 24,000	23%	552	1,104
24,000 to 26,000	22%	528	1,056
26,000 to 28,000	21%	504	1,008
More than 28,000	20%	480	960

report your name to the IRS—so be sure you can justify a high number of exemptions if you so report.

If your taxable income is expected to be substantially higher than taxable income for the previous year, you will probably be better off to set withholdings and/or quarterly payments to equal the prior year's tax liability rather than 80 percent of the projected current year's liability. This will mean payment of more than 20 percent of the liability in April following the tax year but will allow for more potential investment earnings during the tax year.

For individuals who need to make quarterly payments in addition to withholdings—usually self-employed people, individuals with relatively high investment income, or people subject to the Alternative Minimum Tax—the quarterly payment dates are: April 15, June 15, September 15, and January 15.

Social Security taxes are included as part of federal taxes for purposes of determining income tax payment requirements. State income tax payment requirements vary considerably and separate analysis is appropriate for each state which does in fact impose income taxes. It may be better to prepay anticipated state tax balances in December of each year to accelerate federal income tax deductions.

Factors to consider in adjusting and making necessary tax payments:

- Plan for impact of irregular cash inflow such as bonuses or asset sales.
- Treat possible overpayment of Social Security taxes (i.e., if you have more than one job and withholdings are taken for each) as part of the payment toward federal income taxes.
- Include the effect of investment repositionings into tax planning by calculating new tax estimates based upon changes in investment income and/or tax write-offs from tax sheltered or tax oriented investments.
- Be aware of changes in federal income taxation which alter tax liabilities including reductions or increases in rates and withholdings and other items of tax calculation.
- Develop alternate summaries of taxation and tax payment requirements as related to timing realization of income and expenses.

Individuals who own home computers should evaluate the purchase of inexpensive software for tax calculation. Some very good programs are available in the market place.

Some taxpayers prefer to withhold and/or pay taxes in full during the calendar year to avoid payment in April and facilitate budgeting. While "forced" payment avoids expenditure of funds needed for tax payments, it also reduces investment return. If you are inclined to spend extra cash, force yourself to write a check monthly to a special account, such as a money market fund, used exclusively for accumulation of funds needed for taxes. This will enable you to earn interest yet have funds available as needed.

Some individuals feel it is worthwhile to underpay taxes and

FORM 10–1 INCOME TAX PROJECTIONS

	Beginning of The Year	Periodic Projections			
Income					
Income from occupation	$	$	$	$	$
Income from investment					
Other income	$	$	$	$	$
Total income	$	$	$	$	$
Adjustments to Income					
IRA, Koegh	$	$	$	$	$
Other					
Adjusted Gross Income	$	$	$	$	$
Itemized Deductions					
Medical & Dental	$	$	$	$	$
Taxes					
Interest					
Contributions					
Casualty					
Misc.					
Total Itemized Deductions	$	$	$	$	$

Less: Zero* Bracket	$	$	$	$
Net Deductions	$	$	$	$
Personal Exemptions	$	$	$	$
Taxable Income	$	$	$	$
Taxes:				
Federal Income	$	$	$	$
FICA/Self Employment	$	$	$	$
Combined Federal	$	$	$	$
State	$	$	$	$
Local	$	$	$	$
Total	$	$	$	$
Federal Payment Requirements:				
Lesser of prior years tax or 80 % of current years tax	$	$	$	$
Projected planned withholdings & quarterly payments	$	$	$	$
Additional payments needed or projected (overpayment)	$	$	$	$

*If you do not itemize deductions, enter $0; if you file jointly enter $3,540; if you are married and file separately enter $1,770; if you are single enter $2,390–these figures will change with future indexing.

incur interest charges by the IRS, e.g., investment returns available in excess of interest costs. However, extreme caution must be exercised so that additional penalties or fraudulent activities charges are not levied. We discourage underpayment because of the high risks and likelihood of audit. The interest rate on deficient taxes is automatically adjusted semi-annually and is dependent upon general interest rate levels. Penalties vary with degree of infraction and are relatively severe.

AMENDED RETURNS AND TAX AUDITS

In the event you discover after filing your federal income tax return that you have made an error, you may refile with an amended return. You normally have three years from the time at which the original return was filed to claim a refund. With very special exceptions the time period may be extended. Interest is paid on refunds made after 45 days from the date the original return is filed. There is no time limit to amending a return for underpayment and interest may or may not be assessed.

Generally, if your return is audited by the IRS, the notice of audit must occur within three years of the filing due date. Certain misrepresentations can extend the period much longer, particularly if you did not file a return due for one or more tax years or fraud occurred.

It is frequently suggested that tax records be maintained five to seven years. With a neat and orderly filing system, we see no reason why records cannot be maintained for many years. Not all receipts and bills need to be kept for a long time. However, worksheets, summary sheets, and documentation for substantiating major sources of income and deductions, along with copies of returns filed and quarterly tax payments made can be retained without taking up a lot of space. The records may be helpful for tax and other future decision making.

The IRS does not disclose its methods for selecting returns for audit, however, the following are believed to increase your probability of being audited:

- Very high levels of income.
- Unusual sources of income.
- Tax shelter losses.
- Self-employment income and business ownership.
- Unusually high levels of itemized deductions.
- Underpayment of taxes during the year.

- Disorganized or confusing returns.
- Of course, unreported income such as interest and other sources which institutions and businesses are required to report to the IRS on behalf of taxpayers.

FIGURE 10-2   INCOME TAX PLANNING

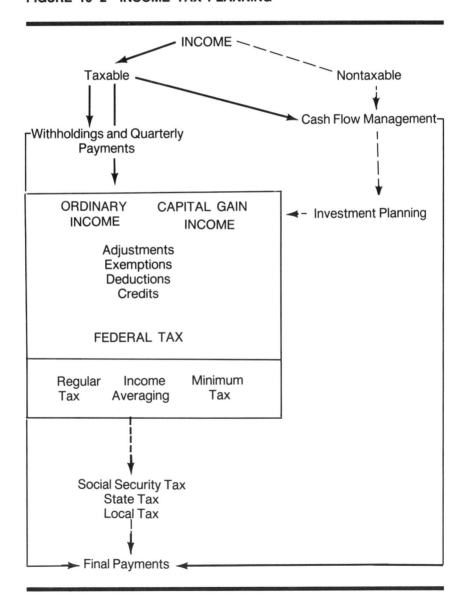

FORM 10-2 KNOW THE TAX IMPACT OF EACH IMPORTANT FINANCIAL OPPORTUNITY/DECISION

Opportunity/ Decision	Gross Income		Adjustments to Gross Income		Itemized Deductions		Exemptions		Tax Credits		Net Tax Change			
											Increase	Decrease		
	Increase	Decrease	Increase	Decrease	Increase	Decrease	Increase	Decrease	Increase	Decrease		Deferral	Elimination
	$	$	$	$	$	$	$	$	$	$	$	$	$
Summation of Combined Opportunities/ Decisions	$	$	$	$	$	$	$	$	$	$	$	$	$

11

REDUCING INCOME TAXES

"Education is to teach men not what to think but how to think."

Calvin Coolidge

A couple we work with from time to time has truly recognized the benefits of coordinated and in-depth planning. She is a corporate executive, earns a nice salary, is covered by a pension plan, participates in a deferred compensation 401(K) plan, and receives stock options and bonuses in addition to other employee benefits. He owns an incorporated small business. He draws a reasonable salary and annually funds pension and profit sharing plans. Their marginal federal tax bracket is 40 percent.

They keep about $10,000 of emergency/opportunity funds in a tax-exempt money market fund. In addition to their savings through employment, they annually fund IRAs and other personal investments. Their IRAs are invested in several growth and growth/income no-load mutual funds. Other personal investments include municipal bond unit trusts and growth and aggressive growth no-load mutual funds.

They live comfortably and their net worth is increasing rapidly. They don't need formal tax shelters. Tax shelters don't fit with their conservative natures, their taxes are reasonable, and much of their wealth is inside the qualified retirement plans, compounding on a tax-deferred basis.

Some people, however, are more aggressive risk takers and like investments that produce tax losses. We categorize investments that are designed to produce tax losses as either formal tax shelters or as tax-oriented investments.

TAX SHELTERS

Formal or deep tax shelters are aggressive in the sense of write-offs sought and are usually obtained through "private placement" partnerships with high financial requirements. Tax-oriented investments provide tax write-offs (although usually more limited in extent and reportable over a longer period of time) and, as with deep shelters, can provide tax-free cash flow and possible appreciation.

Tax-oriented investments usually have lower risk and are more appropriate for most people than deep shelters. Most tax-oriented investments can be obtained through "public" partnerships and investor financial requirements are usually moderate. Investors with marginal tax brackets of less than 40 percent do not belong in deep tax shelters. Some use of public programs for write-off may be appropriate.

With deep shelters, the write-offs normally comprise a major portion of the investment return. That is, tax savings have monetary value. But the savings are dependent upon your tax bracket. To generate savings at tax rates of 50 percent has significant value, while savings at rates of 15 percent are not nearly as valuable.

Tax shelters can be classic examples of improper tax planning. Besides over-sheltering with legitimate shelters, we often find that individuals invest in phony shelters or are unaware of "recapture" from legitimate shelters. Purchasing shelters will significantly increase your chances of being audited and if shelter losses are disallowed, heavy penalties and interest charges can be levied.

Promoters, or general partners, of tax shelters which are expected (with deductions and credits) to provide investors approximate write-offs of 2 to 1 or more during the first five years, are required to register shelters with the Internal Revenue Service. Investors, in turn, must include the shelter registration number on their personal income tax returns.

"At risk" rules apply to tax sheltering. Often nonrecourse debt is used to finance a portion of investment cost. Since an investor is

TABLE 11-1 TAX SHELTER INVESTING

Investment	Risk*	Multiple Write-Offs	Length of Write-Off Period	Cash Flow Distribution Potential	Appreciation Potential
Real Estate	Moderate	Yes	Extended	Good	Very Good
Equipment Leasing	High	No	Short	Good	Very Limited
Oil and Gas Drilling	High	No	Short	Good	Good
Research and Development	Very High	No	Short	Good	Good
Cattle Feeding/ Breeding	High	No	Very Short	Limited	Limited
Movies	Very High	No	Short	Very Good	Limited
Franchising	High	No	Moderate	Good	Very Good

*Within the risk realm of tax sheltering investing.

not personally liable for nonrecourse debt, the investor is not at risk for the debt. With the exception of real estate, tax reportable losses are limited to funds at risk (actual invested dollars plus future dollar commitments plus recourse debt, if any). Real estate, which is excluded from "at risk" rules can provide multiple write-offs on invested amounts. Other shelters, such as equipment leasing, oil and gas, or research and development projects are limited to write-offs of 100 percent of funds at risk (usually up to 1 to 1 on cash invested).

Tax savings from write-offs of 1 to 1 on cash invested for a 50 percent marginal bracket taxpayer are fifty cents on the dollar. The true net investment is 50 percent of invested income. Real estate, depending on structure, can provide write-offs of 2 to 1 or more, meaning net investment of 0 for a 50 percent marginal bracket taxpayer.

Some shelters provide tax write-offs over a very short period of time, examples include oil and gas exploratory drilling and equipment leasing. Other shelters, such as real estate, provide tax write-offs over an extended period of time.

The fact that the cost basis of an investment can fall over time because of reportable expenses leads to the concept of "recapture" as related to tax shelters. Recapture results in taxable income on the sale of an investment following reduction in the cost basis. The income can be both ordinary income and capital gain income depending upon length of time held, expense reporting methods, and other factors.

The idea of a "burned-out" shelter is common and means expenses have been fully reported and used and taxable income will be incurred. Most shelters provide losses because of "paper" expenses and eventually the expenses are used up (such as accelerated depreciation) and investors incur "paper profit" on which taxes are due. This is referred to as "turnaround" or "crossover." Payment of the taxes can be burdensome if cash distributions are not made from the investment. Shelters without good economics become costly. All tax shelter investing should be viewed as tax deferral, not tax elimination. Tax savings should be invested for possible use in later tax payments.

In a relative sense, there are very few good tax shelters, private or public. Typically a certain type will do well for awhile and then there is a flood of new promoters into that arena. Look at what has happened in oil and gas or trading of government securities futures; many, many people have lost a lot of money. Horse trading has recently become a very "hot" investment. Don't invest in any "exotic" deals.

We are concerned about the huge increase in real estate partnerships. We still consider real estate, in general, a favorable investment medium, but be very careful who you deal with and what type of investment you select. Often the up-front "take-out" by promoters totals 25 percent or more of funds raised. That means investors put up $100 for every $75 of net interest in a deal. We consider that too much in fees and commissions.

The very best tax shelters are usually private, small deals done on a local basis, with quality people. Again, though, make sure you are dealing with successful, honest people—retain tax and legal counsel.

We suggest you avoid deals where "take-out" is more than 15 percent and profit splits between partners are not equitable. If general partners in a limited partnership have not invested a substantial amount of their own money, they should receive no more than 30 percent of profits earned after limited partners' investment has been returned in full; and any management fees should be very reasonable. Watch out for hidden fees and charges.

In seeking tax shelter investments, analyze the following:

- the amount of your investment which will actually go into the deal (not to promoters);
- the appropriateness of participation as related to your marginal tax bracket (a low bracket means write-offs have low tax savings value);
- your tolerance for risk as most shelters are high risk investments;
- the time period for which you will need shelter—the time period you expect to be in a high tax bracket;
- the "economics" of a tax sheltered investment; tax savings alone do not make participation worthwhile; an investor is better off in a high yielding taxable investment than in a tax shelter with poor economics (income and gain potential);
- the extent of overall investment portfolio development—too often we see investors holding only shelters and no or too few pure investments.
- management of the shelter—be it yourself on an individual property or a management team for a partnership;
- management cost or fees and profit and cash flow distribution splits;
- projected income, expenses, and profitability;
- economic and market conditions for the particular investment media;
- the soundness of tax write-offs in terms of current IRS rulings and acceptable compliance and reporting standards; and
- any adverse affects (which may offset benefits of the investment) if a "flat" (or similar type) tax does pass in the United States.

QUALIFIED RETIREMENT PLANS

The three best forms of tax sheltering are: (1) use of growth investments to achieve long-term capital gain taxation; (2) receipt (particularly for high bracket taxpayers) of tax-free income, such as from municipal bond investments; and (3) use of qualified retirement plans.

Qualified retirement plans allow both for current shielding of income from taxation and for accumulation of tax-deferred income. Because of the deferral, it is wise to be conservative when investing qualified retirement plan money. You can make investments that otherwise might not be appropriate for you, such as investments with high income yield. Qualified retirement plan investing is discussed in the next two chapters.

As you are well aware, the Social Security program is rapidly deteriorating. It appears that Congress will continue to encourage use of qualified plans and will approve expanded types of qualified retirement plans and raise funding limits.

In the last chapter, we discussed IRAs—a type of retirement plan for which everyone with earned income qualifies.

Several other forms of retirement plans have been approved by Congress. Typically, the availability of these depends upon the form of business organization with which you are affiliated. Note, that as with IRAs, funding of the plans is related to earned income. For example, a passive investor in a limited partnership is not considered to have earned income. An employee of a partnership would have earned income.

Business organization can take one of several forms, some common ones are:

- *Proprietorship*—treated as individual taxpayer, with owner reporting profits or losses as personal income.
- *Partnership*—two or more individuals, with owners splitting profits or losses and reporting the income as personal income.
- *Corporation*—a separate legal entity subject to corporate income taxation on profits. Owner/employee reports compensation as personal income. Owners report dividends (profit distributions) as personal income. Corporations can be "publicly" owned (stock actively traded) or "privately" owned (stock not available to the public).
- *SubChapter S Corporation*—separate legal entity not generally subject to corporate income taxation. Owners split profits or losses and report the income as personal income.

Corporations are often preferred forms of business ownership because they offer the advantages of both limited liability and favorable employee benefits programs. Partnerships can also limit liability with formation of limited partnerships. A limited partnership must have at least one general partner (unlimited liability) and only general partners can participate in management. Often tax sheltered and tax-oriented investments are structured as limited partnerships to allow investors to report tax write-offs personally.

Corporations are allowed to implement pension and profit sharing programs. Employer contributions are tax deductible to the corporation and tax-free to employees until actually received. Several alternatives exist for implementation of a qualified retirement plan; including defined benefit pension, defined contribution pension, and profit sharing plan. The difference is that defined benefit means a projected annual income at retirement; defined contribution is a percent of current compensation. The maximum annual benefit which can currently be funded, under a defined benefit pension, is $90,000.

In a combined profit sharing/defined contribution pension plan, annual contribution limits per employee are the lesser of 25 percent of compensation or $30,000 (with a limit of 15 percent for profit sharing, 25 percent for defined contribution pension, and 25 percent combined limit). Profit-sharing plans offer greater flexibility because contributions are based on profitability and contributions do not have to be made annually.

A popular variation of profit sharing is the 401(K) deferred compensation plan. Employees can typically agree to contribute 10 percent to 15 percent of their annual compensation to the plan. The contributions are not subject to current income taxation and earn investment return on a tax-deferred basis. Employers normally match a portion of the employees' contributions.

In many instances, employees are able to make "voluntary" contributions to pension and profit sharing plans, which are not tax deductible. However, earnings accumulate and compound on a tax-deferred basis.

Employee Stock Ownership Plans (ESOPs) are also popular today. These plans provide another form through which employees own stock in their corporate employer. ESOPs are sometimes fully funded by the corporation; but in some instances employee contributions are required or allowed.

Each type of pension, profit sharing, and stock program carries restrictions with which you should become familiar. Any contribution by you should be viewed as long-term investing. Plan withdrawal rights may be limited or subject to penalties, and loans may or may not be allowed. And there are overall limitations to participation depending on the combination of programs.

Self-employed individuals (including proprietorships and partnerships) can establish Keogh plans—another form of qualified retirement plan. Placement of funds in Keogh plans provides tax write-offs and tax savings as well as accumulation of earnings on a tax-deferred basis. Maximum funding of defined contribution Keogh plans is the lesser of $30,000 or 20 percent of net self employment income. The maximum annual benefit which can currently be funded with a defined benefit Keogh plan is $90,000. Provided the provisions of a plan allow voluntary contributions, additional nondeductible contributions can be made to Keoghs.

SubChapter S corporations are also allowed corporate retirement programs (pension or profit sharing), but are subject to Keogh limitations.

If you are both a corporate employee and self-employed (i.e., part-time business) it is possible for you to be a participant in a pension plan, a profit sharing plan, a Keogh plan and an IRA. Of course, the extent of participation depends on affordability. Also, in the case of plans where you do not control investments or investment options are very limited, the availability of investments and performance, thereof, is very important.

PERSONAL INVESTING

Personal investing, or investing with title in your own name (not that of a qualified retirement plan), requires careful consideration of tax ramifications. As noted before, tax shelters and tax-oriented investments are not for everyone, and qualified plan use is subject to limitations.

It is necessary for goal achievement to build up other investments. Table 11–2 indicates the general tax favorability of various forms of personal investment income. Its use is strictly limited. The table, for example, does not suggest that a high bracket taxpayer would not want taxable profits. Rather, it indicates that a large portion of the profits will be subject to tax. Even so, this may be preferable to many other investments, including deep shelters.

It is important, when investing, to remember whether or not returns will be taxed, at what tax rates, and when.

Timing is very important in making investment, income, and expenditure decisions. Receiving current interest income does not allow you any control over the timing of taxation. It's taxed in the year of receipt. With an investment subject to capital gain tax, you can control tax timing by deciding when you want to sell.

Another example of the importance of timing is the exercise of employee stock options. More and more companies are recognizing

TABLE 11-2 INVESTMENT INCOME— GENERAL TAX FAVORABILITY

	Marginal Tax Bracket		
Investment Income Source	Low – Less than 25%	Moderate 25% to 35%	High – More than 35%
Interest (Taxable)	Yes	Yes	No
Interest (Tax Free)	No	Yes	Yes
Dividends (Taxable)	Yes	Yes	No
Dividends (Excluded or Return of Capital)	No	Yes	Yes
Capital Gains (Short-Term)	Yes	Yes	No
Capital Gains (Long-Term)	No	Yes	Yes
Capital Losses (Short-Term)	No	Yes	Yes
Capital Losses (Long-Term)	No	Yes	Yes
Profits (Cash Inflow), Taxable	Yes	Yes	No
Profits (Cash Inflow), Tax Sheltered	No	Yes	Yes
Losses (No Cash Outflow) Public Programs	No	Yes	Yes
Losses (No Cash Outflow) Deep Shelters	No	No	Yes

the motivational benefits of having employees share in ownership of the company.

There are two basic types of employee stock options—qualified and nonqualified. Each gives the holder the right to purchase a certain number of shares at a fixed price for a limited time period. As with qualified retirement plans, vesting (percentage rights to value) is usually spread over several years. If the price of the company stock rises, the options gain value.

Options are not subject to tax at the time of issue. Upon exercise, nonqualified options are subject to ordinary income tax on the difference between exercise cost and market value(market value, in some instances, can be determined either at the time of exercise or six months later). When the stock purchased through exercise is later sold, any gain over value at the time of exercise is subject to capital gain treatment (either short term or long term, depending on how long shares were held).

Qualified options are not subject to taxation upon exercise. Gains in value over exercise cost are subject to capital gain tax upon sale.

Sometimes options can be exercised with use of "stock appreciation rights" by the employee, with receipt of a combination of stock and cash. There are various other restrictions to which options are subject. Timing of exercise and sale is very important from both an investment and taxation point of view.

INCOME SHIFTING

Income shifting is the concept of transferring taxable income from a high marginal bracket taxpayer to a low marginal bracket taxpayer ($10,000 of interest income, for example, nets $5,000 to a 50 percent bracket taxpayer and $8,000 to a 20 percent marginal bracket taxpayer). Reasons for doing so, in addition to tax considerations, include funding children's education costs or supporting older family members. Many techniques for accomplishing income shifting are available; some common basic techniques are:

- *Clifford Trusts*—These are short term trusts through which investment income and taxation flow to the beneficiaries (e.g., children). The trusts lack flexibility because each principal deposit, each of which will ultimately be returned to the trust creator (grantor), must be committed for at least ten years and a day. Clifford Trusts may also trigger adverse estate and gift tax consequences, and use of funds for obligatory support payments (which in some instances may include education) may disqualify the tax advantages.
- *Spousal Remainder Trusts*—Similar to Clifford Trusts in that taxable investment income can be shifted to a lower bracket taxpayer; however, the duration of the trust can be shorter (often four years), but principal must go to your spouse upon termination of the trust.
- *Direct Gifting*—Allowable annual gifting without gift taxes, is $10,000 per year per donee ($20,000 if both husband and wife join in gifting). Investment return on gifted assets is taxable to the donee at his or her tax rates. Minor children can be gifted to under the Uniform Gifts to Minors Act (UGMA), with a close family friend or relative as designated custodian (someone other

than the donor). Realize, though, that in most states, under UGMA, children will have full rights to funds at age 18. To delay these rights, some people instead gift through what is referred to as a 2503 (C) trust. This is an irrevocable trust which can delay distribution and provide greater investment flexibility, but also may be costly and difficult to manage.

Interest-free loans to family members used to be a popular form of income shifting. However, the benefits have been practically eliminated because lenders are subject to "imputed" interest and possibly to gift taxes. There are exceptions, though. Up to $10,000 can be lent to a family member interest-free, without income tax consequences to the lender, provided the borrower does not use the proceeds to purchase investments which produce income. Under similar use restrictions, the loan amount can be extended to $100,000 provided the borrower does not have more than $1,000 of annual investment income.

The value of income shifting includes payment of expenses with pre-tax dollars instead of after-tax dollars as well as lower taxation on investment earnings. Like many tax concepts, though, income shifting is often "over-sold" and is not for everyone nor at all economic times. Income shifting should be evaluated closely in conjunction with the level of established financial security and the marginal tax bracket of the donors. In general, income shifting is more attractive during periods of high investment return on fixed investments—or, in other words, high interest rates. During favorable growth (capital gain opportunities) periods, potential donors can in effect achieve income shifting by making growth investments on their own behalf. If anticipated growth returns are achieved, assets can be gifted to donees and liquidated at their lower tax rates.

Use of SubChapter S corporations or family partnerships, as income tax and estate tax shifting vehicles, are more complex examples of income shifting. SubChapter S corporations, for example, can be funded for business activities and/or for making economically sound and profitable, passive type investments. Sub S corporations can be used for family investing, management fees and profits can be distributed to allocate compensation, and future stockholders can be accepted as desired (either on an equity or gifting basis). Extreme care must be taken in structuring family corporations or partnerships.

OTHER TAX SAVINGS OPPORTUNITIES

There are many techniques for reducing taxes, from the very conservative to the very aggressive. Appropriateness of a particular technique is dependent on your personal circumstances. Your neighbor's or friend's use of tax planning may not be right for you. Be cautious and thorough. The following are demonstrative of some of the many tax saving opportunities available.

- Whether you are an employee or a business owner, opportunities may exist for legitimately converting expenses to payment with pre-tax dollars rather than after-tax dollars. Someone in the 40 percent bracket must earn $100 to pay an after-tax expense of $60. If the expense is paid with before-tax dollars, only $60 must be earned to cover the cost. Or in other words, earning $100 will leave $0 after tax and expense if the expense is not tax qualified, whereas $24 will remain if the expense is qualified—only $40 of the $100 will be taxable. Programs through which expenses can qualify for this tax treatment include "cafeteria" plans and business expense reimbursement plans. "Cafeteria" or flexible benefit programs enable employees to submit a variety of qualifying expenses (child care, insurance premiums, legal fees, etc.) for tax-free reimbursement; thus in effect converting payment from after-tax dollars to pre-tax dollars.

- Use of the normal annual exclusion of $100 ($200 on a joint return) from dividends received (directly or through mutual funds) from U.S. corporations. Dividends beyond $100 per year ($200 on a joint return) are taxable as ordinary income, unless inside some type of tax qualified plan (stock purchase, pension, etc.) or specifically treated as non-taxable.

- Use of the special and additional utility dividend exclusion. With utilities, an exclusion of $750 per year ($1,500 on joint returns) is available on all dividends reinvested. The dividends effectively received in stock instead of cash escape current income taxation and will have a zero basis so that when sold, the full proceeds will be taxed at capital gains rates. Avoid using utility dividends treated as "return of capital," and therefore, already tax-free. The utility dividend exclusion is scheduled to end in 1985.

- Controlling owners of corporations can take advantage of the 85 percent dividend exclusion on dividends received from ownership by the corporation of stock (including through mutual funds) in other U.S. corporations. This is of particular value if a corporation is subject to high corporate income taxes because of high profits, and the corporation has excess funds to invest.

- Installment sale can be used when selling appreciated property. Negotiate with the buyer to make purchase payments over several years. Capital gain taxes are payable as proceeds are received. Deferring gains over several years may reduce taxes in two ways; payment with inflation eroded (cheaper) dollars and payment at lower marginal tax rates in comparison to possible rates if all gain is reported in one year. The measurement of value of an installment sale should include analysis of interest which can be charged to the buyer on the unpaid balance. Low interest will partially negate the benefits of tax savings from an installment sale. It is important to note that "recapture" (e.g., ordinary income because of accelerated depreciation write-offs) attributable to sale of real or personal property is reportable in the year of sale regardless of amounts collected for that year under an installment sale.

- Tax-free exchanges for property of "like-kind" can avoid taxation. That is, a "swap" could be made for property which is more favorable to you and, if the properties have equal value, no gain will be incurred. If values differ, a gain could be incurred. The cost basis of the first property will become the basis of the second property and gain will be deferred until realized (i.e., upon actual sale). Many types of assets can be exchanged tax-free, such as real estate for real estate. A major exception, though, is securities—stocks and bonds cannot be exchanged tax-free unless special qualifications are met.

- In some instances, charitable contributions are best made with assets, rather than cash, or through trusts. The same charitable objectives can be accomplished with greater tax benefits or less cost.

Suppose a 50 percent taxpayer wishes to provide a charity with $20,000 and could either give cash or appreciated stock, purchased for $6,000 several years ago, now worth $20,000. If the stock was liquidated, the taxpayer would have long-term capital gains tax due of $2,800—a net after tax liquidation value of $17,200. If the stock were instead donated, a $20,000 deduction would save $10,000 in taxes—in effect on $17,200 of cash value. Whereas a direct cash contribution would have to be $20,000 to save $10,000 in taxes. In essence a charitable contribution saving the taxpayer $10,000 in taxes and providing a charity with $20,000 in value could be accomplished on a lower net basis to the taxpayer by donating the appreciated stock rather than cash.

An example of a charitable deduction method which is used relatively infrequently is the charitable lead trust. We favor a format for a charitable lead trust, whereby, a donor gifts an immediate income interest in property to a charity for a period of years (which can vary by desire). The charity receives the investment income and the donor takes a current tax deduction on the present worth of an annual annuity to the charity and then has investment principal revert back to him at the end of the term. The annual income received by the charity is taxable to the donor, however, tax liabilities can be avoided by using tax exempt municipal bonds instead of property producing taxable income. This technique is particularly effective for a taxpayer who wishes to make charitable contributions but wants to retain investment property, and/or who expects to be in a lower tax bracket in future years.

Tax considerations should be reviewed thoroughly and options explored with tax professionals to select the best alternatives for tax management.

SOME INCOME TAX DO'S

- Plan your taxes several times each year and coordinate tax planning with other financial planning areas.
- Get into the habit of asking yourself the tax impacts of financial decisions.
- Make full use of investment opportunities for reducing taxes; starting with qualified retirement plans and employment programs.
- Take advantage of tax-deferred earnings such as with voluntary (nondeductible) pension and profit sharing contributions.
- Seek tax deferral opportunities in addition to tax elimination—pay with cheaper, future dollars.
- Choose economically favorable investments (even if taxable) over tax shelters providing low economic returns.
- Become familiar with concise sources of information on new tax changes and planning techniques; tax laws change frequently.
- Seek more sophisticated tax planning options as your financial position becomes more complex and more resources are available.

- Integrate business and personal activities for optimal tax planning;

  time vacations to coincide with tax deductible seminars;
  hire your spouse and children if you are self-employed to shift income and increase qualified plan contributions;
  turn hobbies into businesses to realize tax advantages;
  put as many expenses as possible through a business;
  as an employee, understand deductible expenses such as entertainment, education costs, and extra car mileage; and
  realize that employment compensation comes in many forms, some of which are more tax favorable than others.

- Pick tax-oriented investments managed by individuals with good long-term track records.
- Have professional advisors review investment deals if you are unsure; the cost will be worthwhile.
- Look for favorable ways out of burned-out tax shelters such as gifting.
- Take advantage of year-end securities trading which reduces taxes such as swapping bonds or selling stocks with losses but holding stocks with gains.
- Realize that some assets take a stepped-up basis at death; meaning capital gains taxes can be eliminated on appreciated assets.
- Take advantage of opportunities such as tax-free gains on home sale and use of private annuities during retirement years.

SOME INCOME TAX DON'TS

- Let tax savings opportunities slip by, even if small (many small savings add up to large savings).
- Purchase tax shelters or tax-oriented investments solely on the advise of commissioned salespeople; trade through these people after receiving objective advice.
- Buy tax shelters which are exotic or offer unrealistically high write-offs.
- Participate in very unusual tax reduction techniques (e.g., tax trusts or nonprofit, self-owned institutions) until getting the opinion of several reputable tax experts.
- Get caught up in the band-wagon effect on new tax or investment ideas unless you are sure the ideas are legitimate.
- Assume sophisticated techniques (e.g., offshore banking, etc.) are for you if you do not have a lot of money or financial complexity.

- Realize imputed (non-cash) income unless it is prudent to do so (e.g., employer paid life insurance above $50,000, life insurance inside qualified retirement plans, tax shelter recapture, etc.).
- Confuse the investment appropriateness for personal investing with qualified retirement plan investing.
- Purchase highly leveraged or other inappropriate investments inside qualified retirement plans because tax qualification can be lost due to unrelated business income treatment.
- Over-fund qualified retirement plans.
- Over-shelter such that tax write-offs from investments only save taxes at low marginal bracket rates.
- Let poor timing of expense incurrence waste itemized deductions which cannot be carried forward to future years.
- Lose deductions because of tax traps (e.g., a security loss on sale can't be taken if the same security is repurchased within 30 days).
- Commit to income realization, such as employment contracts or asset sales, until you know existing tax alternatives.
- Get trapped in "tax shelter syndrome"—continually buying new shelters to avoid tax due to recapture or turn-around of old shelters.

TAX SHELTER RETURNS

There are many techniques for evaluating financial return from an investment in a tax shelter. We favor the following present value method. Importantly, a worthwhile shelter must have both tax savings benefits and economic (income and gain) potential.

Taking a simple example to demonstrate calculation, assume the conditions in Table 11–3.

(Use present value factors in Table 11–4.)

$ INVESTMENT PRESENT VALUE (8% DISCOUNT)

$20,000 now	$20,000
$10,000 1 year from now	9,259
TOTAL	$29,259

NET ANNUAL $ RETURN PRESENT VALUE (8% DISCOUNT)

$10,000 1 year from now	$ 9,259
$ 5,000 2 years from now	4,287
$ 2,500 3 years from now	1,985
$ 2,500 4 years from now	1,838
$18,500 5 years from now	12,591
TOTAL	$29,960

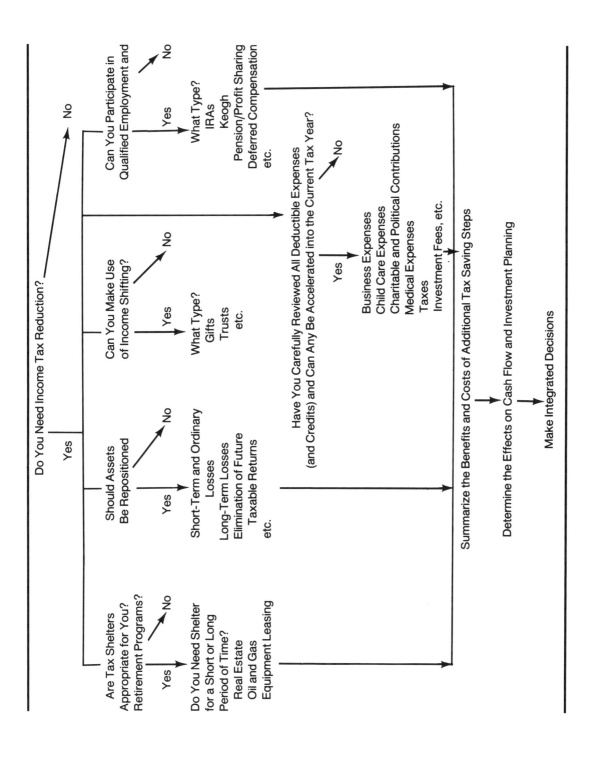

Do You Need Income Tax Reduction?

Yes

No

Are Tax Shelters
Appropriate for You?
Retirement Programs?

Yes → No

Do You Need Shelter
for a Short or Long
Period of Time?
Real Estate
Oil and Gas
Equipment Leasing

Should Assets
Be Repositioned

Yes → No

Short-Term and Ordinary
Losses
Long-Term Losses
Elimination of Future
Taxable Returns
etc.

Can You Make Use
of Income Shifting?

Yes → No

What Type?
Gifts
Trusts
etc.

Can You Participate in
Qualified Employment and

Yes → No

What Type?
IRAs
Keogh
Pension/Profit Sharing
Deferred Compensation
etc.

Have You Carefully Reviewed All Deductible Expenses
(and Credits) and Can Any Be Accelerated into the Current Tax Year?

Yes → No

Business Expenses
Child Care Expenses
Charitable and Political Contributions
Medical Expenses
Taxes
Investment Fees, etc.

Summarize the Benefits and Costs of Additional Tax Saving Steps

→ Determine the Effects on Cash Flow and Investment Planning

→ Make Integrated Decisions

FORM 11-1 TAX SHELTER RETURN*

	A	B	C	D	E
		Projected Tax Savings (Increase)	Projected Cash Distributions + from Operation +	Projected Net Proceeds from Asset Sales =	Net Annual
Year	$ Investment				$ Return
——	$_____	$_____	$_____	$_____	$_____
——	_____	_____	_____	_____	_____
——	_____	_____	_____	_____	_____
——	_____	_____	_____	_____	_____
——	_____	_____	_____	_____	_____
——	_____	_____	_____	_____	_____
——	_____	_____	_____	_____	_____
——	_____	_____	_____	_____	_____
——	_____	_____	_____	_____	_____
——	_____	_____	_____	_____	_____

*Follow steps in Form 11-2.

FORM 11-2 STEPS TO CALCULATING TAX SHELTER RETURN

1. Enter Projected Figures from Investment Prospectus
    A. $ Investment Commitment
    B. Tax Savings (Increase) Based on Assumed Fixed Marginal Rate or Following Steps for each Year

Projected taxable income without shelter	$_____
Projected tax without shelter	$_____
Projected taxable income with shelter deductions (income)	$_____
Projected tax with shelter deductions (income)	$_____
Net change in taxable income	$_____
Net change in tax—tax savings (increase)	$_____
New marginal tax bracket	_____%

Form 11–2 *(concluded)*

  C. Projected Cash Distributions from Business Operations
  D. Projected Proceeds from Investment Property Sale—Based on Reasonable Assumed Appreciation
  E. Summation of Tax Savings (Increase) + Projected Cash Distribution + Net Proceeds from Investment Property Sale

2. Using Present Value Tables—Assume a Discount Rate Equivalent to Your Average Investment Rate of Return—Separately Determine Present Value of $ Investment Column (A) and Net Annual $ Return Column (E)

3. If Present Value of $ Investment Column (A) Exceeds Present Value of Net Annual $ Return Column (E) Do Not Consider Investing

4. If Present Value of $ Investment Column (A) Is Less than Present Value of Net Annual $ Return Column (E) Do Consider Investing

5. If Reasonable and Complete Projection Figures—Based on Conservative Assumptions—Are not Made Available, Do Not Consider Investing

---

TABLE 11–3

Year	$ Investment	Tax Savings (Increase) +	Cash Distributions +	Proceeds from Asset Sale =	Net Annual $ Return
1	$20,000	$10,000	$ 0	$ 0	$10,000
2	10,000	5,000	0	0	5,000
3	0		2,500	0	2,500
4	0		2,500	0	2,500
5	0	(7,500)	1,000	25,000	18,500

TABLE 11-4 PRESENT VALUE FACTORS

DISCOUNT RATE

Years Until Payment	6%	8%	10%	12%	14%	16%	18%	20%	22%	24%
1	.9434	.9259	.9091	.8929	.8772	.8621	.8475	.8333	.8197	.8065
2	.8900	.8573	.8264	.7972	.7695	.7432	.7182	.6944	.6719	.6504
3	.8396	.7938	.7513	.7118	.6750	.6407	.6086	.5787	.5507	.5245
4	.7921	.7350	.6830	.6355	.5921	.5523	.5158	.4823	.4514	.4230
5	.7473	.6806	.6209	.5674	.5194	.4761	.4371	.4019	.3700	.3411
6	.7050	.6302	.5645	.5066	.4556	.4104	.3704	.3349	.3033	.2751
7	.6651	.5835	.5132	.4523	.3996	.3538	.3139	.2791	.2486	.2218
8	.6274	.5403	.4665	.4039	.3506	.3050	.2660	.2326	.2038	.1789
9	.5919	.5002	.4241	.3606	.3075	.2630	.2255	.1938	.1670	.1443
10	.5584	.4632	.3855	.3220	.2697	.2267	.1911	.1615	.1369	.1164
11	.5268	.4289	.3505	.2875	.2366	.1954	.1619	.1346	.1122	.0938
12	.4970	.3971	.3186	.2567	.2076	.1685	.1372	.1122	.0920	.0757
13	.4688	.3677	.2897	.2292	.1821	.1452	.1163	.0935	.0754	.0610
14	.4423	.3405	.2633	.2046	.1597	.1252	.0985	.0779	.0618	.0492
15	.4173	.3152	.2394	.1827	.1401	.1079	.0835	.0649	.0507	.0397
16	.3936	.2919	.2176	.1631	.1229	.0930	.0708	.0541	.0415	.0320
17	.3714	.2703	.1978	.1456	.1078	.0802	.0600	.0451	.0340	.0258
18	.3503	.2502	.1799	.1300	.0946	.0691	.0508	.0376	.0279	.0208
19	.3305	.2317	.1635	.1161	.0829	.0596	.0431	.0313	.0229	.0168
20	.3118	.2145	.1486	.1037	.0728	.0514	.0365	.0261	.0187	.0135
21	.2942	.1987	.1351	.0926	.0638	.0443	.0309	.0217	.0154	.0109
22	.2775	.1839	.1228	.0826	.0560	.0382	.0262	.0191	.0126	.0088
23	.2618	.1703	.1117	.0738	.0491	.0329	.0222	.0151	.0103	.0071
24	.2470	.1577	.1015	.0659	.0431	.0284	.0188	.0126	.0085	.0057
25	.2330	.1460	.0923	.0588	.0378	.0245	.0160	.0105	.0069	.0046

CONCLUSION
Consider investing and conduct full evaluation of investment managers; market conditions, IRS acceptability, and other pertinent factors. The greater the excess of net annual $ return present value over $ investment present value the better. If you feel you want a net investment return spread over inflation by a certain percent, make the discount on net annual $ return present value that much higher than the discount on $ investment present value.

12

SELECTING INVESTMENTS

"Not what we have, but what we use, not what we see, but what
we choose, these are the things that mar or bless the sum of
human happiness."

Joseph Fort Newton

An accountant once called upon us to review the investments of one
of his firm's executive clients. The executive was worth about
$500,000—$150,000 in home equity, $25,000 in passbook savings,
and most of the balance in stock (both inside and outside of qualified plans) of his employer. He preferred the company stock because he believed in the potential of the company and because he
had previously been "burned" on other investments. He had lost
$20,000 in a managed commodities account in two days, $60,000 in a
government securities trading company that went bankrupt, and
about $25,000 when a broker convinced him to write naked options.

It's easy to understand why the company stock and passbook
savings appealed to him. However, unless you are building your
own company where great financial commitment is required for
high return, it's important to be diversified. Even building a business is not for the less than aggressive investor. The executive
actually preferred moderate risk and did not understand the high
risk he was incurring by holding such a large portion of his wealth in

the stock of one company. In today's world, just about any company can go bankrupt.

Far too often we have met people who have been successful in their careers, but depended on outsiders to handle their investments and ended up losing money either through poor performance or simply being "taken." Career success means the ability to oversee matters. You can also effectively oversee your investments.

There are many aspects to successful investing. A prerequisite, though, is to view investing from a "total approach." See your various investments and opportunities as part of an integrated plan; giving attention to specific matters without losing sight of the whole picture.

BLENDING THE PLANNING AREAS

Investment choices must be blended with all financial planning areas. Cash flow management, income tax planning, and estate planning should be addressed in the process of making investment decisions. Overall risk management should also be considered. Ask yourself the following questions:

Cash Flow Management

- Is there a need to generate cash income from investments for living expenditures?
- Are you in a position to commit to investments which may require future cash outlays?

Income Tax Planning

- Is income tax reduction a stated objective now; in the next several years?
- What is your marginal income tax rate?
- What portion of investment income is paid in taxes?
- Should taxable or nontaxable investments be sought?

Estate Planning

- Which family members should own investments and which investments should they own?

- Do estates between husband and wife need to be equalized?
- Should titling of assets be joint, outright, in trust, custodial accounts, etc?

Risk Management

- How comfortable are you with risk?
- How well are disability income funding, retirement funding, and estate funding covered?
- How much risk should be accepted at this time, in the future?
- Have you established appropriate levels of liquidity, balance, and diversification in your investment program?

INVESTMENT STRATEGIES SUCCESS

In addition to blending investment planning with other financial planning areas, investment strategies success requires the integration of specific goals, investment needs, and available investment media alternatives. This integration can be summarized in these steps:

1. Determine savings levels, capacities, and investable assets.

    The need to save must be evaluated in conjunction with expenditure goals; cash flow analysis will determine the ability to save.

    Consideration should be given to forced savings techniques as well as planned, voluntary savings.

    Savings should be placed in investment control accounts for later placement in more appropriate investment media.

    Savings placement will add to the investment portfolio and should be made in line with strategies for goal achievement.

2. Define individual investment objectives including short-term objectives and amounts required, and long-term objectives and amounts required. Remember that amounts required are a function of personal needs and inflation.

3. Evaluate investment needs.

    These include growth, income, tax reduction, liquidity, diversification, balance, and safety.

    Identify your individual comfort levels—psychological needs and profiles should be included along with economic and monetary returns in setting up an investment program.

4. Select investment alternatives with integration of goals and investment needs.

Good market information on availability of investment media is necessary.

A clear understanding of the various investment media should be obtained.

Match available investment media with goals and investment needs and select the amounts of participation in various investments.

5. Monitor investments selected and repeat the process as goals, investment needs, and investment alternatives change or are altered by other variables such as economic conditions (see Figure 12–1).

INVESTMENT PLACEMENT

Table 12–1 (Comparison of Investment Alternatives) summarizes the applicability of many different investment media to investment needs. Ratings for the chart are:

FIGURE 12–1 INVESTMENT STRATEGIES SUCCESS

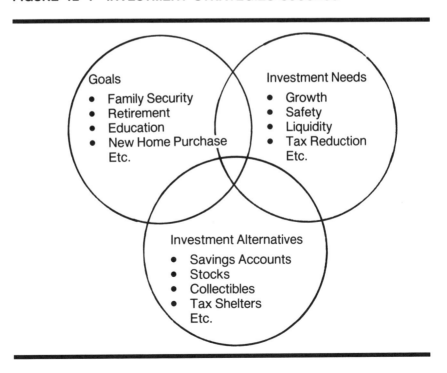

Liquidity	Safety	Potential Investment Return, Income & Growth	Personal Management Attention	Diversification
Excellent	Very high	Very high	Extensive	Extensive
Good	High	High	Moderate	Moderate
Fair	Moderate	Moderate	Little	Little
Poor	Poor	Low		None
Very poor	Very poor	Very low		
	Low	None		
	Very low			

To assist you in reviewing the chart, we have included appropriateness, defined in these tiers:

Tier 1 Investors   Most people; still developing an investment base; not yet close to complete financial security; limited amount of funds; accumulating funds at a moderate rate.

Tier 2 Investors   Good investment base; recognize that financial independence is a very realistic goal; moderate accumulation of funds; accumulating funds at a rapid rate.

Tier 3 Investors   Extremely well-developed investment base; have achieved financial independence; extensive accumulation of funds.

We do not recommend many of the investments listed on the chart. However, for various reasons, you may either have or prefer some of the investments listed. In reviewing the chart, keep in mind that your status may change and different strategies may need to be pursued.

After determining investment alternatives which are appropriate for you, answer the following questions for each investment possibility:

1. Who will manage the investment, yourself or a management team? Is the management team good (be it yourself, a mutual fund management group, corporate officers, or managers of a limited partnership)?

TABLE 12-1 COMPARISON OF INVESTMENT ALTERNATIVES

Investment Alternatives	Liquidity	Safety	Potential Investment Return		Taxability	Personal Management Attention	Diversification	Appropriateness Tier
			Income	Growth				
Annuities & Life Insurance Cash Values	Fair	High	Low	None	Deferred	Little	None	1
Bonds (Corporate) Individual Purchase	Fair	Moderate	Very High	Low	Full on Income	Extensive	Little	3
Mutual Funds & Unit Trusts	Good/Fair	High/Moderate	Very High	Low	Full on Income	Moderate	Extensive	1, 2, 3
Bonds (Municipal) Individual Purchase	Fair	Moderate	Moderate	Low	None on Income	Extensive	Little	2, 3
Mutual Funds & Unit Trusts	Good/Fair	High/Moderate	Moderate	Low	None on Income	Moderate	Extensive	2, 3
Bonds (Federal Government) Individual	Fair	Very High	High	Low	Full on Income	Moderate	Little	3
Mutual Funds & Unit Trusts	Good/Fair	Very High	High	Low	Full on Income	Moderate	Extensive	1, 2, 3
Business Ventures Individual Purchase	Very Poor	Very Low	Depends	Very High	Full on Income/Capital Gain	Extensive	None	2, 3
Pooled Purchase	Poor	Low	Depends	High	Full on Income/Capital Gain	Moderate	Moderate	2, 3
Cash & Savings Accounts (Banks & Financial Institutions)	Excellent	Very High	Moderate	None	Full	Little	None	1

Cash & Savings Accounts (Money Market Funds) Regular	Excellent	High	High	None	Full	Little	Extensive	1, 2, 3
Federal Gov't Securities	Excellent	Very High	High/High	None	Full	Little	Extensive	1, 2, 3
Municipal Securities	Excellent	High	Moderate	None	None	Little	Extensive	2, 3
Collectibles & Hard Assets	Poor	Moderate	None	High	Capital Gains	Moderate	Little	2, 3
Commodities Individual Purchase	Poor	Very Low	None	Very High	Special	Extensive	Little	3
Pooled Purchase	Poor	Very Low	None	High	Special	Moderate	Moderate	2, 3
Equipment Leasing (Public Programs)	Poor	Poor	Moderate	Very Low	Income Sheltered	Little	Moderate	1, 2, 3
Equipment Leasing (Private Programs)	Very Poor	Very Poor	High	Low	Income Sheltered	Moderate	Little	2, 3
Oil & Gas (Public Programs) Developmental	Poor	Poor	High	Moderate	Income Partially Sheltered	Little	Moderate	1, 2, 3
Exploratory	Poor	Very Poor	Depends	High	Income Partially Sheltered	Moderate	Moderate	2, 3
Oil & Gas (Private Programs) Developmental	Very Poor	Very Poor	Very High	Moderate	Income Partially Sheltered	Moderate	Moderate	2, 3
Exploratory	Very Poor	Low	Depends	Very High	Sheltered	Moderate	Little	2, 3
Options (Purchase) Commodities & Futures	Poor	Very Poor	None	Very High	Full	Extensive	Little	3

Investment								
Stocks	Fair	Poor	None	High	Full	Extensive	Little	2, 3
Real Estate (Public Programs)								
Commercial & Residential Pools	Poor	Moderate	High	High	Income Sheltered	Little	Extensive	1, 2, 3
Mortgage Pools	Poor	Moderate	Very High	Low	Full / Possible Income Sheltered	Little	Extensive	1, 2, 3
Reits	Fair	Moderate	High	Moderate	Income Sheltered	Moderate	Moderate	1, 2, 3
Real Estate (Private Programs)								
Commercial & Residential Pools	Very Poor	Poor	High	High	Income Sheltered	Moderate	Little	2, 3
Gov't Sponsored Properties	Very Poor	Moderate	Moderate	Moderate	Income Sheltered	Moderate	Little	2, 3
Individual Purchase	Very Poor	Poor	Moderate	High	Income Sheltered	Extensive	None	3
Stocks (Growth)								
Individual Purchase	Fair	Poor	None	Very High	Capital Gain	Extensive	Little	2, 3
Mutual Funds	Good/Fair	Moderate	Very Low	Very High	Capital Gain	Moderate	Extensive	1, 2, 3
Stocks (Growth & Income)								
Individual Purchase	Fair	Moderate	High	High	On Income With Some Exception/ Capital Gain	Extensive	Little	2, 3
Mutual Funds	Good/Fair	Moderate	Moderate	High	On Income With Some Exception/ Capital Gain	Moderate	Extensive	1, 2, 3

2. Are there tax write-offs associated with the investment? What value will the write-offs have? Will there be recapture taxes at some point? If so, will cash income be available to pay the taxes?

3. If there will be taxable income, will it be ordinary income, long-term capital gain income, or other specially taxed income?

4. What annual income, after taxes, can be expected from the investment?

5. What annual growth rates will be expected from the investment?

6. Will the investment mature? If so, when?

7. Can the investment be sold quickly and at a favorable price, if need be?

INVESTMENT PRINCIPLES

There are a number of factors or investment characteristics that should be considered in choosing investments.

Safety

It is important to protect a major portion of your funds, especially retirement funds, from loss. Yet, investment return must exceed inflation. It is commonly stated that there is a direct relationship between risk and investment return—higher risk, higher return. What is not commonly stated, is that equal returns do not necessarily equate to the same risk. Seek to maximize return while minimizing risk. There is a comfortable balance between return and risk.

Liquidity

Simply stated, liquidity is the ease with which an investment can be converted to cash. Does it take an hour, few days, months, or years? Most of your investment funds, because of available returns and the need for flexibility, should have a liquidity time period of no more than a few weeks. Immediate liquidity results in low investment return and extended liquidity means lack of flexibility.

Balance

Direct investments return comes in two forms: (a) current income (interest and dividends) and (b) capital appreciation or gain (realized upon sale). Current income is like the "bird in hand" theory, yet return is usually limited. Depending on economic and interest rate conditions, interest and dividend payments often range from 5 percent to 15 percent on invested funds. To realize greater return, you must seek growth of investment funds through capital appreciation. But future appreciation is not predictable with high accuracy. Therefore, risk is incurred (but can be managed); gains will be determined at the time of liquidation. Both current income and capital appreciation should be sought. Get some sure return and pursue growth to build financial security.

Diversification

Risk can be substantially reduced by spreading investment funds. Participate in several types of investment media and, furthermore, several different investments within each medium. Risk is further reduced by using several professional money managers, not one but several.

Tax Treatment

Remember that taxation depends on both the form of investment return and the form in which an investment is held. Main breakdowns of the latter are:

- Outright personal investing—usually made with after-tax dollars and returns may be subject to personal income taxation.
- Qualified plan investing—such as IRAs, Keoghs, Pensions, etc; returns accumulate on a tax-deferred basis.
- Business investing—made with business funds or inside business structures, particularly corporations; returns may be subject to corporate income taxation.

Size of Investment Media

Some investments require very sizeable investment commitments, such as $100,000. Other investments have no minimum requirements. Be extremely cautious of large investment commitments as these can distort investment planning and hinder goal achievement. On the other hand, extremely small investments may be relatively costly if commission charges are assessed.

Amount of Attention Required

Most people do not have much time to allocate to investment management because of other time commitments. Yet, you cannot afford to let your financial matters go unattended. It is important to develop a system for investing and monitoring investments, which can be easily implemented and maintained, with good results realized.

INVESTMENT THEORIES

There are many, many investment theories—new ones, old ones, good ones, bad ones. There are the fundamentalists, technical watchers, doomsayers, chartists, contrarians, gold bugs, market timers, inside traders, and so forth.

Who is right? Excluding quackery, there is some value to most theories. Never be totally devoted to any one theory or one type of investment media. What if you follow only one theory or make only one type of investment, and it is wrong? Develop an investment strategy which uses many theories.

We do not adhere to a particular investment theory. We analyze economic conditions and investment markets and evaluate which investment techniques will be most applicable.

While economic conditions and investment conditions have always been closely linked, the interrelation, although not always direct, is probably closer than ever. At the same time, investment opportunities have increased greatly.

Traditionally, historical comparison of investment returns has been used for evaluating investment placement. This assumes past conditions or patterns will repeat; we do not agree with this assumption. It is important to recognize that there are many investment theories practiced today and at various times different techniques will be successful.

We prefer an investment approach which we refer to as *aggressive conservatism* —"play it safe but seek high return." You should place most of your investment funds in pooled investments run by professional money managers (actual money managers, not stockbrokers). Only small portions of portfolios should be placed in speculative investments such as individual stocks, collectibles, or market options.

Individual investment markets (especially securities) have become increasingly dominated by large institutional investors. Consequently, selection for individual investors is difficult. For example, if institutions quickly pull out of a stock, the individual investor can take a beating. Individual securities (stocks and bonds) can offer needed growth and income, but associated risk is very high.

Risk is substantially reduced by pursuing stock and bond type investments through "no-load" mutual funds and "pooled" type investments. Mutual funds and other pools are able to diversify to a much greater extent than individual investors, thus, safety is increased without foregoing income or growth objectives. By utilizing several mutual funds, several professional management teams are retained.

Investment risk in other media, such as real estate, can also be reduced through "pooled" participation rather than individual property speculation. Personal management attention is an investment characteristic that carries substantial value. Any individual investment, be it a security or a rental property, requires a good deal of time to be successful. Many investors are better off to spend their time on their own professional expertise and let professional investors manage investments.

Usually managers of bond and stock mutual funds have particular philosophies they follow, and some "time" market conditions (i.e., liquidate bonds and stocks and invest the proceeds in cash-type investments when they think adverse market conditions will be forthcoming).

In utilizing professional money managers, do not entrust all your money to one manager or management team; use several professional managers. While the professionals far outperform most individuals, it is rare, even among managers with outstanding track records, to find a manager who consistently performs at a high level. We carefully track investment managers and use those funds which we think will perform optimally over selected time periods. Timing market conditions and switching mutual funds accordingly is extremely important. You can sit tight and hold positions for long-term and average very acceptable returns, but you will not do as well as you can by switching.

**POOLED
INVESTMENTS**

The "pooled" investment approach encompasses many different investment areas. We prefer a variety of mutual funds, use of unit trusts for those seeking fixed income, and, in some instances, limited partnerships.

Unit trust investing and limited partnership investing should be viewed as lacking the flexibility available with mutual funds (which can be quickly liquidated). Resale markets do exist for unit trusts and sometimes for limited partnerships, but the sale can be time consuming and there is no assurance that a liquidating investor will receive his or her true net interest in the program and commission expenses will have already been incurred.

Mutual funds are pools of funds managed by professional money managers. Investors invest by buying shares in a fund. We prefer "open-ended" funds which trade at net asset value per share. If fund investments perform well, net asset value per share will increase; and with most funds there are periodic distributions of income or profits to investors (these distributions can usually be automatically reinvested in the fund).

Mutual funds are required by law to state investment objectives in a prospectus. Investment objectives of funds can generally be categorized in three basic areas: funds that seek income, seek both income and growth, or seek only growth. Fund objectives can be further subdivided into very specific goals; such as, funds that invest in international stocks, "blue chip" stocks, small growth oriented companies, natural resources, particular industries, options, merger candidates, etc. A small number of funds are non-diversified; that is investments are limited to a few holdings. We suggest avoiding these funds. For purposes of later portfolio discussion, we use the following main categories:

- **Money Market Funds** invest in short-term debt securities to earn current income. Regular money market funds invest in investments which produce taxable income. Some specialize in purchasing only federal government securities. Tax-free money market funds purchase short-term debt of states and municipal governments. Income is not subject to federal income tax and sometimes not subject to state income tax.
- **Income Mutual Funds** seek current income in contrast to capital appreciation. Investments can include corporate bonds, United States Government bonds, and high dividend, quality stocks. Some income mutual funds specialize in fixed income (i.e., bonds of corporations and/or governments). Municipal

bond funds seek tax-free income but position funds in obligations with longer maturities than those purchased by money market funds. Some bond funds specialize in intermediate maturities, some long-term maturities, and some are mixed.

- **Growth/Income Mutual Funds** usually seek growth, income, and stability. Investments normally include common stocks, preferred stocks, and bonds.
- **Long-Term Growth Mutual Funds** invest mainly in common stocks, with good potential for appreciation. Distributions to shareholders by these funds are normally treated as capital gain to the shareholder. Distributions may be infrequent and if over time the shareholders net asset value per share increases, the shareholder will incur additional capital gain (loss) upon sale.
- **Maximum Capital Gains Mutual Funds** are more aggressive and purchase higher risk stocks than purchased by long-term growth funds. The funds may also use speculative investing techniques. Distributions to shareholders, if any, are similar to that for long-term growth mutual funds.
- **Gold and Precious Metals Mutual Funds** specialize in purchasing shares in mining companies and, sometimes, purchase metals or contracts for metals in commodity markets.

No-load mutual funds should be sought. No-load means there is no sales charge at time of purchase or withdrawal (be careful, as some funds marketed by brokerage firms are referred to as no-load but carry "back-end" withdrawal penalties). Load funds generally have a sales charge ranging from 6 percent to 8 percent at the time of purchase. For example, with $20,000 placed in load funds, $1,200 to $1,600 could go to commissions—meaning a net investment of only $18,400 to $18,800. Use of no-load funds would result in all $20,000 working for you. Contrary to what many salesmen say, load funds do not outperform no-load funds. Some funds have small loads such as $\frac{1}{2}$ percent to 2 percent to cover trading costs; we also find these acceptable.

Be careful of so-called 12b–1 funds. In addition to management fees assessed to shareholders (which are generally less than 1 percent per year), some funds have other charges which cover advertising costs. We don't think 12b–1 is a major problem, just that the managers should perform a little better than those without the charge to offset the charge. Mutual fund prospectuses must state policies and charges.

For some investors, we favor placement of a portion of their investment funds in unit trusts which invest in a fixed portfolio of bonds. Generally the trusts distribute income frequently (such as on a monthly basis). The trusts are similar to mutual funds in the sense that investors' funds are pooled, however, unlike mutual funds, the bonds purchased with investors' money are usually not traded. The bonds are purchased and held until they mature. The trusts, in turn, mature and funds are distributed to investors. The major advantage of investing in unit trusts is that instead of purchasing a single issue (such as of one corporation or government unit), an investor is purchasing a pro-rata interest in many bonds. This decreases risk attributable to possible default by the bond issues. Several other aspects of unit trusts are as follows:

- Maturity is usually on a staggered basis with investment principal returned to investors over time. Investors can select short-term, intermediate, or long-term trusts. Interest rates will vary depending upon length of the trust.
- If you do not wish to receive current cash distributions, you can usually participate in accumulation programs; i.e., distributions are automatically placed in other similar type, programs.
- Trusts specializing in corporate bonds, federal government bonds, or tax-free municipal bonds are available.
- Trusts are assembled, and sold, by brokerage firms. The issuers of trusts normally charge commissions of 3 percent to 5 percent, but the convenience and diversification offered by the trusts may make the commissions well worth paying.

Banks and similar financial institutions have been greatly expanding their services. Some have formed joint marketing and management agreements with mutual fund organizations. Some trust departments have lowered minimum requirements for participation in managed pools of stocks and bonds; and the performance of many trust department investment managers has improved substantially as banks have become more progressive.

We expect that no-load type bond trusts, partnerships, and similar investments will be available through banks. Get familiar with progressive banks in your area.

Limited partnerships, public and private, are created for investment in many types of media. Public partnerships usually require only a one time investment. Private partnerships can require payment over a period of several years. Some partnerships are specifi-

cally designed for personal investing, some for investing with qualified retirement plan funds. Never confuse the objective. For
example, many partnerships borrow money to pool with investor
funds. These "leveraged" partnerships should not be purchased for
investment of qualified retirement plan funds.

In limited partnerships, limited partners risk only the amount
they commit (cash plus recourse debt) to a program and are not
liable for debt or mismanagement. However, investors do not have
management participation. It is important that the general partners (those with management rights) be experienced and have good
past performance records and affiliations. In many states, investors can have managers removed, but this is a very time consuming process.

Be extremely cautious about partnership investing. Many partnerships have steep commissions and charges, and a great many
have had poor performance. You might be better off to create your
own partnership with people you know and trust, and hire a manager to run it for you.

Real estate partnerships are probably the most conservative
form of partnership investing for tax write-offs. Real estate can
also offer tax sheltered cash flow and potential for appreciation.
Pooled programs are frequently structured to invest in residential
real estate, such as apartment complexes, and/or commercial real
estate, such as office buildings and shopping centers. Some partnerships only buy one property. These carry much higher risk than
those which purchase many properties.

An arrangement used in some private placement partnerships
involves use of several subpartnerships combined under an
"umbrella" partnership. These usually are more attractive than
single property private placements.

There are many types of partnerships such as for oil and gas,
equipment leasing, horse trading, research and development, etc.
We have seen very few investors do well in these programs. The
vast majority of the partnerships available to the public simply are
not worth investing in. If for example, oil and gas prices rise
sharply, you will probably make more money buying oil stocks or
mutual funds heavily invested in oil stocks, than you would by
buying into an oil partnership available to the general public.
Understand that specialists that are involved in real estate or oil
and gas partnerships, for example, save the best properties for

themselves. They don't share interests in the really good ones.

INVESTMENT MISCONCEPTIONS

With the increasing complexity and confusion in investment markets, misconceptions are becoming more common. The following are examples of some of the ones we frequently encounter.

- *Federal government debt purchase (notes, bills, and bonds) are the safest available investment because they are backed by the federal government.* We reject this because of difficulties in federal government financing and because if the economy and businesses collapse, so too will government financing. The currency is no longer backed by anything valuable. You will be better off to own your own resources.
- *Bank and thrift institutions deposits are very safe because these are insured by the FDIC and other government-backed companies.* With increasing frequency, banks and financial institutions are going bankrupt, and while insured accounts have been protected, financing of the insuring organizations is very weak and payments would be very limited (or useless) in the event of widespread financial institution bankruptcy. We do believe, though, that the U.S. banking industry is stabilizing and will be stronger when currently weak banks are closed or merged.
- *U.S. industry is dying and most large companies will not last.* Yes, this is the service age, but we believe Americans prefer not being vulnerable. Free-trade will expand and with it, programs that will protect the United States from vulnerability. Also, many U.S. manufacturers will expand into service businesses to protect themselves.
- *You should seek to pay absolutely the minimum amount of income taxes possible.* Often, formal "tax shelters" are a sucker investment and many people "overshelter" (wasting deductions and losing economic return). You are often better off to make taxable economic investments, pay taxes, and keep the balance.
- *"Dollar cost averaging" is a good investment technique.* This is the idea that if you regularly purchase an interest in the same investment, the average market value will exceed the average cost basis, because you get more shares (for example with stock) at lower prices than higher prices, and, therefore you will make a profit. Two major things are wrong with this technique: (1) foregone investment returns from switching out when the price

begins falling are not considered and (2) this type of technique impedes diversification.
- *"Index" funds are a good investment.* Why invest for average return, when many investments are available at any given time that will outperform the averages?
- *That psychological factors should not be considered in making investment decisions, and decisions should be based solely on profit potential.*
- *Wealthy people do not make poor investments or that speculators make money most of the time.* In fact, successful speculators frequently make most of their money on a very small percentage of their trades.
- *Rich people don't have to be concerned about money.* Actually they must watch their money very carefully. There is always someone trying to take it.
- *"Get Rich Quick" formulas work; such as many of the current promotions in the commodities industry.*
- *That insurance companies or full service brokerage firms really sell no-load (no charge) financial products.* Instead of a direct commission, there may be a "back-end" load, investment structure fee, or reduced return. In any case, it is usually still a very substantial charge (sales people have to be paid).

Application of our investment management techniques will greatly reduce your susceptability to misconceptions.

GENERAL INVESTMENT THOUGHTS

Investment targets should be realistic and investments should be made only after considerable thought and evaluation. Keep the following points in mind as investments are selected.

- Diversification should be sought within each selected medium as well as among the different investment media.
- Recognize the impact of inflation and seek growth investments to the extent necessary.
- The time value of money is very important—a dollar today is worth much more than a dollar several years from now.
- Do not incur investment debt such as margin accounts or commitments to annual payments to investment deals unless you have already established significant financial security (Tier 2 and Tier 3).

- Use investment debt only if there is a very high probability that cash investment return and/or tax savings will be sufficient to finance debt payments.
- Good recordkeeping improves investment management.
- Always know your investment position and funds available for investing. Keep your money working. Good recordkeeping improves investment management.
- Do not invest in anything you do not understand.
- In making investments, never turn money over directly to an individual, or make checks payable to an individual for an investment. Make your checks out to the investment.
- Many investments have minimum investment amounts; make sure you are aware of the minimum dollar amounts before selecting an investment.
- Some investments have financial criteria such as levels of income and net worth, you should be aware of this information.
- Many investments have sale charges, fees, and commissions— know these costs, and determine the percent of your funds that will actually be put to work for you.
- Seek investments with no sales costs or low sales costs (examples include no-load mutual funds and use of discount stock brokerage services).
- Be very skeptical of any investments "pushed" heavily by salesmen, or investments which seem to offer unusually high rates of return or tax write-offs; don't deal with any unsolicited salesmen.
- Don't be misled by the tax benefits of tax-deferred annuities. The underlying investments are often not good and tax penalties are imposed on withdrawals before age 59 1/2.
- Do not buy gold bullion or precious metals for storage with someone else; if you want these, take possession and set up your own storage.
- Be certain of the value you are buying; for example, stocks may trade at prices different than true asset value per share whereas no-load mutual funds trade at net asset value per share.
- Be aware of the impact placement of additional savings will have on your investment portfolio.
- Avoid inappropriate investments such as holding tax-oriented investments inside qualified retirement plans.
- Do not accept risk levels, if investment return equivalents can be achieved with lower risk investments; only accept higher risk if it

is appropriate and the investment offers higher return than investments with lower risk.

- Seek the highest return possible for the level of risk you are willing to accept; for example, equally safe investments to life insurance cash values can be obtained and usually offer much higher return.
- Pick your own investments, but do so after assessing professional opinions and consensus.
- Become aware of accurate and concise sources of investment information.
- If you seek advice from a financial planner, watch out for the "bait and switch" technique; a low fee is charged and then high commission products are recommended.
- Don't use contractual investment programs.
- Periodically review your investment philosophies.
- If funds will be professionally managed, use several managers rather than relying on one manager.
- When learning about new investment alternatives, make sure to evaluate the investments in terms of your goals and investment needs.
- Always be certain as to whether you are taking on ownership status or creditor status as investments are made and get returns accordingly.
- Continually recognize the impacts of investment performance on your investment objectives and the other financial planning areas.
- Do not understate the value of freedom from constant investment management, such as with individual real estate investments.
- Take precautions with respect to assistance your spouse and heirs may need in money management.
- Seek effective "income tax shifting" methods for providing money to individuals, including children and relatives.
- Realize that at any given time you may have to seek several different investment objectives.
- Stay current of economic developments and the impact the developments will have on your investments.
- Establish proper levels of convenience in managing and purchasing investments.
- Do not be afraid to "take" profits on an investment or "cut" losses.

- Make sure you are knowledgeable of and comfortable with your portfolio selections.
- Make the best use of your funds.
- Use the process of decision trees, or similar analysis, in making investment decisions so that all relevant factors will be considered and evaluated.
- Do not consider your home, personal property, or life insurance as investment vehicles.

13

DEVELOPING AND REFINING AN INVESTMENT PORTFOLIO

"Life's greatest achievement is the continual remaking of yourself so that at last you know how to live."

Winfred Rhodes

An entrepreneur we were familiar with went through years of struggle to build a service business. His spouse worked outside of the home to support the family while he built up the business. After about 10 years the business became very successful. Five years later he sold the business, netting out about $600,000 after taxes. He signed a consulting agreement with the new owners, but shortly after became disenchanted and left. He did not work for about 12 months. Then a friend approached him about buying a small manufacturing company. Together they put down one million dollars in cash and financed the balance of the five million dollar purchase price by pledging the company's assets as collateral. The first year was good and they paid themselves nice salaries. In the second year, things began to deteriorate, profits stopped, and heavy losses began. By the fourth year, they filed for bankruptcy. He was virtually broke.

There are many ways to accumulate wealth. If there is one best way—it probably is to start a business which requires low capital funding, make the business grow rapidly, set up and heavily fund qualified retirement plans, sell the business, and then build another one.

Obviously, this is not easy, nor is it for the less than aggressive risk taker. Even the aggressive risk taker should seek to diversify investments. Use wealth to protect yourself. You don't want to spend a lifetime building something, and then watch it collapse with everything you own in it.

Too often we see people with all their wealth tied up in a few holdings. Whether you are an employee or business owner, force yourself to make personal and qualified plan investments for long-term security. Establishing multiple investments and multiple sources of income are the most important steps to achieving financial well being.

ANALYZING YOUR CURRENT POSITION

Analyze your current investment position and possible alternate positions for liquidity, balance, and diversification.

Some liquid assets will not be subject to investment value fluctuation (e.g., cash), some values will be subject to change because of interest rate fluctuations (e.g., corporate bonds), and other liquid assets may change in value because of market conditions (e.g., stocks). Other assets, such as real estate, may take considerable time to sell and should not be considered liquid. Do not treat qualified retirement plan investments, or investments owned by your business, as liquid even though holdings may be in things such as money markets or stocks. Frequently there are penalties or taxes imposed on withdrawals, and we do not encourage borrowing from qualified plans or your own business unless it is very necessary.

Using Form 13–1, total all your investments, net of investment debt, and calculate percents of total investments. Each category should be calculated separately and the totals for each liquidity, balance and diversification should equal total net investments. Then enter the desired targets for investment placement with consideration for needs and appropriateness.

Optimal targets vary considerably with variation in personal needs, goals, level of wealth, and lifestyle. Set your own targets and build to these targets over time, making adjustments as necessary. The targets should be based on the assumption of normal economic conditions (i.e., steady growth). Unusually high or unusually low

FORM 13-1

	$ Amount	% of Total Invested Funds		Desired Targets for % of Total Invested Funds	
Liquidity					
Instant Liquidity	————	————————		————————	
Interest Rate Sensitive	————	————————		————————	
Market Sensitive	————	————————		————————	
Liquid Funds	————	————————		————————	
Non-Liquid Funds	————	————————		————————	
Total Investments	$	100	%	100	%
Balance					
Investments with growth potential	————	————————		————————	
Investments with no growth potential	————	————————		————————	
Total Investments	$	100	%	100	%
Diversification					
Cash & equivalents	————	————————		————————	
Stock type investments	————	————————		————————	
Bond type investments	————	————————		————————	
Real estate	————	————————		————————	
Business interests	————	————————		————————	
Other	————	————————		————————	
Total Investments	$	100	%	100	%

periods of economic growth should be responded to by temporarily shifting investments.

Evaluation and target setting should be very thorough. For example, if you desire very rapid accumulation of wealth, can you afford to risk funds on very aggressive growth opportunity investments and, if so, with what portion of your investment portfolio? Frequently review your current position and revaluate future targets.

Some very general guidelines are:

- Try to maintain at least 40 percent of your investment funds in liquid form.
- The closer you are to retirement, the less the proportion of funds with growth potential should be—to the extent that at retirement, perhaps 40 percent of funds are invested for growth and 60 percent for income. (Note: there may be economic time periods during which you may be better off with most of your funds invested in income investments, regardless of your age.)
- Cash and equivalents for emergencies and opportunities should typically average about 5 percent of investments; other investment mixes should depend on your personal circumstances and objectives.

SAMPLE PORTFOLIO

Investing is an extremely important part of the financial planning process. Placement of investment funds applies both to current and future savings. Investment placement changes are needed as more wealth is accumulated, goals change, and investment market and economic conditions change.

Different tactics and placement are appropriate for the different types of investing. Listed below are the types along with general objectives.

- Outright Personal Investing—emergency/opportunity funds, funding short-term expenses, funding intermediate-term expenses, funding long-term expenses, long-term security, speculation, and tax savings.
- Qualified Plan Investing—long-term security and tax savings.
- Business Investing—growth of actively owned and operated businesses and/or use of excess business funds to take advantage of special tax planning opportunities.

The investment mix which is right for someone else is not the same as that which is right for you. By reviewing an example, though, we can point out important principles of investing and appropriate investments; both of which you can apply to your own situation.

Example: Married couple (each 38 years old), two children (ages 6 and 4), she is a self-employed professional, he is an executive with a major corporation. They own a home which is 75 percent financed and they have accumulated $133,000 of investments—$3,000 in savings accounts for each of the children (UGMA), $16,000 in IRAs (split equally), $12,000 in her Keogh plan, $10,000 in his 401(K) deferred compensation plan, she has invested $15,000 in her business, and the balance of their investments is in a bank money market account. He is also covered by a defined benefit pension plan provided by his employer. They maintain an average checking account balance just sufficient for monthly expenditures. Together they make about $100,000 per year, and save $10,000 per year in addition to IRA, Keogh, and 401(K) contributions. Her business is well established and additional investment of money should not be necessary. They are in the 42 percent marginal federal income tax bracket and have a $4,000 tax payment due soon. They would like to make an addition to their home in about four to five years, at an estimated cost of about $10,000.

Risk Comfort—both consider themselves to be moderate risk takers. They know they make a good income, are well insured, and would like to increase investment return. They live comfortably and would like early retirement, but do not want to risk a great deal in an attempt to become rich quickly. They enjoy reading about investments and want to begin making investment decisions, some of which will be purely for excitement.

Economic Conditions.   The economy is 24 months into an upturn, with additional, but slower growth expected. Corporate profits are good and expected to stay favorable. Other major world economies are also on an upswing. Inflation is low but expected to increase and interest rates are relatively high (the prime rate exceeds inflation by about 5 percent).

First, let's break out their various investment objectives.

- *Emergency/opportunity funds*—cash reserves
- *Short-term expenses*—taxes

- *Intermediate-term expenses*—possible home addition
- *Long-term expenses*—children's college education
- *Long-term security*—retirement
- *Speculation*—fun and possible high return
- *Tax savings*—keep taxes reasonable

The investment positioning which would be appropriate for them is shown on the next page. Importantly, the portfolio includes a great deal of flexibility to respond to changing conditions or unforseen events.

After investment repositioning they have the spread between liquidity, balance, and diversification shown on Form 13–1a. We have excluded $4,000 which will be used soon for the income tax payment.

General Comments

- They should deposit future savings to the tax-exempt money market fund for later investing, including IRAs, the Keogh, and personal investing.
- They should not make additional gifts to the children until they are more comfortable that when the children gain control of the funds at age 18, the funds will actually be used for college expenses. Instead, they should accumulate assets in their own names for possible later gifting to the children.
- She should keep idle business funds in an interest bearing account.
- She might consider incorporating her professional practice to reduce liability exposure; with incorporation, evaluation should be given to establishing a combination profit sharing plan/defined contribution pension plan or a defined benefit pension.
- As their financial security increases, they can increase investment aggressiveness.
- She should investigate the feasibility of purchasing a small office building with other professionals for use, tax write-offs, and possible gain.
- Keep the children's savings accounts for their use to familarize themselves with money management.

Investment To Use

No-load and lo-load mutual funds should be researched and reviewed prior to use. Most libraries carry good publications which

TABLE 13–1

Investment	Amount	Reason
Children's Savings		
Two growth/income mutual funds	$ 3,000	Low tax brackets; long term funding; therefore, some possible down periods can be tolerated for overall growth.
Two growth mutual funds	3,000	
Personal Investing		
Her business	15,000	Maintain current position; additions are not needed.
Tax-exempt money market fund	10,500	Cash reserves and tax payment; because of marginal tax bracket, they are better off in a tax-free fund than in a taxable interest account.
Intermediate tax-exempt fund	7,500	Home addition; higher return than tax-exempt money market fund, but principal could fluctuate some in value.
Three maximum capital gains mutual funds	15,000	Favorable economic conditions suggest good potential for diversified approach to aggressive growth; seek long-term capital gain taxation.
Three long-term growth mutual funds	16,000	Growth with more stability; seek long-term capital gain taxation.
Two gold and precious metals mutual funds	10,000	Expected increases in inflation suggest likely favorable impact on gold and precious metals prices; hedge in event adverse economic conditions develop.
Insured municipal bond unit trust	10,000	Take advantage of unusually high real interest rates and tax-free income.
Common stocks	5,000	Speculation and fun.

TABLE 13–1 *(concluded)*

IRAs		
Two corporate bond unit trusts	5,000	Tax qualified benefits of plans suggests receipt of
One income mutual fund	3,000	high income; income fund
Two growth/income mutual funds	5,000	also could gain if interest rates fall, growth to achieve
One growth mutual fund	3,000	retirement goals.
Keogh		
Growth mutual fund	5,000	Current income; growth and appreciation potential to
Income real estate program	7,000	achieve retirement goals.
401(K) [1]		
Elect 25% company stock, 25% guaranteed fixed income and 50% growth and income pool	10,000	He believes company has good potential for future growth; growth and income to achieve retirement goals.
	$133,000	

[1] Common choices in 401(K) programs are money market, guaranteed fixed income, company stock, and growth and income pool or growth pool. Each 401(K) program is independently structured and investment options vary. All investments should be analyzed for quality and potential performance.

both explain mutual funds and monitor the performance of mutual funds. *Forbes* and *Money* magazines, among others, rate mutual funds. Many newsletters make recommendations for mutual fund use.

There are many financial information sources available, and we expect many new ones in the future. Carefully review good ones and make your own decisions after obtaining a consensus view.

There are hundreds of mutual funds and not all funds perform well. Mutual funds, as with any investment medium, must be carefully analyzed, selectively chosen, and monitored. Know who the manager or management team is. These people will be investing your money.

A manager's performance can decline for many reasons—maybe

FORM 13–1a

	$ Amount	% of Total Invested Funds
Liquidity		
Instant Liquidity	$ 6,500	5
Interest Rate Sensitive	7,500	6
Market Sensitive	46,000	36
Liquid Funds	$ 60,000	47
Non-Liquid Funds	69,000	53
Total Investments	$129,000	100 %
Balance		
Investments with growth potential	$ 94,500	73
Investments with no growth potential	34,500	27
Total Investments	$129,000	100 %
Diversification		
Cash & equivalents	$ 6,500	5
Stock type investments	62,500	48
Bond type investments	28,000	22
Real estate	7,000	5
Business interests	15,000	12
Other	10,000	8
Total Investments	$129,000	100 %

he is handling too much money, his philosophies may not work well in current markets, or his investment specialty area (if any) may be out of favor. Don't hesitate to change funds if a manager no longer performs well or if a manager leaves a fund.

Look for managers who are progressive and make use of new financial instruments, such as financial futures indexes. Also, we prefer diversified mutual funds over nondiversified. Diversified means that no more than 5 percent of a fund's assets can be in one issue.

Be careful in making purchases in personal name that a fund is not about to make a distribution which will be taxable to you. Wait until the total distribution amount is set aside by fund managers (usually price per share will fall), then invest. Distributions by funds usually retain their character for personal taxation (i.e., dividends, interest, short-term or long-term capital gains).

For the sample portfolio, we would select the following types of mutual funds.

- *Children's funds*—large, conservatively managed funds, which invest a large portion of funds in "blue chip" type securities. The selected managers should have different investment philosophies. Two of the four managers should "time" investments; that is, at times be fully invested in cash, at times be fully in the bond and stock markets, and at other times have some securities and the balance cash.
- *Personal investing*—both of the tax-exempt funds should be large, well-diversified funds, with yields at or near the top of their classes. For maximum capital gains funds, we would select one large fund and one small fund—each specializing in small growth oriented companies—and one fund specializing in a particular sector of the stock market (such as technology stocks). For growth mutual funds, we would consider one international fund, and two good performers where the manager specializes in a particular type of investing (such as finding merger candidates or under valued stocks). For gold and precious metals funds, we would pick one fund which invests only in gold related investments, and one which makes gold and other precious metals investments. With the exception of the tax-exempt funds, all the funds should seek long-term capital gains.
- *Qualified retirement plan funds*—the income fund would be one specializing in both dividend income from common and preferred

stocks and interest from intermediate-term debt instruments. The growth/income funds should be balanced type funds, providing good income with growth secondary. For growth funds, we would look to funds managed specifically for qualified retirement plans (i.e., look for gains regardless of whether or not the gains are short-term or long-term).

The unit trusts should consist of quality bonds with ratings of A or better. The sponsor of the trusts should be a financially strong, high-quality organization. New trusts are offered very frequently. Interest rates on the trusts should be very competitive and close to rates offered on individual bond issues. For a small reduction in the interest yield, trusts which are insured are available.

The municipal bond trust and the corporate bond trusts suggested in the sample portfolio should be intermediate-term trusts. We also favor intermediate terms when using federal government bond trusts.

Your intention when purchasing unit trusts should be to hold them until maturity. However, for a variety of reasons, you may need or want to liquidate the trusts before maturity. Intermediate trusts are less subject to change in principal value as market interest rates change than are long-term trusts. Unlike bond mutual funds, unit trust portfolios are usually not actively managed or traded. Principal is repaid in full upon maturity. Bond mutual funds, because they are actively traded, offer greater potential for capital gain; particularly if interest rates are expected to fall.

As mentioned previously, there are many bad partnership investments and relatively few good partnership investments available to the general public.

The income real estate program we would choose for the sample portfolio would be specifically designed for qualified retirement plan investing. The program would invest, on a cash only basis (no debt), in a mix of residential and commercial properties. Rental income and appreciation projections would be good and realistic. The general partners would be quality people with proven track records. Fees and commissions should be low so that there is a high net of investor dollars into purchase of the properties.

Shop carefully for all investments, including unit trusts and partnerships. Check with brokerage firms, banks, and other established financial institutions. Finding a quality deal is worth the effort.

Accounts to Use

Banks and full-service brokerage firms should be used only for a very limited portion of your investment placements.

Each no-load or lo-load mutual fund can be purchased directly from the fund or liquidated by contacting the fund. No salesperson is needed. However, while this would keep implementation costs to a minimum, paperwork can be substantial and there may be some short time lags in making withdrawals. For very reasonable transaction charges, accounts can be set up with discount brokerage firms that handle no-load and lo-load mutual funds. Accounts at discount brokerage firms are usually well insured for protection against fraud or bankruptcy of the firm.

An account should be set up for each person and type of investing involved in your investment program. In the sample portfolio, an account should be set up for each child, one personal account for each husband and wife (see the estate planning chapters regarding joint titling), an account for his IRA, an account for her IRA, and an account for her Keogh. Monthly statements would be received from the discount brokerage firm for each account and would show consolidated investment positioning. Each account could be set up so that any temporarily idle funds are automatically placed in a money market fund.

Savings can be sent by check to the proper account and held in a money market fund for later placement in more favorable investments. Orders for purchase and sale can be made by phone.

Some advisors encourage the "family of funds" approach to mutual fund investing. That is, find a group which sponsors many different types of funds and switch among the funds as your needs or market conditions change. We do not like this method for the simple reason that some very good funds are not in a "family" and most groups with many funds have some good funds, but they also have some poor performing funds. You are better off to use the best possible funds available regardless of the group or organization with which they are associated.

Discount brokerage firms can also be used for speculative investing, such as purchase of individual securities or options.

If you already have accounts at full service brokerage firms or financial institutions, exercise caution in switching. First, consider tax consequences of liquidating. You might prefer to switch, but hold current investment positions until liquidation will be more favorable. Discount brokerage firms accept cash and securities, and some accept mutual fund investments, If you have given a broker discretionary trading authority over your funds, send the broker a written note indicating that there are to be no more trades. Then contact the discount brokerage firm of your choice and they will handle account transfers for you.

Many investment account alternatives are available and new ones are continually being offered. When choosing investment accounts, consider fees and charges, quality of servicing, convenience, and the availability of various investment media. Having different investment accounts helps segregate funds for achievement of your investment objectives.

COMPANY STOCK   Many corporate benefit plans now in use include investments on behalf of or by employees in the stock of the company. These plans can be good for building security, saving taxes, and assuring savings. But they are good only if the stock value will increase. If a company performs poorly, the stock price could fall, even possibly becoming worthless. Don't be deluded by tax savings or forced savings; and don't get too closely tied with your employer by having most of your wealth in the company stock.

There are many ways to analyze a company and evaluate investment in its stock. Some stocks are riskier than others. Start by looking at your own feelings. You are there every workday. Are things going well or poorly for the company? Be willing to view investment in company stock as a long-term investment.

Listed below are some factors we like to see when seeking stock for purchase.

- High level executives of the company own a substantial amount of the stock and are buying more.
- Management is relatively stable and considered progressive.
- The company has good ratings by outside financial services.
- The company is in a growing industry and has good, long-term market potential.
- The company has good annual growth with increasing earnings.
- The company has good cash flow and does not borrow heavily.
- Market price per share is below book value per share.
- The company has undervalued assets on its balance sheet (such as real estate at cost rather than market price).

HIGH RISK/
HIGH RETURN

There are many high risk investments, some of which do not have high enough return potential to justify investment. New investment products are being created at a rapid rate. Don't be fooled by marketing hype about returns or features of an investment. Two examples to consider in this regard are commodity funds and zero coupon bonds.

It has been estimated that less than 10 percent of commodity investors make money. Those who do make money, though, can make big, big money. Expansions of the commodity markets and the increase in the number of investors willing to take high risk lead to the formation of many commodity pools. Very few have performed well, most have not. High risk combined with poor performance is unacceptable.

We are not suggesting that zero coupon bonds are in the risk category of commodities, at least not most of them anyway. But many zero-coupon bond investors have been mislead regarding security of the investment.

Zero-coupon bond investing, whether in individual bonds or through pools, does not produce income to investors on an annual basis. Purchase price is set low and at maturity, usually quite a few years out, investors receive a lump sum payoff. Many people purchased zero-coupon bonds on the mistaken notion that principal value was very safe (i.e., not subject to fluctuation). Liquidating, or selling before maturity, subjects an investor to market value fluctuations. In many instances people who have had to liquidate early have not received nearly what they anticipated. Furthermore, some people purchase these bonds without realizing that the IRS requires annual reporting of "accrued" interest. This is not a problem if the bonds are in a qualified retirement plan; but, if held personally, taxes are incurred with no cash distribution for payment of the taxes.

Realizing that speculation can produce very high returns and can be fun for people who can tolerate high risk, we do consider the following to be appropriate for a small percent of portfolio funds— with the understanding that loses can be substantial.

Option Purchase.   Purchase of call options on anticipation of rising values or put options on anticipation of falling values. Options may be purchased on publicly traded common stocks, stock indexes, and other investment media. Besides for speculation, options can also be used to act as a hedge for protection of a portfolio.

Returns on options can be dramatic. For example, $5,000 invested in IBM July 110 puts in winter, 1984, was worth over $200,000 in spring of that year. Its easy to lose money in options, though. Be careful if you should have good fortune. Don't get unrealistic about possible losses and invest too much money in options. Stick with purchase of options. Leave writing options to professional portfolio managers unless you have your position covered or wish to close a purchase position.

Common Stocks. Individual stock purchase can also provide high return. We suggest you limit yourself to purchase of stocks in companies with which you are familiar (such as your employer, local companies, suppliers to your company, or competitors), or to companies which you can carefully research and thoroughly evaluate. We like the following criteria for selection of individual stocks for speculation.

- The stock is traded in the over-the-counter (OTC) market.
- The company is in a growing industry.
- Less than 20 percent of the stock is owned by institutional investors.
- The company has had the same management team for several years.
- Market price per share of stock is less than $20.
- Earnings per share has increased in each of the last three years.
- The P-E ratio (price per share divided by earnings per share) is less than 10.
- Average return on equity has exceeded 15 percent for each of the last three years.
- The Current Ratio (current assets divided by current liabilities) is at least 1.5 to 1.
- Long term debt is less than 50 percent of book value of the company.

Other opportunities for speculation may be available to you. Don't do anything you don't understand and haven't thoroughly evaluated, including how much an investment would impact your overall financial situation. Avoid investments (such as futures contracts) on which "calls" or other demands for additional funds can be made. Know your risk exposure (potential loss) before committing to any investment.

MAKING INVESTMENT DECISIONS

Develop an effective pattern and decision making process that integrates your goals and investment needs with available investments. Employ the following step in developing an investment program for yourself:

1. Always know your investment position and funds available for investing. Keep your money working. Depend on a structured cash management system for savings flow.

2. Clearly establish investment objectives and maintain an ultimate use perspective on funds placement (i.e., from short-term expenditures to long-term financial security).

3. Seek multiple financial planning needs, considering cash flow planning, tax planning, insurance protection and estate planning.

4. Always maintain emergency/opportunity funds.

5. Use professional money management sources but do so in ways such that commissions and fees are incurred only when necessary and appropriate, and then on a lowest cost basis.

6. Distinguish between different types of investing such as personal investing and qualified retirement plan investing.

7. Seek appropriate levels of liquidity, balance, and diversification.

8. Maintain flexibility so you can respond to changes in goals, economic conditions, and new investment opportunities.

9. Understand the risk/reward ratio of any investment and obtain a given return for the least possible risk or highest return for any given level of risk.

10. Continually review and monitor your investment position and investment needs.

Develop and utilize a system of investment decision making for yourself which accounts for all critical factors of investment decision making. A technique we often find useful is an investment decision making tree (Figure 13–1). Decision trees can be broad based for general investment decisions or narrow in scope for very specific investment decision making. For example purposes, find decision trees for general investing and Individual Retirement Account (IRA) investing.

FIGURE 13-1   GENERAL INVESTING

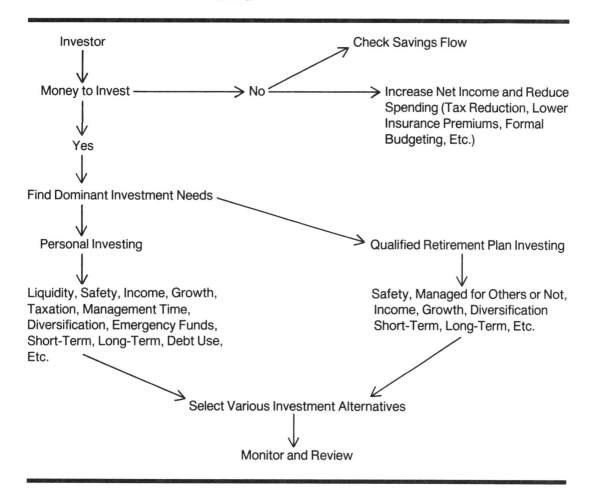

MONITORING INVESTMENTS

Upon completion of investment selections, choices should be carried out. Timing schedules should be established and should include dates for initial and future deposits, anticipated dates for investment returns, and possible dates for investment liquidation or termination.

All investments should be reviewed for performance and appropriateness at least every six to nine months; some more frequently. Do not hesitate to change investments if there are changes in economic conditions or your personal circumstances, or if new and

FIGURE 13-2 IRA INVESTING

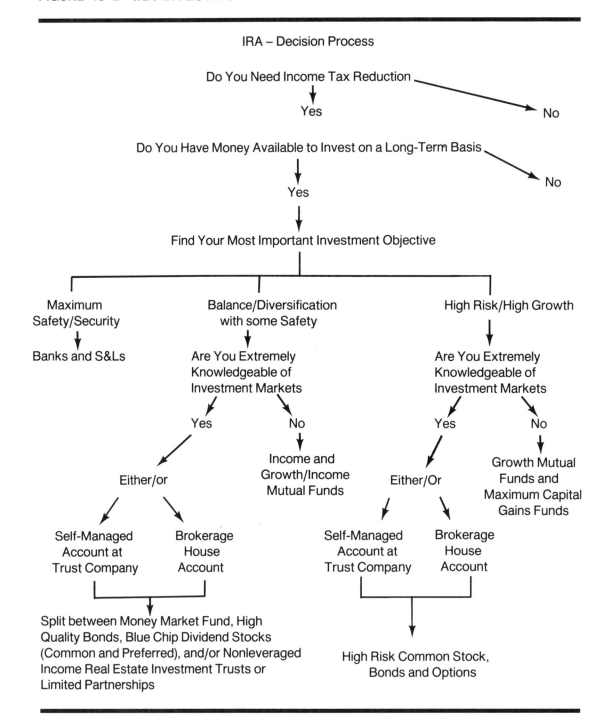

better investment opportunities become available. If you follow our investment techniques, you can effectively evaluate new opportunities. Keep all planning needs in mind and make decisions accordingly (such as year end sales of investments with losses to achieve tax savings and acquire better investments).

Future savings should be placed in line with long-term strategies, but placement should be made only after revaluation of investment needs and market conditions. Decisions to make major purchases should be evaluated in conjunction with investment planning.

In the sample portfolio, a movement of the economy toward recession would mean that, at a minimum, the personal investments in maximum capital gains funds and the growth mutual funds should be liquidated, with proceeds placed in the money market fund until economic activity improves.

Some of the better mutual funds have long-term average compounded returns in excess of 20 percent per year. This means they have some spectacular years mixed in with poor years. If you avoid their down years and participate in their up years, your gains can be very sizeable; and you are in diversified investments.

Investment performance can be evaluated in many ways. In addition to actual dollar return, investors should be certain that factors (including investment management teams, investment market conditions, and investment media structuring) are still favorable. The following terms and calculations are important in the performance evaluation process:

$$\text{YIELD} = \frac{\text{INCOME DISTRIBUTIONS OR ACCUMULATIONS}}{\text{INVESTED AMOUNT}}$$

$$\text{GROWTH} = \frac{\text{DOLLAR VALUE INCREASE}}{\text{INVESTED AMOUNT}}$$

COMBINED RETURN = YIELD + GROWTH

REAL RATE OF RETURN = COMBINED RETURN – INFLATION RATE

Investment rates of return are normally stated and compared on an annual basis. Therefore, computed returns must be converted to an annual basis for both yield and growth. Do so separately.

ANNUAL RETURN = COMPUTED RETURN X THE NUMBER OF TIME PERIODS IN A YEAR FOR WHICH THE RETURN IS CALCULATED

Everybody wants to know what a good rate of return is. Above 15 percent in combined return is good, above 20 percent is very good, and above 25 percent is excellent. In a more important measurement form, an annual real rate of return in excess of 5 percent is good.

Of course, the higher the risk undertaken, the higher the rate of return potential should be. Acceptable return levels also depend on your objectives; your tax bracket; your desires for safety, income, growth, and liquidity; and the extent of personal management attention your investments require.

Following calculations of returns on your investments, analysis should be conducted on progress made toward achievement of your investment objectives. Time framework for objectives must be kept in mind; different objectives require different time periods. Dollar targets should be established, and re-established following evaluation of investment performance. Tables 13–2 to 13–7 can be useful for target analysis.

At the end of this chapter is a sample worksheet (Form 13–2) for recording mutual fund investments. Similar sheets should be used for each of your various investments.

Sample Uses (Table 13–2)

1. Future value of current lump sum investment:

    FUTURE $ VALUE OF FUNDS = DEPOSIT AMOUNT X FACTOR

2. Lump sum investment needed today for future value accumulation:

    $$\text{DEPOSIT AMOUNT} = \frac{\text{FUTURE \$ VALUE OF FUNDS}}{\text{FACTOR}}$$

3. Annual income needed at retirement with consideration for inflation (use investment rate of return column for inflation):

    ANNUAL INCOME AT RETIREMENT =
    INCOME IN TODAY'S $S X FACTOR

4. Period of time it will take to accumulate a future value on a current lump sum investment:

    $$\text{(A) FACTOR} = \frac{\text{FUTURE \$ VALUE OF FUNDS}}{\text{DEPOSIT AMOUNT}}$$

(B) YEARS = FIND INVESTMENT RATE OF RETURN ROW AND LOOK ACROSS TO FIND FACTOR, THEN YEARS COLUMN HEADING

5. Investment rate of return it will take to accumulate a future value on a current lump sum investment:

(A) $\text{FACTOR} = \dfrac{\text{FUTURE \$ VALUE OF FUNDS}}{\text{DEPOSIT AMOUNT}}$

(B) INVESTMENT RATE OF RETURN = FIND YEARS COLUMN AND LOOK DOWN TO FIND FACTOR, THEN INVESTMENT RATE OF RETURN ROW HEADING

Sample Uses (Table 13–3)

1. Future value of equal annual investments:

FUTURE $ VALUE OF FUNDS =
ANNUAL DEPOSIT AMOUNT X FACTOR

2. Equal annual investments needed for future value accumulation:

$\text{ANNUAL DEPOSIT AMOUNT} = \dfrac{\text{FUTURE \$ VALUE OF FUNDS}}{\text{FACTOR}}$

3. Future value of equal annual investments beginning in the future with consideration for inflation during the interim (use investment rate of return column for inflation):

(A) SEE PREVIOUS TABLE SAMPLE (3)

(B) FUTURE $ VALUE OF FUNDS = STEP (A) X FACTOR

4. Period of time it will take to accumulate a future value with equal annual investments:

(A) $\text{FACTOR} = \dfrac{\text{FUTURE \$ VALUE OF FUNDS}}{\text{DEPOSIT AMOUNT}}$

(B) YEARS = FIND INVESTMENT RATE OF RETURN ROW AND LOOK ACROSS TO FIND FACTOR, THEN YEARS COLUMN HEADING

5. Investment rate of return it will take to accumulate a future value with equal annual investments:

(A) $\text{FACTOR} = \dfrac{\text{FUTURE \$ VALUE OF FUNDS}}{\text{DEPOSIT AMOUNT}}$

TABLE 13-2 GROWTH FACTORS FOR A ONE TIME DEPOSIT

Investment Rate of Return	3	5	10	15	Years 20	25	30	35	40
6%	1.1910	1.3382	1.7908	2.3966	3.2071	4.2919	5.7435	7.6861	10.2857
8%	1.2597	1.4693	2.1589	3.1722	4.6610	6.8485	10.0627	14.7853	21.7245
10%	1.3310	1.6105	2.5937	4.1772	6.7275	10.8347	17.4494	28.1024	45.2593
12%	1.4049	1.7623	3.1058	5.4736	9.6463	17.0001	29.9599	52.7996	93.0510
14%	1.4815	1.9254	3.7072	7.1379	13.7435	26.4619	50.9502	98.1002	188.8835
16%	1.5609	2.1003	4.4114	9.2655	19.4608	40.8742	85.8499	180.3141	378.7212
18%	1.6430	2.2878	5.2338	11.9737	27.3930	62.6686	143.3706	327.9973	750.3783
20%	1.7280	2.4883	6.1917	15.4070	38.3376	95.3962	237.3763	590.6682	1469.7716
25%	1.9531	3.0518	9.3132	28.4217	86.7362	264.6978	807.7936	2465.1904	7523.1641

TABLE 13-3 GROWTH FACTORS FOR EQUAL ANNUAL DEPOSITS

Investment Rate of Return	3	5	10	15	Years 20	25	30	35	40
6%	3.1836	5.6371	13.1808	23.2760	36.7856	54.8645	79.0582	111.4348	154.7620
8%	3.2464	5.8666	14.4866	27.1521	45.7620	73.1059	113.2832	172.3168	259.0565
10%	3.3100	6.1051	15.9374	31.7725	57.2750	98.3471	164.4940	271.0244	442.5926
12%	3.3744	6.3528	17.5487	37.3797	72.0524	133.3339	241.3327	431.6635	767.0914
14%	3.4396	6.6101	19.3373	43.8424	91.0249	181.8708	356.7869	693.5727	1342.0251
16%	3.5056	6.8771	21.3215	51.6595	115.3798	249.2140	530.3177	1120.7130	2360.7593
18%	3.5724	7.1542	23.5213	60.9653	146.6280	342.6035	790.9480	1816.6516	4163.2130
20%	3.6400	7.4416	25.9587	72.0351	186.6880	471.9811	1181.8816	2948.3412	7343.8579
25%	3.8125	8.2070	33.2529	109.6868	342.9447	1054.7912	3227.1743	9856.7615	30088.6560

TABLE 13-4 GROWTH FACTORS FOR ANNUAL DEPOSITS WHICH INCREASE 5% PER YEAR

Investment Rate of Return	Years								
	3	5	10	15	20	25	30	35	40
6%	3.5	6.6	17.1	33.6	58.9	95.9	150.6	230.0	344.1
8%	3.7	6.9	19.1	39.3	72.2	124.6	206.6	333.6	528.6
10%	3.8	7.3	21.2	46.2	89.6	163.8	288.8	496.9	840.8
12%	3.9	7.8	23.6	54.3	111.8	217.8	410.2	756.5	1376.2
14%	4.1	8.2	26.3	64.0	140.4	292.2	590.6	1172.7	2303.3
16%	4.2	8.7	29.3	75.8	177.2	395.3	859.7	1843.3	3919.5
18%	4.5	10.9	32.7	89.8	224.6	538.1	1262.1	2927.1	6747.2
20%	4.6	12.0	36.5	106.6	285.4	736.1	1864.4	4681.2	11701.8
24%	4.9	13.4	45.6	150.9	464.7	1391.1	4114.8	12109.8	35561.1

TABLE 13-5 GROWTH FACTORS FOR ANNUAL DEPOSITS WHICH INCREASE 10% PER YEAR

Investment Rate of Return	Years								
	3	5	10	15	20	25	30	35	40
6%	3.7	7.2	21.3	47.2	93.2	173.4	310.3	541.0	926.8
8%	3.8	7.6	23.5	54.2	111.6	215.2	398.9	719.1	1270.9
10%	4.0	8.3	26.5	68.4	155.2	290.6	610.5	1150.2	2175.4
12%	4.1	8.5	28.7	72.6	163.4	345.3	700.6	1383.0	2676.3
14%	4.3	9.0	31.7	84.4	200.0	445.4	954.4	1994.9	4093.3
16%	4.4	9.5	35.1	98.4	246.2	580.7	1322.5	2942.7	6446.9
18%	4.6	10.0	38.9	115.0	304.8	764.6	1857.1	4173.5	10400.6
20%	4.7	10.5	43.2	134.8	379.3	1014.7	2639.1	6750.8	17094.1
24%	5.1	11.7	53.1	186.1	594.6	1822.0	5468.1	16234.1	47922.4

(B) INVESTMENT RATE OF RETURN = FIND YEARS COLUMN AND
     LOOK DOWN TO FIND FACTOR, THEN INVESTMENT RATE
     OF RETURN ROW HEADING

Sample Uses: Select the Appropriate Table (Table 13–4 to 13–5)

1. Future value of annual investments:

FUTURE $ VALUE OF FUNDS =
          FIRST YEAR DEPOSIT AMOUNT X FACTOR

2. Beginning annual investment amount needed for future value
accumulations:

$$\text{FIRST YEAR DEPOSIT AMOUNT} = \frac{\text{FUTURE \$ VALUE OF FUNDS}}{\text{FACTOR}}$$

3. Period of time it will take to accumulate a future value with
increasing annual investments:

$$\text{(A) FACTOR} = \frac{\text{FUTURE \$ VALUE OF FUNDS}}{\text{DEPOSIT AMOUNT}}$$

(B) YEARS = FIND INVESTMENT RATE OF RETURN ROW AND
           LOOK ACROSS TO FIND FACTOR, THEN YEARS
           COLUMN HEADING

4. Investment rate of return it will taske to accumulate a future
value with increasing annual investments:

$$\text{(A) FACTOR} = \frac{\text{FUTURE \$ VALUE OF FUNDS}}{\text{DEPOSIT AMOUNT}}$$

(B) INVESTMENT RATE OF RETURN = FIND YEARS COLUMN AND
     LOOK DOWN TO FIND FACTOR, THEN INVESTMENT
     RATE OF RETURN ROW HEADING

Sample Uses (Table 13–6)

1. Annual amount which can be withdrawn and have accumulated
funds last a desired period of time:

VALUE OF EQUAL ANNUAL WITHDRAWALS =
               ACCUMULATED FUNDS VALUE × FACTOR

2. Accumulation of funds needed to provide for equal annual
withdrawals over a desired period of time:

$$\frac{\text{ACCUMULATED}}{\text{FUNDS VALUE}} = \frac{\text{VALUE OF EQUAL ANNUAL WITHDRAWALS}}{\text{FACTOR}}$$

3. Period of time an accumulation of funds will last if making a desired amount of annual withdrawals:

(A) $\text{FACTOR} = \dfrac{\text{VALUE OF EQUAL ANNUAL WITHDRAWALS}}{\text{ACCUMULATED FUNDS VALUE}}$

(B) YEARS = FIND INVESTMENT RATE OF RETURN ROW AND LOOK ACROSS TO FIND FACTOR, THEN YEARS COLUMN HEADING

4. Investment rate of return needed on accumulated funds if making a desired amount of annual withdrawals:

(A) $\text{FACTOR} = \dfrac{\text{VALUE OF EQUAL ANNUAL WITHDRAWALS}}{\text{ACCUMULATED FUNDS VALUE}}$

(B) INVESTMENT RATE OF RETURN = FIND YEARS COLUMN AND LOOK DOWN TO FIND FACTOR, THEN INVESTMENT RATE OF RETURN ROW HEADING

TABLE 13–6 FACTORS FOR DETERMINING AMOUNT OF ANNUAL WITHDRAWAL IN EQUAL AMOUNTS OF ACCUMULATED FUNDS

Investment Rate of Return on Balance not Withdrawn	Years Payments Are to be Received						
	3	5	10	15	20	25	30
6%	.3741	.2374	.1359	.1030	.0872	.0782	.0726
8%	.3880	.2505	.1490	.1168	.1019	.0937	.0888
10%	.4021	.2638	.1627	.1315	.1175	.1102	.1061
12%	.4163	.2774	.1770	.1468	.1339	.1275	.1241
14%	.4307	.2913	.1917	.1628	.1510	.1455	.1428
16%	.4453	.3054	.2069	.1794	.1687	.1640	.1619
18%	.4599	.3198	.2225	.1964	.1868	.1829	.1813
20%	.4747	.3344	.2385	.2139	.2054	.2021	.2008
25%	.5123	.3718	.2801	.2591	.2529	.2509	.2503

Personal Economics

TABLE 13–7 TAXABLE INVESTMENT RATE OF RETURN
EQUIVALENT TO TAX-FREE OR TAX-
DEFERRED RATE OF RETURN

Tax-Free Rate of Return	Marginal Tax Bracket				
	16%	25%	33%	44%	50%
6%	7.14	8.00	8.96	10.71	12.00
8%	9.52	10.67	11.94	14.29	16.00
10%	11.90	13.33	13.93	17.86	20.00
12%	14.29	16.00	17.91	21.43	24.00
14%	16.67	18.67	20.90	25.00	28.00
16%	19.05	21.33	23.88	28.57	32.00
18%	21.43	24.00	26.87	32.14	36.00
20%	23.81	26.67	29.85	35.71	40.00
25%	29.76	33.33	37.31	44.64	50.00

Sample Use (Table 13–7)

Many investment rates, for comparison, are quoted on an annual gross basis. Before deciding between a tax-free investment return (or tax-deferred, like IRA investing) and a taxable investment return, convert the tax-free return to taxable equivalent return in the above table and compare the investments on a gross taxable equivalent return basis.

FORM 13-2

MUTUAL FUND CONTROL SHEET
SUMMARY OF TRANSACTIONS
FOR 19____

Name of Fund _____
Account # _____
Original Purchase Date ____/____/____
Amount of Original Investment _____
Initial Share Balance _____

Fund Objective _____
Telephone # _____
Registered Owner _____
Distribution Option _____

Summary of Share Balances and Values

| Month of Activity | Beginning Mo. Share Balance | Additions to Shares | | | Deletions to Shares | Ending of Mo. Share Balance | Nav or Sell Price Per Share | $ Value of Total Shares |
		By Purchase	By Cap. Gain Distribution	By Dividend Distribution	By Withdrawal			
Jan.							$	$
Feb.								
Mar.								
Apr.								
May								
June								
July								
Aug.								
Sept.								
Oct.								
Nov.								
Dec.								
Annual Summary								

Share Reconciliation _____
Beg. of Year Balance _____
Additions   + _____
Deletions   – _____
End of Year Bal. _____

FIGURE 13-2 IRA INVESTING

FORM 13-2a *(Continued)*

Summary for Current Year Taxes*

Total Capital Gain & Dividend Distributions Paid or Reinvested	Month	Made Up of the Following			Memo	
		Long Term Capital Gain Distribution	Short Term Capital Gain Distribution	Income Dividend	Dividends Qualifying for Exclusion	Dividends Not Qualifying for Exclusion
$ ___	___	$ ___	$ ___	$ ___	$ ___	$ ___
___	___	___	___	___	___	___
___	___	___	___	___	___	___
___	___	___	___	___	___	___
TOTAL* ___		___	___	___	___	___

*This information will also be available and provided to you by fund at year end by form 1099.

Adjusted Cost Basis if Reinvesting Distributions*

Cost Basis of Share Purchases by Direct Investment (Initial Investment + Cash Additions)	Plus	All Previous Years' Capital Gain/Dividend Distributions Reinvested (Cumm. Balance)	Plus	This Year's Capital Gain & Dividend Distributions Reinvested (Total from Above)	Equals	Adjusted Cost Basis
$ ___	+	$ ___	+	$ ___	=	$ ___

*This information is important for tracking the cost basis of Mutual Funds for individuals reinvesting distributions. If you are reinvesting a portion (e.g., capital gains only) use the above to record those reinvestments only.

14

ESTIMATING ESTATE TAXES

"It requires a great deal of boldness and a great deal of caution to make a great fortune, and when you have got it, it requires ten times as much wit to keep it."

Rothschild

A young family was involved in a tragic accident. The father was killed in the accident, the mother and four children survived. Fortunately the father had a will, but in it left everything to his wife. There was about $150,000 in assets. He was also covered with $500,000 of life insurance.

The mother died about two years later from complications caused by the accident. The probating of her estate was very expensive and substantial estate and inheritance taxes were paid. The amount of money left for the children and their care was greatly diminished. The parents hadn't seen any reason to structure their estate planning differently. That was unfortunate because, with a different structure, expenses and taxes could have been greatly reduced.

Often we encounter a negative attitude towards estate planning. Perhaps most of us don't like to think about death, or perhaps life insurance salesmen eager for commission income have over-sold the concept of estate planning. There are certainly valid reasons for carrying insurance, but needs for estate liquidity and family security have changed greatly in light of revisions in federal estate taxation laws.

Individuals have much greater interest in "living" areas of financial planning—cash flow management, income tax planning, and investment planning. The transition from these high interest areas to estate planning is an easy one when employing the concepts of comprehensive financial planning. To determine, for example, family income needs in the event the main income earner dies is an off-shoot of cash flow, insurance, and net worth summaries. Asset titling, another important area of estate planning, can be addressed at the time new investments or asset purchases are made.

Incorporating estate planning into other financial planning activities not only assures a broad-based approach to financial planning, but also makes the estate planning process itself easier.

Estate planning is best treated matter-of-factly, just as are getting a physical or other important life routines. Estate planning is as important as other areas of financial planning and should be viewed accordingly.

Poor estate planning can result in:

- undesirable asset distributions to heirs;
- net estate size reduction because of unnecessary taxes and expenses;
- time delays in distribution of funds to heirs;
- financial mismanagement by heirs or others involved in an estate;
- unsatisfied dependent needs; and
- missed opportunities for preparatory planning for incapacity or severe disability.

Estate plans can be simple or complex depending on personal preferences and financial positions. Substantial opportunity exists to create the type of overall estate plan one wants, yet minimize estate taxes and death expenses and provide for coordinated financial management.

FEDERAL AND STATE TAXATION   State laws and regulations vary greatly with respect to death taxes. Some states do not impose death or inheritance taxes and, thus, become attractive as states of residency in later years of life. States that do impose death taxes usually have inheritance taxation in contrast to estate taxation. Estate taxes are taxes imposed on an estate based on the amount of assets considered taxable. Inheritance taxes are determined on the basis of allocated shares of an estate to heirs. Normally different classes of heirs (usually based on family or nonfamily relationship) are subject to different levels of taxes, with closer heirs such as a spouse or children receiving the lightest taxation.

The United States has both "common" law states and "community property" law states. Without pursuing precise technical variations from state-to-state, community property law states assume husband and wife have equal ownership of assets, regardless of title, unless property was acquired prior to marriage or through inheritance. The majority of states are common law states and treat ownership according to asset titling. If property is titled jointly with right of survivorship between spouses, it is assumed each owns one-half and upon the death of one person, the property automatically passes to the survivor. Property titled jointly as tenants in common means each party owns a specified (not necessarily equal) interest, which they can leave upon death to any heir(s) they want. Joint ownership interest between nonspouses is based on relative contribution to cost by the various parties. In common law states, assets titled separately (i.e., one name) can be left to any desired heir whether or not the heir is a surviving spouse. The same is true for community property states on true separate property and nonjoint community property shares.

Become familiar with the regulations of your particular state, and states of optional residency which might appeal to you. Discuss the regulations with your attorney and base your estate planning on federal and state laws. Estimate your estate and inheritance taxes attributable to your estate distributions with your current estate plans in effect and under various scenarios which you wish to consider for estate planning.

The federal government does not levy inheritance taxes but does impose estate taxes. The taxes are based on gross assets includable in a decedent's estate less certain deductions, and are calculated according to progressive tax rates. Forms 14–1 through 14–3 are useful in estimating estate taxes which would be incurred in the event of death. Estate taxes should be estimated to plan for liquidity and family security needs.

FORM 14-1 ESTATE ASSETS AND LIABILITIES*

Assets	Title	Value	Husband's Estate	Wife's Estate
		$	$	$
Total Assets		$	$	$

Liabilities	Title	Amount	Husband's Estate	Wife's Estate
		$	$	$
Total Liabilities		$	$	$
Net Assets Subject to Estate Taxes			$	$

*Include life insurance ownership and proceeds (if cross ownership of cash value life insurance is used, then, for example, a wife owning life insurance on her husband would subject any net cash value to taxation if she predeceases him, but the death benefit of the policy would not be includable in her taxable estate); also include qualified retirement plans (retirement plans distributable to beneficiaries on an annuity basis—such as a defined benefit pension—are subject to estate taxation on the present value of the expected distributions); in common law states, split joint property 50/50; in community property states, allocate true separate property and split joint and non-joint community property 50/50; single individuals should use either one of the two estate columns.

FORM 14-2   ESTIMATED FEDERAL ESTATE TAXES AND EXPENSES (SINGLE)

Net Assets Subject to Tax	$_____
− Administrative Costs	_____
= Adjusted Gross Estate	$_____
− Charitable Bequests	_____
= Taxable Estate	$_____
Gross Federal Tax	$_____
− State Tax Credit	_____
− Unified Tax Credit	_____
= Net Federal Tax	$_____
+ Net State Tax	_____
+ Administrative Costs	_____
= Taxes and Expenses	$_____

ASSETS SUBJECT TO TAX

- All assets, less debts, which you own, including shares of jointly owned property are subject to tax. If assets have been irrevocably placed in trust or gifted (with associated qualifications met), do not include these.
- Do include life insurance policies (net value) which you own; unless placed in an irrevocable trust or properly gifted.
- The first $100,000 of combined qualified retirement plan benefits (Keogh, Pension, Profit Sharing Plan, etc.) which will be distributed to heirs because of irrevocable elections is not subject to estate tax, if benefits collection began before January 1, 1985. If collection did not begin before then, this exclusion does not apply. The $100,000 estate tax exclusion is lost if any qualified plan proceeds are used to pay estate taxes.

ADMINISTRATIVE COSTS

Your attorney should be able to give you an estimate of approximate legal fees, court costs, funeral, and other expenses.

Commonly a rule of thumb of 5 percent of assets subject to tax is used to estimate the costs. However, if most of your assets are joint, held in trust, and/or consists of life insurance and retirement plans with designated beneficiaries, we suggest the rule of thumb percentage be decreased to 2 percent. This is because transfers of

FORM 14-3 ESTIMATED FEDERAL ESTATE TAXES AND EXPENSES (MARRIED)

	Husband Predeceases	Wife Predeceases
First Estate		
Net Assets Subject to Tax	$_____	$_____
− Administrative Costs	_____	_____
= Adjusted Gross Estate	$_____	$_____
− Marital Deduction	_____	_____
− Charitable Bequests	_____	_____
= Taxable Estate	$_____	$_____
Gross Federal Tax	$_____	$_____
− State Tax Credit	_____	_____
− Unified Tax Credit	_____	_____
= Net Federal Tax	$_____	$_____
+ Net State Tax	_____	_____
+ Administrative Costs	_____	_____
= Total Taxes and Expenses	$_____	$_____
Second Estate	Wife	Husband
Net Assets Subject to Tax	$_____	$_____
+ Assets Received from First Estate	_____	_____
− Administrative Costs	_____	_____
= Adjusted Gross Estate	$_____	$_____
− Charitable Bequests	_____	_____
= Taxable Estate	$_____	$_____
Gross Federal Tax	$_____	$_____
− State Tax Credit	_____	_____
− Unified Tax Credit	_____	_____
= Net Federal Tax	$_____	$_____
+ Net State Tax	_____	_____
+ Administrative Costs	_____	_____
= Taxes and Expenses	$_____	$_____
Total Taxes and Expenses	$_____	$_____

property are less expensive and easier under these types of circumstances.

MARITAL DEDUCTION

The current Unlimited Marital Deduction allows a decedent who predeceases his or her spouse to leave the surviving spouse up to 100 percent of qualified assets without estate taxes.

The assets can be left directly to the surviving spouse, or in trust for the surviving spouse. The surviving spouse does not have to be provided full control over the assets. Normally, income from trust assets is paid to the spouse along with principal—either at the spouse's or an independent trustee's discretion.

Plans can be structured so that assets, upon the second spouse's death, pass to heirs according to the desires of either spouse, whichever is preferred. See the discussion of Qualified Terminable Interest in Chapter 15.

CHARITABLE BEQUESTS

Death gifts to qualified charitable institutions are deductible from the taxable estate. Acceptable donees include charitable organizations, nonprofit institutions, and governmental units.

Bequests may be direct or delayed distributions effective upon death or bequests arranged prior to death such as use of Charitable Remainder Trusts.

GROSS FEDERAL TAX

Tax, before applied credits, calculated on the Taxable Estate figure according to Table 14–1.

STATE TAX CREDIT

The federal government allows a credit (subject to the maximums in Table 14–2) for all estate, inheritance, legacy or succession taxes actually paid to a state. To determine the maximum credit allowed, subtract $60,000 from the Taxable Estate and calculate the credit according to Table 14–2.

UNIFIED TAX CREDIT

The federal government allows the credit in Table 14–3 (which increases by year) to be used to offset estate and/or gift taxes. To the extent the credit is not used during lifetime against taxes due on gifts subject to gift taxes, it applies to estate taxes to determine estate taxes due.

TABLE 14-1 FEDERAL ESTATE AND GIFT TAX SCHEDULE

Taxable Estate	Before 1988			1988 and Thereafter		
	Base Amount +	Marginal Rate	On Excess Over	Base Amount +	Marginal Rate	On Excess Over
Less than $10,000	$ 0	18%	$ 0	$ 0	18%	$ 0
10,000–20,000	1,800	20	10,000	1,800	20	10,000
20,000–40,000	3,800	22	20,000	3,800	22	20,000
40,000–60,000	8,200	24	40,000	8,200	24	40,000
60,000–80,000	13,000	26	60,000	13,000	26	60,000
80,000–100,000	18,200	28	80,000	18,200	28	80,000
100,000–150,000	23,800	30	100,000	23,800	30	100,000
150,000–250,000	38,800	32	150,000	38,800	32	150,000
250,000–500,000	70,800	34	250,000	70,800	34	250,000
500,000–750,000	155,800	37	500,000	155,800	37	500,000
750,000–1,000,000	248,300	39	750,000	248,300	39	750,000
1,000,000–1,250,000	345,800	41	1,000,000	345,800	41	1,000,000
1,250,000–1,500,000	448,300	43	1,250,000	448,300	43	1,250,000
1,500,000–2,000,000	555,800	45	1,500,000	555,800	45	1,500,000
2,000,000–2,500,000	780,800	49	2,000,000	780,800	49	2,000,000
2,500,000–3,000,000	1,025,800	53	2,500,000	1,025,800	50	2,500,000
3,000,000 and Above	1,290,800	55	3,000,000	1,025,800	50	2,500,000

TABLE 14-2 STATE TAX CREDIT SCHEDULE

Reduced Taxable Estate	Base Credit	+	Marginal Rate	On Excess Over
Less than $40,000	$ 0		0 %	$ 0
40,000–90,000	0		.8	40,000
90,000–140,000	400		1.6	90,000
140,000–240,000	1,200		2.4	140,000
240,000–440,000	3,600		3.2	240,000
440,000–640,000	10,000		4.0	440,000
640,000–840,000	18,000		4.8	640,000
840,000–1,040,000	27,600		5.6	840,000
1,040,000–1,540,000	38,800		6.4	1,040,000
1,540,000–2,040,000	70,800		7.2	1,540,000
2,040,000–2,540,000	106,800		8.0	2,040,000
2,540,000–3,040,000	146,800		8.8	2,540,000
3,040,000–3,540,000	190,800		9.6	3,040,000
3,540,000–4,040,000	238,800		10.4	3,540,000
4,040,000–5,040,000	290,800		11.2	4,040,000
5,040,000–6,040,000	402,800		12.0	5,040,000
6,040,000–7,040,000	522,800		12.8	6,040,000
7,040,000–8,040,000	650,800		13.6	7,040,000
8,040,000–9,040,000	786,800		14.4	8,040,000
9,040,000–10,040,000	930,800		15.2	9,040,000
10,040,000 and Above	1,082,800		16.0	10,040,000

NET STATE TAX The amount of net state tax depends on the particular state in which a decedent had residency; some states do not impose death taxes. Many states have a tax structure which is tied into the federal government allowable state tax credit. The states using this approach levy inheritance or other taxes at legislated rates and impose additional taxes, which apply in some circumstances, to the extent the allowable federal state tax credit exceeds the levied state taxes.

Inheritance or other death tax rates for state taxes are available from the state governments and often can be obtained from lawyers, accountants, insurance agents, or bankers.

Married couples should estimate death taxes and expenses for

TABLE 14-3 UNIFIED TAX CREDIT

Year	Credit	Estate Asset Exemption Equivalent
1985	$121,800	$400,000
1986	155,800	500,000
1987 and thereafter	192,800	600,000

both the first and second death, and revise the order of death, to determine combined overall taxes.

With an understanding of estate taxation, you can proceed to effectively plan your estate. As with income taxes, become familiar with the various reforms in estate and inheritance taxation which are passed by legislators and analyze the impact of such changes on your personal financial planning.

15

PROVIDING AN ESTATE

"A well-ordered life is like climbing a tower; the view halfway up is better than the view from the base, and it steadily becomes finer as the horizon expands."

William Lyon Phelps

Over a period of about a year, we repeatedly met with a widow. She was in constant emotional turmoil. She was attending financial classes and meeting with many advisors, but becoming more confused all the time. She was angry with her deceased husband because she did not know what to do with the money she had inherited and feared that with mismanagement she could end up in poverty.

The husband had left her a very sizeable inheritance, mostly securities which he had actively managed prior to his death. She had complete discretionary control over the money. A large portion of it was with a brokerage firm her husband had used for trading. Following her husband's death, there was no management of the portfolio and it fell substantially in value. She was afraid to confront the broker for fear of offending him. She asked her accountant for investment advise, but he really could not offer any. A family friend was a co-trustee on a small family trust, but he too lacked investment knowledge. Her fear, and lack of money management knowledge, inhibited her from decision making.

The husband would have saved his wife from tremendous emotional pain had he left his wealth to trusts (for the benefit of his wife), with qualified trustees to oversee money management. The widow would have been far happier if she did not have to make investment decisions.

We have encountered many, many situations of family problems following death of a member; particularly because of insufficient financial resources to care for survivors, spouses left without knowledge and understanding of family finances, and family estate arguments.

Estate planning involves living as well as post-mortem planning. As with other areas of planning, it is important to understand the basics of estate planning and to know where competent and objective, professional advice can be found. Estate document drafting is best handled by attorneys and we recommend against do-it-yourself kits, or "holographic" type documents. Make sure the attorney you hire specializes in estate planning. We find in many instances that general practitioner-type attorneys are not up-to-date on optimal estate planning techniques.

Estate plans should be reviewed every two to four years or upon major changes, including federal or state death tax laws; family births or deaths; marriages or divorces; business changes; and residence relocation to another state. Although it is necessary for attorneys to use precise legal language, you should understand your estate plans and the contents of estate documents; that is, in working with your attorney, you should be able to explain your plans in simple language. It may be helpful to diagram and summarize the plans on a sheet of paper.

DECIDING ON AN APPROACH

Several important concerns arise in thinking through the best approach for planning any particular estate. Married couples should decide estate issues simultaneously.

1. *Family Security* Will there be enough assets to provide for family income needs? Chapter 5 included an estate funding analysis to answer this question. First look to accumulated investments and vested retirement plans which have death payout provisions. Make up projected deficits, if any, with life insurance coverage, purchasing the lowest cost protection possible. Estate taxes and death expenses, which depend on the

structure of estate planning, will affect overall family security as these expenses will consume assets at death.

2. *Estate Liquidity*   Will there be enough liquid assets (easily converted to cash) to pay estate taxes and other death expenses? Liquidity is an important factor in structuring investment portfolios and estate liquidity, as well as liquidity needs while living, should be incorporated into investment planning. Life insurance is a source of liquidity, although for most individuals death taxes and expense will be substantially less than costs incurred by estates in the past because of legislative changes in death taxes. Liquidity and expense payments can be provided for through estate documents in many ways.

3. *Asset Management*   In the event of the death (or incapacity due to disability) of the main income earner of the family, who will manage family assets, or if you are single, your assets? Sometimes a family member other than the main income earner manages the finances and has full knowledge of family finances. This person most likely can continue to effectively handle and manage financial affairs. In other instances, the main income earner manages the finances and upon his or her death other family members may need assistance with financial management. Assistance is available in several ways; most commonly through professional advisors or trustees of trusts.

4. *Assets to Heirs*   Who do you wish to receive your assets following your death? You can direct assets to anyone you desire. Normally distributions will be to a surviving spouse, children, siblings, other relatives or friends, and charities. Death without estate documents—referred to as intestate—means assets will be distributed according to state law which may be in conflict with what a decedent would have desired. Poor estate planning results in distributions to governmental units in the form of taxes beyond that necessary.

5. *Asset Form to Heirs*   Do you want your heirs to receive your assets with full control over the assets? If so, do you want immediate or delayed distributions? Some individuals prefer that heirs receive only the use of assets (e.g., a home or investment principal to produce income) rather than receiving full control of the assets to do whatever the heirs please (sell, liquidate, consume, etc.). Some people like to include provi-

sions in their estate plans regarding remarriage of a surviving spouse or education of children. There are many alternatives. It depends upon how you feel about your personal circumstances. You may decide you would like heirs to receive all of your assets, but on a delayed basis, such as distributing stated portions to children at certain ages.

After thinking through the above mentioned estate concerns, summarize your conclusions in writing. (See Form 15–1.) Knowing your desires and conclusions, you can proceed to determine the best choices in structuring your estate plans. If you have estate documents, review these to see if the documents conform with your desires and are up-to-date with current laws.

GIFTING

As discussed in Chapter 11, gifting assets to others can reduce income taxes. It can also reduce estate taxes. Gifting reduces estate taxes because qualifying asset gifts made before death are not included in the donor's taxable estate.

To qualify for exclusion from estate taxes, a gift must be a so-called gift of present interest in contrast to a gift of future interest. In simple terms, the donor must relinquish control over the gifted asset and the gift must have current value. Generally a gift of future interest is the right to use property in the future, but the fact that an asset is payable in the future does not necessarily

FORM 15–1

Concern:	Conclusions:
Family Security	
Estate Liquidity	
Asset Management	
Assets to Heirs and Others	
Asset Form to Heirs	

constitute future interest ownership. If for example, income on gift trust property is accumulated instead of being paid out, it becomes (in many instances) a gift of future interest rather than present interest. There are several ways of accomplishing the relinquishment of control requirement for a gift of present interest, including outright pure gifting or, in some cases, retaining some type of qualifying lifetime use following an irrevocable gift to be completed upon death. Complex gifting (i.e., private annuities, irrevocable trusts, charitable remainder trusts, etc.) should be handled through a specialized attorney.

Most gifts are not "brought" back into a donor's taxable estate upon his or her death. Gifts of life insurance, "retained interest" (income payments to or control by the donor) gifts, and some other exceptions, made within three years of death are brought back into a donor's estate.

Gifts to nonqualifying donees are subject to gift taxes, payable by the donor. Gifts to qualifying donees, which are not subject to gift taxes, include interspousal gifting, charitable and nonprofit institutions, government units, direct educational tuition payments made on behalf of other individuals, and medical payments made for others.

The donor of taxable gifts must file a gift tax return, if taxes are due, for the year in which the gift(s) is made and submit the return to the IRS along with his or her income tax return. There is allowable annual gifting, without gift taxes, of $10,000 per year per donee ($20,000 if both husband and wife join in gifting—written consent is required by a nongifting spouse if one spouse provides all gifted assets). Taxable gifts to donees beyond these allowable amounts are subject to the same tax rates as shown for estate taxes in the previous chapter. However, the federal Unified Tax Credit can be used during lifetime to offset payment of gift taxes. To the extent the credit is used during the lifetime, it cannot be used upon death against estate taxes.

A donee assumes the same "cost basis" for an asset as the donor had immediately prior to the gift. The concept of "stepped-up" in basis which can apply at death does not apply to lifetime gifts. "Stepped-up" basis means heirs take on a new cost basis equal to the fair market value of an asset at a decedent's death. Thus any appreciation of asset value between the time of purchase and inheritance escapes capital gain income tax.

In gifting assets, careful evaluation needs to be given to which assets will be gifted. Assets retained for purposes of achieving a "step-up" in basis following death of the owner may result in more estate taxes than income tax savings from a "step-up" in basis. Maximum marginal estate tax rates reach 55 percent (50 percent in 1988), while the maximum income tax rate on long-term capital gains is a net 20 percent. This suggests, particularly for high wealth—income tax payers, greater favorability of removing assets from a taxable estate over avoiding capital gain taxation. With estates, which will not be subject to a high level of estate taxation, a "step-up" in basis can be very favorable. Gifts should be made only to produce tax savings and/or after family financial security and independence have been established. The funding analyses in Chapter 5 provide good guidelines for determining levels of financial security and independence.

Minor children can be gifted to under the Uniform Gifts to Minors Act (UGMA). A custodian must be named to handle management of the assets on behalf of a child; and to avoid inclusion of gifted assets in the donor's estate, the custodian should be someone other than the donor. In most states, the children have full rights to, and control of, gifted assets at age 18.

Children, and other donees, can also be gifted to through trusts. To remove gifted assets from a donor's taxable estate, the trusts must be irrevocable. Gifts may not be rescinded. Revocable gifts or placement of assets in trust does not qualify for estate exclusion because control over assets is not relinquished.

An irrevocable 2503(C) trust is sometimes preferable (but more costly) to UGMA gifting because income can accumulate along with principal for a child until the child reaches age 21 (and sometimes longer). Assets are still removed from the donor's taxable estate.

Clifford Trusts (short-term trusts) are revocable and do not remove assets from a donor's taxable estate. These trusts are popular for accomplishing income tax shifting. The trusts must be for terms of at least 10 years and one day (extended for each additional principal deposit beyond the initial deposit). Assets are transferred to the trust to generate investment earnings for beneficiaries with principal reverting back to the grantor at the end of the trust period. Transfers are subject to gift taxes on the basis of the present value of the income stream to the beneficiaries.

**ESTATE
DOCUMENTS**

The selection of estate documents to be used should be dependent on several factors, including:

- personal desires for lifetime and death asset distributions;
- personal financial circumstances (complexity, wealth, asset composition, dependent needs, etc.);
- family financial planning and management capabilities, both currently and anticipated after death; and
- federal and state laws in effect at the time documents are drafted.

Everyone should have a will and many people should create a living and/or testamentary trust(s). Death, without a will in effect, can result in many unfavorable consequences:

- Assets will be distributed to heirs according to state laws (some of which are rather adverse to surviving spouses).
- No specific burial instructions.
- Court appointed administrator of the estate.
- Court appointed guardian for children.
- Unnecessary delays and costs.
- Assets open to creditors.
- Lack of specific asset management.
- Lack of privacy.
- Problems with the purchase, sale, or lease of property, and continued operation of a business.

Commonly used estate documents are:

- Simple Will
- Testamentary Trust Will
- Pour-Over Will
- Living Revocable Trust
- Living Irrevocable Trust

Estate document provisions determine, among many other things, the flow and distribution of most assets. Two important exceptions, which supersede estate document provisions, are joint (with right of survivorship) titling of assets and beneficiary designations of life insurance and retirement plans. Other assets pass according to estate document provisions.

Trusts can be created (and possibly funded) during lifetime and/or upon death. Trusts which go into effect upon death are referred to as testamentary trusts. Often wills and trusts are interlinked. Wills can carry provisions for creation of trusts upon death and/or for flows of assets to trusts.

Wills usually carry provisions for payment of death expenses and taxes, distributions of assets outright to individuals and/or to trusts, designations for guardians of minor children, and naming of executor/executrix (personal representative or administrator)—individual(s) responsible for handling the estate, including filing of the estate tax return.

Simple Will   Distributes assets outright to heirs and does not involve trusts.

Testamentary Trust Will   May distribute some assets outright to heirs, with the balance going to trust(s) created, and taking effect, upon death; the trust(s) carry provisions for asset distribution to heirs.

Pour-Over Will   May distribute some assets outright to heirs, with the balance going to trust(s) created before death.

Living Revocable Trust   Effective and often funded while living (assets actually placed in and titled in trust name); can be changed by the grantor at any time prior to death; frequently carrying provisions for management of assets in event of severe disability of the grantor or simply if the grantor does not have time or ability to manage assets; also carrying provisions for management and distribution of assets to heirs following death of the grantor. Funding of living revocable trusts does not reduce estate taxes but does reduce probate expenses and time delays for asset distributions and provides for estate planning; living trusts can be designated beneficiary of life insurance policies and retirement plans; and can receive assets from the grantor's estate or the estates of other individuals.

Living Irrevocable Trust   Effective while living and most frequently funded with life insurance; cannot be changed by the grantor; carrying provisions for management and distribution of assets to heirs following death of the grantor; this type of trust is also used in conjunction with charitable bequests and can provide for income to the grantor while living; assets placed in trust (provided legal requirements, including three-year rule, are met) are

FIGURE 15–1 PASSING ASSETS TO HEIRS

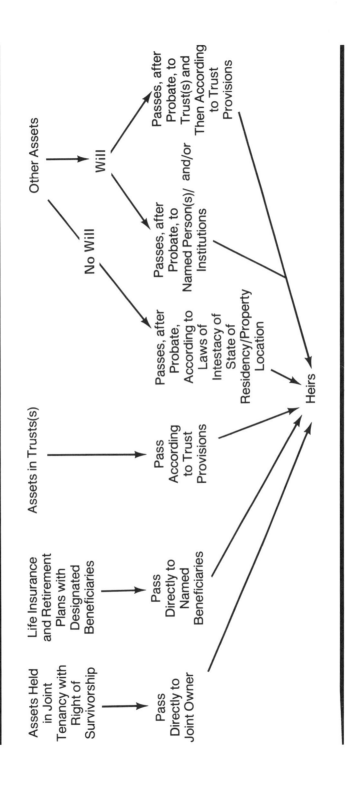

not includable in the grantor's taxable estate, but can be used to provide estate liquidity to the grantor's estate.

As suggested, there are many factors to be considered in selecting estate documents for use. Choices should be made only with the assistance of an attorney. Table 15–1 provides suggestions for consideration based on estate size.

ESTATE DOCUMENT PROVISIONS

In order to conform to federal and state laws and accomplish personal desires, estate documents must include many important features. Of extreme importance is the distribution of assets to

TABLE 15–1   ESTATE DOCUMENTS TO CONSIDER*

	Estate Size of Single Individuals or Combined Size of Married Couples		
	Less Than $600,000	$600,000 To $1,200,000	More Than $1,200,000
Married-no dependents	Simple will or pour-over will and living revocable trust	Simple will or pour-over will and living revocable trust	Pour-over will and living revocable trust; charitable living irrevocable trust
Married-dependents	Simple will or testamentary trust will or pour-over will and living revocable trust (including contingent life insurance funding)	Testamentary trust will or pour-over will and living revocable trust (including contingent life insurance funding)	Pour-over will and living revocable trust; living irrevocable trust (including life insurance funding); charitable living irrevocable trust
Unmarried-no dependents	Simple will or pour-over will and living revocable trust	Simple will or pour-over will and living revocable trust	Pour-over will and living revocable trust; charitable living irrevocable trust
Unmarried-dependents	Simple will or testamentary trust will or pour-over will and living revocable trust (including contingent life insurance funding)	Testamentary trust will or pour-over will and living revocable trust (includng contingent life insurance funding)	Pour-over will and living revocable trust; living irrevocable trust (including life insurance funding); charitable living irrevocable trust

Notes:
A will may be either a simple will, testamentary trust will, or a pour-over will.
A trust may be either a testamentary trust, living revocable trust, or a living irrevocable trust.
*Based on the 1987 (and thereafter) Unified Federal Estate Tax Credit, earlier years have lower suggested amounts—consult your attorney for proper flexibility.

heirs, in conjunction with minimization of estate taxes to maximize net after-tax estate size.

Married couples should maintain perspective on the amount of combined overall estate taxes resulting from the deaths of both spouses. Care must be taken in structuring estate planning not only to minimize taxes at the first death but also at the second death. Suppose a husband has an Adjusted Gross Estate of $500,000 and his wife $300,000, the husband dies in 1987 with the wife's death shortly thereafter. Estate taxes upon his death can be easily avoided, however, the approach taken affects taxes at the wife's subsequent death. For example (ignoring state taxes and expenses):

A. If he leaves all assets to his wife.

HIS ADJUSTED GROSS ESTATE	$500,000
– MARITAL DEDUCTION	–500,000
TAXABLE ESTATE	$ 0
GROSS FEDERAL TAX	$ 0
–UNIFIED TAX CREDIT	N/A
NET FEDERAL TAX	$ 0
HER ADJUSTED GROSS ESTATE	$800,000
TAXABLE ESTATE	$800,000
GROSS FEDERAL TAX	$267,800
– UNIFIED TAX CREDIT	–192,800
NET FEDERAL TAX	$ 75,000

B. If he leaves $400,000 to a family trust for the benefit of his wife and the balance of $100,000 outright to his wife.

HIS ADJUSTED GROSS ESTATE	$500,000
– MARITAL DEDUCTION	–100,000
TAXABLE ESTATE	$400,000
GROSS FEDERAL TAX	$121,800
– UNIFIED TAX CREDIT	–192,800
NET FEDERAL TAX	$ 0
HER ADJUSTED GROSS ESTATE	$400,000
TAXABLE ESTATE	$400,000
GROSS FEDERAL TAX	$121,800
– UNIFIED TAX CREDIT	–192,800
NET FEDERAL TAX	$ 0

Example B results in combined death tax savings of $75,000 (or $75,000 more to heirs) in contrast to example A because in B advantageous use of the Federal Estate Unified Tax Credit is made. $400,000 of assets are left upon the husband's death to a family (or residuary) trust and this amount does not qualify for the allowable Marital Deduction. However, the credit is more than sufficient to offset taxes. To avoid inclusion of the funds left to trust in the wife's subsequent taxable estate, trust provisions must be such that the wife does not have full control over the assets. Income from trust investments can be paid out to her regularly and principal can be distributed to her, at the discretion of an independent trustee, for maintenance of her accustomed standard of living. She can be a co-trustee (along with an independent trustee) of the residuary trust.

In either case A or B, the amount left directly to the wife, could instead be left to a marital trust on her behalf and the funds would still qualify for the Marital Deduction. Full control over assets can be given to her but such powers do not have to be granted.

In lieu of full control over marital trust assets, the wife could receive a Qualified Terminable Interest (QTIP). A Qualified Terminable Interest allows a decedent who predeceases his or her spouse to leave the surviving spouse use of qualified assets without estate taxes and upon the death of the second spouse (at which time assets will be taxed), assets can pass to heirs according to the desires of the first spouse to die (that is, the surviving spouse does not have to have a power of appointment to qualify assets for the marital deduction). Use of Qualified Terminable Interest Trusts is common today because of the high rate of divorce, remarriage, step children, and general desire of spouses to direct the ultimate distribution of their assets yet also minimize estate taxes. To qualify assets for the Marital Deduction on the death of the first spouse, and leave the surviving spouse a Qualified Terminable Interest, the following requirements must be met:

- The estate executor must make an election for a Qualified Terminable Interest on the estate tax return of the first spouse to die and the election is irrevocable.
- The property intended for the Qualified Terminable Interest must be placed in trust.
- The surviving spouse must be given full rights, for life, to the income earned on trust assets.

- The income earned on trust assets must be paid to the surviving spouse at frequencies of no less than once per year.
- Principal of the trust cannot be paid out for the benefit of anyone other than the surviving spouse while the surviving spouse is still living.

The surviving spouse does not have to be, but can be, a trustee of the QTIP. He or she should be given trustee status only on a co-trustee basis with an independent trustee. The surviving spouse should not be allowed to withdraw trust principal on a completely discretionary basis. Withdrawal powers by the surviving spouse at his or her own discretion, should be carefully structured and re-stricted. The surviving spouse cannot withdraw principal for the benefit of anyone other than himself or herself. Therefore, careful consideration and planning needs to be conducted prior to drafting and executing a QTIP, as principal may be needed for individuals other than the surviving spouse and assets may be better placed outside of a Qualified Terminable Interest Trust.

Use of QTIPs should also be carefully evaluated in conjunction with state death tax laws. In some states, the advantages of federal QTIP use could be partially offset with adverse state tax conse-quences.

The decision to leave assets outright or in trust to heirs should be based both on an individual's ultimate asset distribution desires and the financial management capabilities of heirs. Intention could be to leave only the use of assets to some heirs with principal ultimately flowing to other heirs. Any type of trust should carry provisions for the management of assets. Competent initial and successor trustees should be selected and designated. Sources of trustees include:

- self (self-trusteed living revocable trust);
- spouse;
- adult children;
- close friends and relatives;
- lawyers;
- professional tax and investment advisors;
- banks; and
- trust companies.

Some people prefer the objectivity and security offered by using large institutions as trustees. Other individuals dislike large insti-

FIGURE 15-2   WILL DIAGRAMS

(a)   Simple Will (Single Individual)

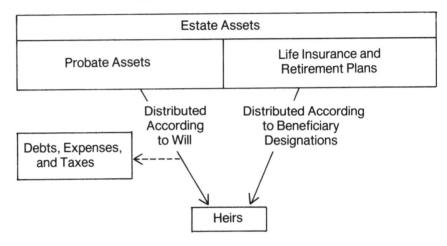

(b)   Simple Will (Married Individual)

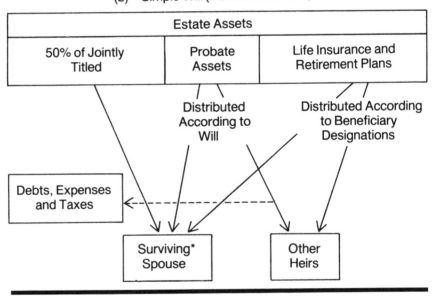

*Not subject to estate taxes at first spouse's death.

tutions and are aware of the relatively poor investment management record of many large institutional trustees. It is a matter of personal preference. Co-trustees, or to use more than one trustee simultaneously, is acceptable. Successor trustees should also be included so that court determined replacement of a trustee is not necessary. Trustees may die, resign, be removed by beneficiaries, or for other reasons be unable to continue. Certain precautions must be taken in selecting trustees to meet estate planning requirements and desires. For example, self-trustee of a trust designed to remove estate assets would not reduce estate taxes because requirements are such that control must be given up by a grantor. Irrevocable trusts, which if properly structured do reduce estate taxes, must be trusteed by an independent party. Similarly, use of residuary (often family) trusts is intended, in addition to asset management, to keep assets out of a surviving spouse's estate. Therefore, while a surviving spouse can be a co-trustee, he or she should not be sole trustee. If he or she has full control and discretion over assets, the assets will be included in his or her taxable estate.

Of course, fiscal responsibility, financial knowledge, integrity, honesty, and reputation, of individuals or institutions are extremely important criteria in the trustee selection process. Trustee's powers can be limited, or specifically directed, but in general need to be broad ranged so as to effectively handle estate matters and manage assets. The powers usually encompass buying and selling assets, making income and principal distributions to trust beneficiaries, providing children with educational and other funding, business ownership matters and decisions, and other important functions.

Table 15–1 outlines suggested estate document use based on asset size. The chart is based on the Federal Unified Estate Tax Credit for 1987 and thereafter. Dollar brackets for years before 1987 should be somewhat lower as credit amounts will be lower. Attorneys writing documents before 1987 can incorporate flexibility into the documents so as to achieve optimal results. In planning document use, also consider that over time, with successful money management, your estate size will increase (although you may offset this with gifting if desired). In reviewing the following summary of objectives and estate sizes, keep in mind that factors other than estate tax minimization may be most important to you. The following is intended to present strategies for minimizing estate taxes. Interpret the dollar levels to be in reference to estate size for a single individual or the combined estate size for married couples.

Estate Size of Less Than $600,000

- In 1987, the Federal Unified Estate Tax Credit will be $192,800, which is equivalent to eliminating scheduled estate taxes on taxable estates of up to $600,000. Assets will pass to heirs free of federal estate taxes.
- A husband, for example, could leave all his assets to his wife (either outright or in trust) or vice versa, without federal estate taxes due upon his death or upon her subsequent death.
- Simple Wills, distributing assets outright, may be appropriate both for single and married individuals.
- Testamentary trusts or living revocable trusts may be desired, if there are dependents such as children, for management purposes and/or to reserve some assets for ultimate distribution to heirs.

Estate Size of $600,000 to $1,200,000

- The first $600,000 of net taxable estate assets will be tax free. The estates of single individuals with assets above $600,000 will incur federal estate taxes.
- Single individuals could gift, using living irrevocable trusts, and make charitable bequests upon death to reduce taxes. Unless an individual is old with a short life expectancy, the need to retain financial security may outweigh the potential advantages of estate tax reduction from gifting or using irrevocable trusts.
- Because the amount of assets is very significant, both single and married individuals should give consideration to the benefits of placing assets in a living revocable trust while living (for management and precautionary reasons) and have assets not placed in trust while living pour over to the trust at death.
- Typically it is most advantageous to leave personal property (including the residence for married couples) outside of trust and place other assets in trust. Careful attention needs to be given to the amount of assets married couples own separately and jointly.
- Married couples should seek planning so that net taxable estate size will not exceed $600,000 at the second death. Upon the first

FIGURE 15-3 TESTAMENTARY TRUST WILL
(SINGLE INDIVIDUAL)

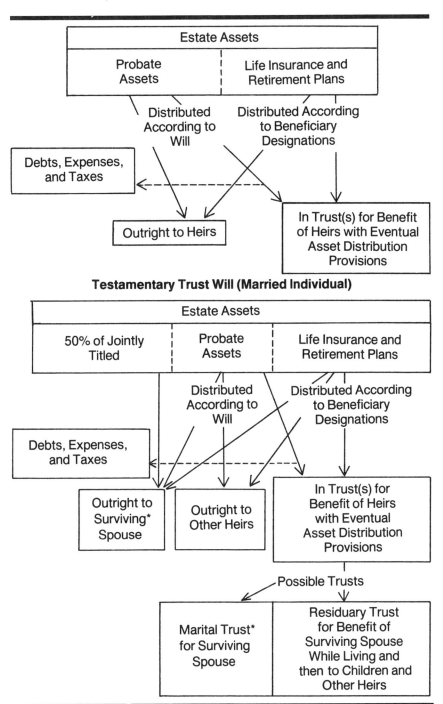

Testamentary Trust Will (Married Individual)

*Not subject to estate taxes at first spouse's death.

death, assets should be placed in a residuary or family trust, if the couple has dependents, to fully utilize the federal estate tax credit. The balance can be left to the surviving spouse to qualify for the marital deduction and eliminate estate taxes. This technique is referred to as "reduce-to-zero" funding.

- Appropriate provisions can be included in either a testamentary trust will or a combination pour-over will/living revocable trust.
- Married couples without dependents could leave all assets to each other, missing out on use of the credit at the first death, and eliminate taxes with use of the marital deduction. The surviving spouse could then exercise planning such as gifting, irrevocable trusts, or charitable bequests to reduce estate taxes.
- Titling of assets between spouses is very important. Joint titling with right of survivorship means assets will automatically pass to the surviving spouse regardless of will or trust document provisions. Too much property in joint titling could reduce funding of a residuary trust and result in lost use of the federal estate tax credit at the first death. We recommend that only personal and household effects, checking account, a small savings account, and the principal residence be titled jointly. Joint titling of assets can be severed and the assets can be titled in the name of the appropriate spouse.
- Married couples with combined estate size in excess of $600,000 should seek estate equalization; that is, title assets so each individuals' estate is about equal in size to the other's estate. If, for example, a husband has a taxable estate of $800,000 (and his wife $100,000) and he died first, estate minimization can be achieved. But if she dies first, estate taxes will be due upon his subsequent death; whereas if assets were titled such that each estate approximated $450,000, federal estate taxes (with credit use) could be eliminated regardless of the order of death between husband and wife.
- Joint titling with right of survivorship between spouses means asset value is split 50/50, upon the death of either, for estate valuation. At death assets take on a stepped-up cost basis. With the death of one spouse, only one-half of jointly titled assets will take on an advantageous stepped-up cost basis. Assets, which have the lowest cost basis relative to appreciated market value, should be titled in the name of the spouse with the shortest life expectancy.

- There is no limitation, or imposition of gift taxes, on interspousal gifting. Joint titling can be severed and assets titled separately. Also assets already titled separately can be gifted between the spouses as appropriate.

Estate Size of More than $1,200,000

- As mentioned, single individuals can leave net taxable estates up to $600,000 without federal estate taxes and married couples (with proper asset titling and estate document provisions) can leave combined net taxable estates to heirs of $1,200,000 without incurring federal estate taxes. Beyond these levels taxes will be due.
- Married couples should be sure that enough assets are kept in the smaller of the two estates to equal the exemption level ($600,000) based on the federal estate tax credit; particularly couples with dependents or those who wish to distribute assets to noncharitable sources.

FIGURE 15-4   POUR-OVER WILL AND LIVING REVOCABLE TRUST (SINGLE INDIVIDUAL)

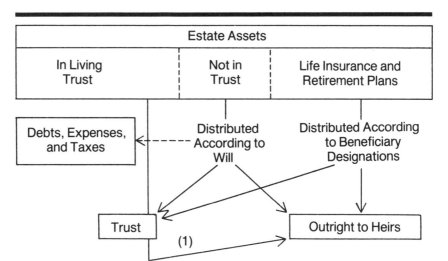

(1) Distributions may be delayed based on age or other factors.

- Use of the marital deduction and/or estate tax credit can eliminate federal estate taxes at the first death.
- We strongly encourage single and married individuals at this wealth level to each establish and fund a living revocable trust in conjunction with a pour-over will. If management capabilities and time commitments allow, self-trustee (with successor trustees) is preferable.
- In addition to living management contingencies for disability occurrence or lack of time for asset management, living revocable trusts offer advantages following death which include privacy (particularly important for those with large wealth levels who do not want asset holdings to be part of public records), reduced probate expenses, reduced time delays in distribution of assets to heirs, and substantial opportunities for postmortem planning.
- Surviving spouses have opportunities to deny inheritance (disclaim) which may be prudent in some instances to reduce overall taxes. Of course, any disclaimers should be made only with the assistance of a qualified attorney.
- Surviving spouses can also utilize gifting, charitable and non-charitable, to reduce estate taxes.
- Single and married individuals can utilize a variety of techniques (gifting, irrevocable trusts, private annuities, charitable bequests, etc.) to reduce estate taxes. All involve decisions of an irrevocable nature. Also, future taxes of heirs can be reduced with use of "generation skipping transfers."
- Irrevocable trusts can be established for the benefit of heirs and/or charitable organizations. Assets can be placed in trust, and if properly structured grantors can be lifetime income beneficiaries with principal excluded from the grantor's taxable estate and flowing to the designated heirs or charitable organizations at death.
- Very often, single individuals and married couples with wealth levels above $1,200,000 do not need life insurance. However, if life insurance makes up a substantial portion of the wealth level and/or is needed for support of dependents, it can be excluded from taxable estates through use of an irrevocable life insurance trust. This is the most common form of irrevocable trust use.
- Having a spouse own insurance can remove insurance from an insured's estate but does not remove the proceeds from the spouse's taxable estate if he or she is beneficiary; and the spouse could predecease requiring ownership to pass to someone else.

- Use of an irrevocable life insurance trust will remove life insurance from a taxable estate (both taxable estates in the case of a married couple), and still have the insurance available to provide for estate liquidity and family security needs.
- An insured can gift life insurance, including employer sponsored group insurance if properly handled, to an irrevocable life insurance trust established with minimal funding. The trust becomes the owner of the insurance on the insured. Gift taxes will not be due on gifted term insurance and may be due on gifted whole life insurance because of cash values (we discourage purchase or retention, except when uninsurable, of whole life insurance). Each year thereafter the grantor (insured) gifts sufficient cash funds to the trust, with which the trust trustee makes insurance premium payments. Trusts are usually structured to provide income to, and limited principal invasion powers to or for the benefit of, the insured's surviving spouse (if the insured is married) following death of the insured, with principal ultimately going to others (remaindermen) after the surviving spouse's death. Insurance proceeds can be used by the trustee to purchase assets from, and provide estate liquidity to, the insured's estate. To qualify irrevocable life insurance trusts for estate tax exclusion, the beneficiaries of the trust must be given the right, while the insured is still living, to withdraw funds deposited annually by the insured. If the beneficiaries do withdraw the funds, the trustee may not be able to make premium payments, causing the lapse of the insurance. The intention, of course, is that beneficiaries will not make withdrawals of funds provided for premium payments. With proper document drafting, the annual gifts of cash funds are gifts of present interest, qualifying for the annual gift tax exclusion. Care must also be taken in structuring the maximums allowable for withdrawal by the beneficiaries.

Again, federal estate planning should be carefully planned and integrated with state death tax consequences so as not to negate strategy steps or miss attractive planning opportunities.

EXECUTORS AND GUARDIANS

Executor/Executrix (personal representative or administrator) and Guardians are two very important designations which should be considered for inclusion in wills. Extreme care should be exercised in selecting executors and guardians as the functions of each are critical. Successor executors and guardians should also be des-

FIGURE 15-5 POUR-OVER WILL AND LIVING REVOCABLE TRUST (MARRIED INDIVIDUAL)

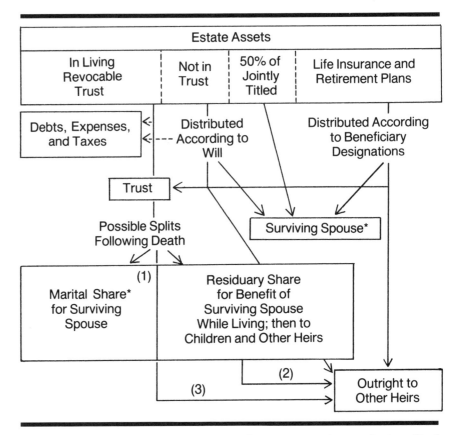

(1) May be outright following death of the first spouse or in trust for benefit of surviving spouse. Upon surviving spouse's death, assets will be distributed according to terms of surviving spouse's estate documents if marital share received with full power of appointment. If trust distribution is made with Qualified Terminable Interest to surviving spouse, assets will be distributed according to terms determined by first spouse. In any event, assets remaining at surviving spouse's death are includable in his or her estate.

(2) Distributions may be delayed based on age or other factors.

(3) Trust may or may not call for marital/residuary split and distributions may be outright or in trust.

*Not subject to estate taxes at first spouse's death.

ignated in case the individuals named first are unable or unwilling to serve.

Every individual should name an executor; frequently a spouse or close relative is named. An executor is in charge of overseeing a decedent's estate; from presenting estate documents to filing insurance claims and tax returns to the distribution of assets to heirs. Many executors need professional and legal assistance in carrying out their functions. A lawyer, bank trust department or officer, or others can be named executor in lieu of a family member. Make sure the person you intend to designate executor is aware that he or she has been named as the task frequently carries substantial responsibility. Using professionals can be expensive, so make sure you are aware of charges before naming one as executor.

People with young children (under 18 years old in most states) and other dependents need to name guardians to care for the dependents. An individual without dependents does not need to designate a guardian. If no guardian is named, the dependents will have a court-appointed guardian. The guardian(s) should know that you intend to name them as they will be responsible for raising and/or caring for the dependents. Financial arrangements for dependent expenses should be made as part of overall financial planning.

BUSINESS OWNERSHIP

Business owners who fail to implement appropriate estate planning cause tremendous difficulties for family members and heirs. Sole proprietorships are especially difficult to handle and manage after an owner's death. Whether a business is a sole proprietorship, partnership, or closely held corporation, an owner should decide what family involvement (if any) is desired after his or her death.

If an owner wants to pass on ownership to family members after death, he or she should be certain the family members want the ownership and very clear transfers of ownership and authority should be outlined.

Frequently family members either do not want ownership or are not prepared (skill or otherwise) for it. For full time or part-time business interests, we recommend that business owners establish buy/sell agreements as part of their estate planning. The agreements can be made with employees, outside parties, or competitors for sole proprietorships, partners in partnerships, and other stockholders in closely held corporations.

Buy-sell agreements can be structured to take effect on death, disability, or participant's option at a predetermined price, which should be periodically reviewed. Disability and death buy-sell agreements (both of which can be funded with insurance) are especially useful in relieving family members of the burden of selling a business, or selling at "fire sale" prices, and providing the owner's estate with liquid assets.

Death buy-outs are often best structured on a lump sum basis. At death, assets take on a "stepped-up" basis and, therefore, capital gains income taxation is not a concern. Disability and other buy-outs may be best structured on an installment basis, with interest, to reduce and spread-out income tax payments.

Income taxation and estate taxation of business ownership in the event of death or sale, especially if other family members will retain an interest, should be thoroughly discussed with an accountant and attorney as tax laws are complicated. If the value of a closely held business exceeds 35 percent of a decedent's Adjusted Gross Estate, the executor can elect to pay the portion of federal estate tax attributable to the ownership over a 15-year period rather than at the normally required estate tax payment time of nine months after death. Special income tax treatment may also apply if proceeds from sale of a decedent's stock in a closely held corporation are used to pay estate taxes, administrative expenses, debts and other estate liabilities.

Most estate assets must be reported for estate tax purposes at "fair market value." However, real property used in farming or in a closely held business may be included in a decedent's estate at its "current use" value rather than at its "best use" value. The maximum reduction from "best use" value to "current use" value is $750,000. Several rules must be met to get "current use" value instead of "best use" value, including the requirement that a "qualified heir" must continue the same use of the property and participate in the business. The property must be so utilized for at least ten years following the decedent's death.

MISCELLANEOUS THOUGHTS FOR ESTATE PLANNING

Original estate documents should be kept by your attorney with copies filed at home. The documents will be needed shortly after death. Sometimes safe deposit boxes are sealed by state authorities following death and, therefore, boxes should not be used to store estate documents.

Your estate documents should be reviewed by legal counsel for possible revisions if the documents are more than two to three years old.

In some instances, estate planning changes can be made by revising current documents rather than having new documents drafted. Revisions are usually less costly than having new documents prepared. The extra money spent on new documents will be a good investment if major changes are needed.

Your will should cover many specifics, including: your name; county-city-state of residence; revocation of previous wills and codicils; payment of death expenses, debts, and taxes; burial in-

FIGURE 15–6 POUR-OVER WILL AND LIVING REVOCABLE TRUST AND LIVING IRREVOCABLE TRUST (SINGLE INDIVIDUAL)

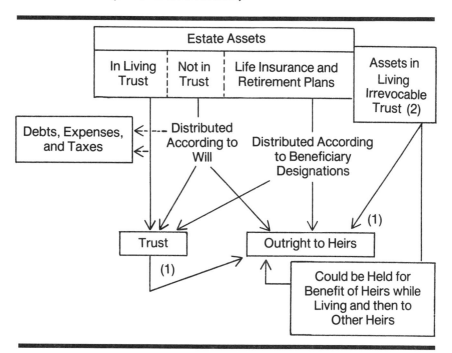

(1) Distributions may be delayed based on age or other factors.
(2) Assets (including life insurance), if properly qualified, are not included in a decedent's taxable estate. Funds may be used to purchase assets from a decedent's estate to provide estate liquidity.

structions; charitable and noncharitable bequests and/or flow of funds to trusts; asset administration provisions; guardian(s) and responsibilities; executor(s); executor's responsibility and compensation; and signature and attestation.

You do not have to provide for heirs or beneficiaries of trusts equally; disproportionate distributions may be called for by you or referenced to on the basis of trustee discretion.

Family members, especially spouses, should discuss estate plans together and be aware of the estate matters which will transpire in the event of death. Family members should be prepared to review, possibly with professional assistance, all financial planning areas and set new goals, objectives, and strategies, in the event of death of a family member. Most likely, cash flow, tax, investment, insurance protection and estate needs will change.

Post-mortem planning is very important both with respect to actions by representatives of a decedent's estate, and surviving family members and other heirs. Mistakes or inadequate planning can be very costly.

Provisions in wills and trusts regarding asset distributions do not have to be made in reference to particular assets. Amounts in dollar or formula (e.g., funding a residuary trust to the maximum extent possible without incurring estate taxes) are most frequently used to describe distributions.

Life insurance proceeds, payable upon a decedent's death, are not subject to income taxes, but may be subject to federal estate taxes if the decedent owned the insurance and may or may not be subject to inheritance tax depending on the state of residency.

Life insurance and retirement plan beneficiary designations should be reviewed to assure coordination of estate planning and management; depending on circumstances it may be desirable to name trusts as beneficiaries rather than individuals. It is often disadvantageous to leave the proceeds to an "estate" in general.

The estate plans of spouses should be carefully integrated, with each using appropriate documents. If, for example, a husband has a large estate relative to the size of the wife's estate, he may need a living revocable trust (with testamentary trusts and provisions) and pour-over will and she a simple will. Her will could direct eventual distribution of her assets to his trust, to be distributed according to the trust provisions.

Wills and/or trust documents should clearly indicate from which

FIGURE 15-7 POUR-OVER WILL AND LIVING REVOCABLE TRUST AND LIVING IRREVOCABLE TRUST (MARRIED INDIVIDUAL)

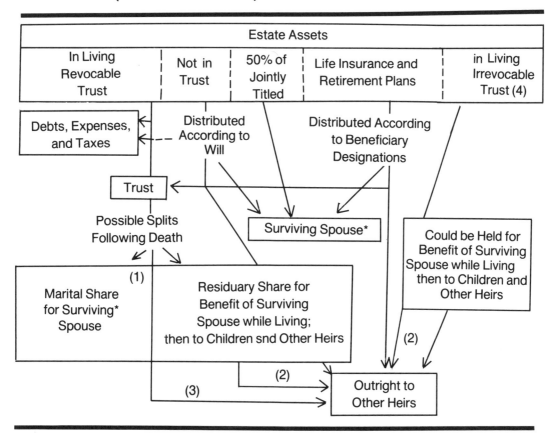

(1) May be outright following death of the first spouse or in trust for benefit of surviving spouse. Upon surviving spouse's death, assets will be distributed according to terms of surviving spouse's estate documents if marital share received with full power of appointment. If trust distribution is made with Qualified Terminable Interest to surviving spouse, assets will be distributed according to terms determined by first spouse. In any event, assets remaining at surviving spouse's death are includable in his or her estate.

(2) Distributions may be delayed based on age or other factors.

(3) Trust may or may not call for marital/residuary split and distributions may be outright or in trust.

(4) Assets (including life insurance), if properly qualified, are not included in a decedent's taxable estate. Funds may be used to purchase assets from a decedent's estate to provide estate liquidity.

*Not subject to estate taxes at first spouse's death.

distributions (or before any distributions) tax payments are to be made. For example, if a husband creates a QTIP trust for his surviving spouse, it may be desirable to state that the trust is to pay her estate taxes before distributing assets to his desired heirs. Her will should also have a similar provision. Another example is if a pour-over will and living revocable trust are used, the tax payments could come from the probate estate and/or funds inside the trust.

Estate liquidity for tax payments and expenses should be planned for and included in the estate planning process.

After invoking estate planning changes (such as, executing trust agreements, retitling assets, making gifts, etc.), estimate estate taxes and expenses again to assure effective planning.

BLENDING THE PLANNING AREAS

"Thinking well is wise, planning well, wiser; doing well wisest and best of all."

Persian Proverb

Optimizing financial well being requires adaptation of the whole financial planning process. Earlier chapters have covered setting goals and objectives, assembling information, interpreting and analyzing the financial position, inputting economics into personal planning, and evaluating alternatives and determining strategies in each financial planning area—cash flow management, insurance protection, income tax planning, investment planning, and estate planning. The planning process is not effective unless decisions are carried out and updated as personal and/or market conditions change.

Before beginning implementation, rethink your goals and review the relation of these goals to financial objectives. Again, financial objectives are targets for goal achievement and are categorized within the major financial planning areas.

Reconsider all the financial resources which you have available, including employee benefits.

**EMPLOYEE
BENEFITS**

Employee benefits are an important component of many individual's/family's total financial resources. Benefits often comprise a substantial portion of employment compensation. The self-employed, particularly if business ownership is structured as a corporation, can also be covered with valuable benefits.

Employee benefits is a broad and loosely used term for employment compensation in addition to salary and other direct monetary payments. In some instances, programs are fully funded by the employer. In other situations, employees may share costs with employees. Some programs are entirely voluntary and employee paid, but may provide special opportunities or conveniences.

Benefit programs may range from the very basic and limited in scope to extended programs with choices and optional elections available. Benefits may or may not be "tax qualified" and may be formal or informal. Most often benefits are favorable in terms of cost effectiveness and income taxation. However, alternatives (i.e., group insurance supplemental options, etc.) should be "shopped" for price comparison and should be participated in only with full awareness of cash flow, income tax, investment, and risk ramifications.

Fully understand your benefit coverages and options. Analyze appropriateness before committing to participation in optional programs. For example, a company-sponsored investment program with employer/employee contributions may be favorable in terms of receiving additional funds from your employer, but investment opportunities may be poor, limited, or inappropriate. Extra compensation from employer matching contributions must be evaluated against alternative personal investment opportunities, personal need, and affordability. Noncommitment to such a program may be best for some individuals. Alternatively, participation with periodic liquidation and investment repositioning may be feasible.

Categorize and summarize your employee benefit coverages and options. Then evaluate these in respect to the various financial planning objectives you have established. Decide which are favorable, and for those requiring employee contributions, which you should participate in. Use a table similar to Form 16–1 or one that fits your needs for summarization and decision making.

After determining programs for participation, make sure you notify your employer and file all necessary forms. Timing may be important for some programs as election may be available only during certain times of the year. Also, be sure that beneficiary designations for death payments from programs are in accordance with your estate planning desires. Evaluate new programs as offered through your employer and periodically review all benefits participation.

IMPLEMENTATION Review each major planning area separately and then look at all areas together to establish an overall, coordinated strategy. Remember the specific concerns identified in the financial profiles and observations portion of the planning process and seek corrective measures.

Decisions should be finalized (with recognition of the need for future flexibility) and a timing schedule set for each action. Make out your own financial calendar. Decide who you will call on for assistance and where you can best implement your decisions.

Summarize in writing the action steps necessary for achievement of objectives. Trade-offs must be made and achievement dates must be broken down between various short-term and long-term time periods. Available funds must be allocated on a priority basis. Use a schedule similar to Form 16–2 to summarize implementation steps and reconstruct the schedule on at least an annual basis in conjunction with monitoring as described in the next chapter.

Supplemental sheets should also be used along with the Planning Implementation Summary. Particularly helpful are a financial calendar (Form 16–3), a detailed summary of investment decisions (Form 16–4), and a review of all investments following planned repositioning (Form 16–5).

Each individual's or family's circumstance is unique and planning steps should be customized accordingly. It is important to remember that you should seek improvements in each financial planning area while simultaneously coordinating and integrating all planning areas. Action steps should be viewed as the beginning steps of long-term strategies.

KNOWING THE IMPACTS Segregate the impact of planning changes in the current year from future years. Assuming all planned changes for the current year are made, answer the following questions:

- What is the net "bottom line" affect on cash inflow/outflow? If additional funds are required, where will they come from? If savings will increase, where will the additions be placed? Following summarization of changes, complete a new budget.
- What is the combined impact of all changes on income taxes? Can taxes be further reduced in future years? Avoid excessive reductions. Project income taxes again following decisions to determine taxes expected for the current (and future) year(s). How much should actually be paid in taxes during the current year? How much will be owed when the tax return is filed?
- Are investment selections appropriate in view of the different goals and various time periods planned for goal achievement? Are all investment decisions made with recognition of both short-term and long-term planning? Will the lowest cost sources of investment implementation be used? How will future savings flow to new investments? Is "forced" savings necessary?
- Is insurance protection adequate and cost efficient? Have insurance beneficiary designations been properly chosen and recorded? Have group insurance alternatives been compared to individual insurance alternatives? How will insurance protection changes affect cash flow? Income taxation?
- Do wills and/or trusts need to be updated? If so, at what cost? Will titling be changed on current asset holdings? How will new asset acquisitions be titled?

With thorough understanding of the impacts of planning steps, note changes which are scheduled for future years and planning alternatives which could not currently be used because of trade-offs and resource limitations. Additional improvements can be made in the future as more funds/resources become available. Double check to be certain that high priority concerns and needs have been addressed in lieu of low priority items.

Recognize the benefits received from making planning changes. This will reinforce current actions and add incentive for continued planning towards attainment of goals.

IMPLEMENTATION SOURCES

Carefully select implementation sources and seek a combination of quality and cost efficiency. Implement directly when feasible and prudent. However, unless you are extremely knowledgeable, avoid self-implementation in highly technical areas such as drafting your own will/trust agreement.

Use advisors as necessary but check their credentials thoroughly. Ask about an advisor's education and practice background, licensing, and method of operation. Get client references and contact the references. Know advisor fees and compensation ahead of time. Be leery of any advisor who seems tied to other outside advisors (e.g., a CPA who always recommends the same tax shelter salesman).

The following represent some of our thoughts on using various advisors.

- *Attorneys*   Seek attorneys who are specialized and hire as your needs dictate. If you are hiring for estate document preparation, use an attorney who specializes in estate planning. The same should be true for other areas of legal work: taxation, business agreements, divorce, etc. Avoid use of general practioner-type attorneys other than for simple legal work such as house closings and small civil suits.

- *Accountants*   Generally we recommend using accountants who are CPAs for business and personal income tax planning. Depending upon a business size and complexity, a CPA may also be desirable for business recordkeeping and auditing. Do expect specific tax advice and suggestions on the need for tax reduction from your accountant, but do not expect specific investment product suggestions.

- *Bankers*   Select a bank with consideration for a combination of: convenience, progressiveness of the bank, services offered, interest rates, investment product availability, and the potential for development of personal relationships (which are important). In some instances, it may be better to conduct personal and business banking at the same bank. Alternatively, to expand banking contacts, personal and business banking might be handled at separate banks.

- *Insurance Representatives*   Deal with reputable and financially stable companies. Get objective input on claims processing and other services. Know the true net cost of various policies. In purchasing life insurance and disability insurance policies, do not use agents who work for only one or a few companies. Use agents who can "shop" the market for you with many different companies. "Buy" insurance, do not be "sold" to.

- *Brokers and Securities Dealers*   Use discount brokerage services for securities purchases if you make your own investment decisions. If discount brokerage services are not appropriate for you—that is, you need full service (specific recommendations, research, etc.)—obtain several client referrals before using a particular stockbroker. It may also be appropriate to see a full-service broker, even if you do use discount brokerage services, to obtain public limited partnerships, new stock issues, or other products not available through discount brokers or banks. Always get a "second opinion" on securities and investment recommendations. Often individual portfolio managers (money managers) have affiliations, or trading agreements, with certain brokerage firms. In these instances, the money manager (who should be on a fee-only basis) will actually make investment decisions rather than a broker.

- *Trust Officers*   Bank trust officers traditionally have been known to be extremely conservative in investing (although this is changing quickly) and consequently have had relatively poor investment performances. Pure trust companies, and individual portfolio managers, may be more aggressive but should be chosen with extreme caution when portfolio management is desired. Some trust companies offer self-directed asset management accounts with consolidated valuation reports. Often, any investment medium can be purchased. Banks and brokerage firms typically limit their consolidated reporting to investment products which they sell. Trust companies may also be indirectly used in conjunction with mutual funds or independent portfolio managers.

- *Financial Planners*   Consider a financial planner if you decide to seek professional counseling in conjunction with your own planning. The term "financial planner" (and similar terms) is widely used today. If you choose to hire a financial planner, make sure he or she is truly a planner and not a salesperson. The individual should be degreed from an accredited college. Professional education programs, such as CFP or ChFC, are increasing in number and quality. However, these programs do not yet have the rigorous standards or professional acceptance associated with M.D., J.D., or C.P.A. We also suggest using "fee-only" planners; that is, individuals who derive income from fees and not commissions. If your planner is licensed to handle commissioned products, it should only be for your convenience and commissions should not represent a large percentage of the advisor's income. You can request, in writing, a statement of services and compensation. Understand all recommendations made by your planner and participate actively in the planning process increasing your knowledge, awareness and self-sufficiency over time.

So-called "one-stop-shop" financial servicing is becoming widespread. Department stores, brokerage firms, banks, and other financial organizations are advertising that consumers can have all financial planning and product needs met by dealing with one financial organization. Some companies do offer a wide array of high quality services. However, it is unrealistic to think that all financial needs can be met in the most efficient manner through one organization. Comparison shop for cost competitiveness and quality service and use the services and products of a particular organization only as they fit your needs. Our economic system is based on competition and organizations typically have a competitive advantage with some products and services but not all. Combine the aspects of convenience offered by using a few organizations, when needed, with the advantages of avoiding total reliance on one organization.

We believe that the financial services industry will be more closely and better regulated in the future by the Securities and Exchanges Commission and other authorities. Organizations offering financial products, services, and advice will be more accountable and responsible, and performance results will be more widely published. This will lead to greater investor sophistication and better deals. Watch for favorable developments but, in the meantime, be very cautious about who you deal with, what you buy, and how much you pay.

SOME GENERAL PLANNING TIPS

- Family members should be aware of major goals; joint decisions are more effective, when practical, than individual decisions; children should be taught about finances at an early age so good habits can be developed.
- Continually review trade-offs which are made to stay in touch with priorities as priorities change; realize that new goals will evolve over time.
- Be well aware of expected results from planning action steps.
- Be patient in trying to satisfy long-term goals.
- Even though you may be very busy, try to use concise and practical sources of information on financial matters (local

newspapers, magazines, educational materials from financial businesses and non-profit organizations, etc.).

- Be on the lookout for new ideas—tax planning techniques, new investment products, new banking services, etc.
- Remember the extreme importance of inputting economics into personal planning.
- Do not rely exclusively on the advice of any one advisor—get a "second opinion"—and develop self-reliance and decision making.
- Use the principles of forced automatic payments and forced savings if appropriate.
- Plan assets transfers, such as gifting or retitling of assets, carefully and take a long-term perspective.
- Maintain an understanding of financial ratio analysis and improvements which you need to make.
- Use credit cards, automatic teller services, and other conveniences as appropriate but do not let such use disrupt budgeting.
- If you have difficulty sorting through choices, develop various decision trees to visualize your alternatives and help you reach conclusions.
- Recognize that planning is based on ballpark numbers, not precise numbers; current and future direction is most important.
- Know what kind of decision maker you are and what information is vital to your decision making process.
- Remember the importance of timing in making planning changes (i.e., securities sales, etc.).
- In making choices in individual planning areas, always think through the effects on other planning areas.
- Review beneficiary designations any time insurance, retirement plans or other programs with death payouts are changed.

PHASING INTO MONITORING

Chapter 17 covers the monitoring of personal economic planning. As with implementation, this is of critical importance for achievement of goals. Organization and consolidated financial management make planning and decision making easier and more successful. Choices must be reevaluated and new objectives determined. Internal and external factors affecting financial security change over time and adjustments and new strategy tactics are needed. Knowledge, desire, and action should be blended in an on-going process (Figure 16–1).

FIGURE 16-1

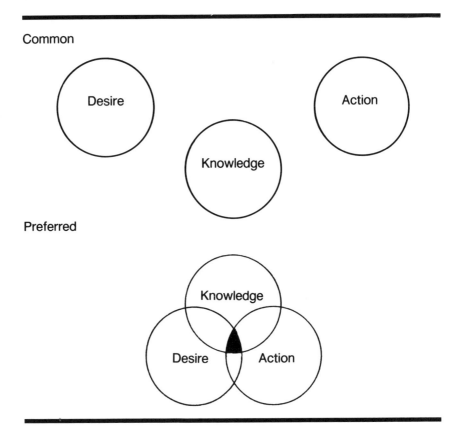

FORM 16-1 BENEFIT PROGRAMS

Benefits	Coverage Yes/No	Employer Paid	Employee Paid	Employer/ Employee Paid	Personal Cash Requirements	Income Tax Consequences	Objectives Area Appropriateness	Participation Decision/ Special Notes
Insurances medical					$			
disability								
life								
automobile								
property & liability								
other								
Qualified Plans IRA								
Keogh								
profit-sharing								
pension								
ESOP/TRASOP								
deferred compensation								
thrift plan								
other								

FORM 16-2 PLANNING IMPLEMENTATION SUMMARY, TIMING, AND COST (SAVINGS)

Action Steps	Timing	Other Objectives Areas Affected	Special Notes	Net Annual ($) Cost (Savings)	Date Completed
Cash Flow					
Insurance Protection					
Income Taxes					
Investments					
Estate Planning					
Employee Benefits/ Business Planning					

Miscellaneous						
automobile expenses						
child care						
club membership						
counseling						
financial						
legal						
psychological						
entertainment expenses						
leaves of absence						
loans						
professional assoc. dues						
seminars & school tuition						
stock options						
stock savings purchase						
travel						
other						
TOTAL			$			

FORM 16-3   FINANCIAL CALENDAR

| Month | Cash Inflows | | | | Cash Outflows | | | | | | | | | | Financial Planning Actions/Reviews |
| | Employment/ Retirement Income | Investment Income | Other Income | | Living Expenses | Debt Payments | Insurance Premiums | Income Taxes | Investment Commitments | | Other Major Expenditures | | Savings | |
			Type	Amount					Type	Amount	Type	Amount		
January	$	$		$	$	$	$	$		$		$	$	
February														
March														
April														
May														
June														
July														
August														
September														
October														
November														
December														
Totals	$	$		$	$	$	$	$		$		$	$	

FORM 16-4   INVESTMENT DECISIONS—SPECIFICATIONS

Funds for New Investments			Description of New Investments					Method of Implementation	Date Completed
Source	Amount	Availability or Timing	General Category	Specific Media	Titling	Amount			
	$					$			
Total	$					$			

equipment leasing—private programs				
oil and gas—public programs—developmental				
oil and gas—public programs—exploratory				
oil and gas—private programs—developmental				
oil and gas—private programs—exploratory				
options—commodities and futures				
options—stocks				
real estate—public programs—commercial and residential pools				
real estate—public programs—mortgage pools				
real estate—public programs—REITS				
real estate—private programs—commercial and residential pools				
real estate—private programs—government sponsored properties				
real estate—private programs—individual purchase				
stocks—growth—individual purchase				
stocks—growth—mutual funds				
stocks—growth and income—individual purchase				
stocks—growth and income—mutual funds				
Other				
Totals	$			

FORM 16-5 NEW INVESTMENT POSITIONING APPROPRIATENESS

Investment	Amount	Percent of Portfolio	Appropriateness	Anticipated Holding Period
annuities and life insurance cash values	$			
bonds (corporate)—individual purchase				
bonds (corporate)—mutual funds and unit trusts				
bonds (municipal)—individual purchase				
bonds (municipal)—mutual funds and unit trusts				
bonds (federal government)—individual purchase				
bonds (federal government)—mutual funds and unit trusts				
business ventures—individual purchase				
business ventures—pooled purchase				
cash and savings accounts—banks and financial institutions				
cash and savings accounts—money market funds—regular				
cash and savings accounts—money market funds—federal government securities				
cash and savings accounts—money market funds—municipal securities				
collectibles and hard assets				
commodities—individual purchase				
commodities—pooled purchase				
equipment leasing—public programs				

17

MONITORING YOUR FINANCIAL PLAN

"Many have been ruined by their fortune, and many have escaped ruin by the want of fortune. To obtain it the great have become little, and the little great."

Zimmermann

We have covered the planning process through implementation. The next and final step is to monitor your financial plan and actions. This entails staying organized, keeping current on financial and economic matters, and periodically repeating parts of the financial planning process.

Some aspects of financial management need more frequent review than others. Success in reaching objectives and goals depends on the quality of attention you give to financial management. It does not have to be tedious or overly time consuming; quality is far more important than quantity. In fact, people who use our management system find that financial management time requirements are reduced, fears are alleviated, and goal achievement enhanced.

Traditionally, average households experience:

- cash flow deficits in early stages, surpluses in middle and later years, and deficits again in retirement years;

- increasing income taxes until retirement years, at which time dollar taxes (not necessarily the burden of payments) decline;
- net worth growth until retirement, with asset depletion in retirement to facilitate income needs;
- debt levels rising through middle years and falling thereafter; and
- deficits in estate funding and family security protection in early and middle years, turning to surpluses in later years.

You, however, can influence greatly the pattern of cash flow, taxation, investing, risk and family protection you will experience. Rapid changes in our economic structure have presented many new profitable employment and investment opportunities. High technological developments and the vast increases in information, make greater financial awareness readily accessible. More leisure time afforded by the growing economy and changing social structure increases time available for learning and attention to personal matters. Most people, today, have more resources at their disposal and better choices available to them. Set your own course of action and strive for financial security. You will find this to be a predictive process with natural progression.

The steps involved in monitoring can be summarized as follows:

1. *Staying Abreast of Financial and Economic Conditions.* Use concise and practical information sources. This may require sampling many sources until you find those you are comfortable with. Do not spend excessive time reading or trying to absorb too many details. Look for key factors, such as economic variables discussed in Chapter 6. Newsletters and major magazines can be very good. Focus on economic developments, tax law changes, and investment opportunities.

2. *Continuing Development of Financial Knowledge and Understanding.* In addition to reading and listening to financial information shows, look for financial education programs. Many community groups sponsor low cost workshops. Community colleges, universities and continuing adult education programs are now offering many personal finance courses. Practical financial books and other publications are growing in popularity and supply. Memberships are available in nonprofit groups and associations which offer financial information. The

FIGURE 17-1 THE MONITORING PROCESS

The financial planning process is a feedback system as summarized below. Decisions affect future outcomes, which in turn affect the need for future decisions. It is a continual process.

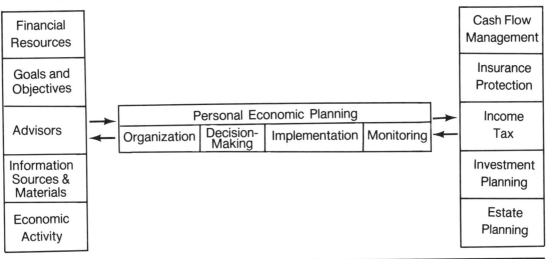

best method of improving financial awareness is continuous involvement in management of your own financial matters.

3. *Maintaining Organization and Recordkeeping.* Organization and recordkeeping should be structured to be a convenient, consolidated, and complete working system; designed to track progress towards achievement of financial goals. Files, worksheets, and possible computer use should cover all aspects of cash flow management, insurance protection, income tax planning, investment planning, and estate planning. Document and receipt storage, goals and objectives, analyses, update information, and new ideas should be included. Frequency of recording and updating tasks varies. Listed in Table 17–1 are the main summary schedules from Chapter 4 along with suggested update timing (some individuals, especially those using personal computers, may desire greater frequency).

To facilitate summary schedule preparation and general financial management, several important records must be kept on a regular basis. Cash flows, income tax matters, and invest-

TABLE 17-1

Schedule	Updating
General information and personal data	Every 6 to 12 months or as major changes occur
Life insurance summary	Every 12 months
Net worth summary	Every 12 months
Investment composition	Every 6 to 9 months
Cash flow analysis	Annually for projections; monthly for budgeting sheets
Death estate	Every 12 months
Tax return analysis	Annually; with several projections during each year

ment transactions must be included in a good recordkeeping system. Specific suggestions are presented later in this chapter on keeping these records current.

4. *Re-evaluating Goals and Objectives.* Goals and objectives should be reviewed at least annually for both appropriateness and progress. Changes in personal circumstances may occur. New goals may replace goals which have been satisfied or are no longer relevant; or additional goals may be added because of increases in financial resources. Objectives are the specific targets set for goal achievement. Review the targets to see if changes should be made and set targets for new goals. Long-term goals which require accumulation of funds should be reviewed in respect to the adequacy of planned funding. Summarize goals in writing, with recognition of the relation of each goal to the various financial objective areas.

5. *Reanalyzing Financial Profiles and Funding Analyses.* Financial ratio calculations and funding analyses should be repeated at least annually to observe progress or deficiencies. With understanding, decisions can be made for improving actions or selected trade-offs. The following calculations, derived from the main summary schedules and miscellaneous information, should be made:

- total liabilities/total assets
- liquid assets/total assets
- savings/cash income
- income tax/cash income
- total investments/net worth
- fixed investments/total investments
- variable investments/total investments
- retirement funding/retirement needs
- estate funding/estate needs
- disability funding/disability needs

After calculating the ratios and analyses, review the results against your preferred targets.

Identify and prioritize areas of desired change and plan appropriate action. Make note of the general progress over calculations for the previous year.

6. *Implementing Additional Action Steps Planned Beyond Initial Steps.* Look at the last Planning Implementation Summary schedule and see which action steps have not been completed. Determine whether or not the actions are still appropriate and reconsider the importance of each. For those still relevant, what is the reason implementation has not been completed? Were the actions planned for later implementation or have circumstances and/or resources changed? Decide if the steps which are still appropriate should be carried out soon. Also review previously planned and implemented action steps for effectiveness and suitability.

7. *Changing Courses of Action.* A multitude of reasons (new goals, economic changes, increased wealth, new information or opportunities, etc.) could account for the need to consider alternative planning steps. After re-evaluating goals and objectives, and reanalyzing financial profiles, select new planning choices as appropriate in each financial area—cash flow management, insurance protection, income taxation, investment planning, and estate planning.

THE PLANNING AREAS

Keep in mind each of the five major financial objective areas. In addition to scheduled monitoring, frequently ask yourself questions and mentally review your financial circumstances, management, and choices.

Cash Flow Management

- Is the budget being maintained?
- What deviations, if any, are occurring in anticipated cash inflows and outflows?
- Should inflow or outflow amounts or types be adjusted?
- Should a new budget be developed?
- Are tax payments and major expenditures being sufficiently planned, with funds reserved?
- Are debt payments in line with financial resources?
- Are savings and accumulation targets being achieved?
- How are savings flowing into additional investments?
- Are investments appropriate for future goals?
- Are the best (considering your needs) cash accounts being used?
- As budgeting choices arise, is thorough evaluation made on a cost/benefit basis?

Insurance Protection

- Are you making provisions for uninsured risks?
- Are all formal insurance protections adequate and cost efficient (life, disability, medical, property, casualty, and liability)?
- Are premium dates optimal for your cash management?
- Who do you purchase insurance from? Have you checked with others?
- Can some formal coverages be safely reduced or terminated?

Income Tax Planning

- What is your current marginal federal income tax rate?
- Are you meeting minimum annual income tax payment requirements and investing reserves for later tax payments?
- How often do you project future income taxes?
- Are your income taxes too high or too low?
- Do you know the tax impacts, if any, of each financial opportunity/decision?
- How do you stay current on federal and state tax law changes?
- Do you use a good system for recording income (losses), adjustments to gross income, itemized deductions, exemptions, and tax credits?

- Are you aware of future tax impacts of current investments?
- If you are a business owner, are you carefully integrating business and personal planning for favorable tax consequences?
- Are you using professional advisors for tax advice?

Investment Planning

- Do you adhere to the investment principles of balance, diversification, and liquidity?
- Do investment risks meet your desired levels of risk tolerance/comfort?
- Have you carefully blended goals, investment needs, and investment media alternatives?
- When did you last review your investment needs?
- Can you specifically identify each investment as related to future goals?
- Are your emergency/opportunity funds adequate but not excessive?
- Should any investments be changed because of personal circumstances, economic conditions, or new opportunities?
- Are investment performance results what you had anticipated?
- How do you stay current of your investments and newly created investment opportunities?
- What methods do you use for investment performance measurement?
- Do you include income, appreciation, and tax savings in your return calculations?
- Do you distinguish between nominal investment return and real investment return (after inflation)?
- Are your investment strategies still appropriate in view of your objectives for cash flow management, insurance protection, income tax planning, and estate planning?
- Are you meeting targets for accumulation of funds toward various goals?
- How often do you review investment balance and diversification?
- How do you record investment transactions (including purchase, sale, income receipt, and additional investments)?
- What sources do you use for purchasing investment products? Are better sources available?

Estate Planning

- Are your estate documents up-to-date (i.e., reflect your current desires, best use considering estate size, comply with current federal and state laws, etc.)?
- How are you titling new asset acquisitions?
- Are all assets titled properly?
- Are insurance and retirement plan beneficiary designations appropriate?
- Have changes occurred which necessitate rethinking of selections for executors, guardians, trustees, or other appointed individuals or institutions?
- Are you comfortable and confident that your assets would be well managed in the event of death or a severe disability?
- If applicable, have pension plan (and other qualified plan) survivor benefit elections been reviewed?
- Are you counting heavily on Social Security and other unpredictable sources of future income for family security?
- Should you be using gifting and/or income shifting techniques?
- When was the last time you estimated death expenses and taxes?
- Do you know the amount of the current federal estate tax credit?
- Have you recently evaluated the tax favorability of titling assets for realization of a "step-up" in basis (as applied to income taxation) versus taxable estate inclusion?
- If you are a business owner, have provisions been made for business management and/or ownership transfer in the event of your death?
- Are accidental death life insurance and miscellaneous death benefits summarized and recorded, with notations for collection procedures?
- Have burial and other death instructions been made and given to family members?

FILING AND RECORD KEEPING

Clear segregation and consolidation should be sought to maintain good accounting of transactions and to conveniently store important information. Computerization can certainly be helpful for many filing and recordkeeping functions. However, even with computerization, good systems will be needed for storage of important documents and computer printouts. Visualize filing and recordkeeping as a flow of activities:

- receive incoming bills, statements, checks, receipts and other forms which must be held for payment, deposit, recordkeeping, or return;

- following payment, deposit, or review, make proper recordings and store (if necessary) forms for later use or reference;
- keep on-going records of current transactions affecting cash flow, insurance protection, income taxation, investing and estate planning;
- have ready access to listings of goals and objectives, summary schedules, ratio and funding analyses, evaluation of alternatives, and other "work-ups";
- assemble general financial, economic, and other goal affecting information along with new planning ideas for referencing; and
- maintain a current file of important documents (wills, past tax returns, securities, etc.).

We recommend a system based on the following:

1. A binder or file for permanent storage of documents and information.

2. A binder for on-going recordkeeping.

3. Folders or files for storing receipts, statements, cancelled checks, and other materials held for precautionary purposes.

Time commitments are greatest in structuring a good system. Thereafter, time allocation to retrieving needed information from records will be significantly lower than without an effective system. Make sure the system you choose coordinates all practical facets of financial management. This will make planning and decision making much more efficient. The results derived from setting up and maintaining a system will be worth the effort. A haphazard or "shoe box" approach makes goal attainment very difficult. Build in flexibility to the system so changes can be made to incorporate implementation of new planning choices (e.g., new bank accounts, investment repositionings, different income sources, etc.).

The following categorization suggestions will be useful in forming a base for your organization and recordkeeping system. Make adjustments as necessary to facilitate your needs and efficient management.

Permanent Storage of Documents and Information

Important documents and information pertaining to your personal finances should be carefully organized and placed. Most may be kept at home or office if reasonable privacy and safety against theft, fire and other damage can be provided.

Some items (such as coins, securities, stamps, personal property inventory list and photographs, collectibles, important papers, and other valuables) should be transferred to a bank safe deposit box or to publicly available storage facilities. Special insurance policies can be purchased on safe deposit box contents not covered under other policies.

Instead of holding stocks and bonds or mutual fund shares personally, the securities can be held by brokerage firms or transfer agents.

We suggest that documents and information held personally be assembled in a binder or file structure for easy access. If some items are not held personally or are removed from the binder/files, retain a list of the items along with notations for where they have been placed. Professional advisors should have duplicate copies of some documents—wills and trusts with your attorney, tax returns with your accountant, investment statements with your financial advisor, etc.

The following divisions are useful for organizing important documents and information in a binder/file structure.

- Financial Management

  main summary schedules (general information and personal data, life insurance summary, net worth summary, investment composition, cash flow analysis, death estate, tax return analysis)

  goals and objectives

  financial profiles and funding analyses

  implementation summary schedules

  general planning observations

- Assets and Liabilities   Residence deed and cost basis information, car titles, warranties on major purchases, bank books, securities certificates, investment confirmation statements, credit card listings, mortgages, debt notes, special payment obligations, gifting plans and programs, etc.

- Cash Flow Management   Past years' budgeting sheets, various cash expenditure analyses, income/use application summaries, cash management ideas, etc.

- Insurance Protection   All insurance policies (life, disability, health, automobile, homeowners, liability, and title), potential new policies and quotes, summaries of insured and uninsured risks, personal property inventory and pictures, insurance claims procedures, records of claims, etc.

- Income Tax Planning   Past years tax returns (federal, state, and local), communications with tax authorities, pending tax matters, analyses of tax alternatives and consequences, tax savings ideas, etc.
- Investment Planning   Investment record sheets from past years or past investments, investment decision analyses, summaries of investment funds, allocations to goals, accumulations to date, potential or alternate investment opportunities, etc.
- Estate Planning   Estate documents and summaries, estate assets and liabilities summaries, estate tax calculations, death instructions, estate planning ideas, etc.
- Employment   Benefits booklets and summaries, employer provided statements, benefits selection analyses, compensation agreements, etc.
- Business Ownership   Stock purchase agreements, buy/sell agreements, general records pertaining to the family, etc.
- Outside Information Sources   Financial and economic articles and presentations, programs for development of financial knowledge and understanding, etc.
- Miscellaneous   Documents describing potential inheritances or trusts, nonfinancial matters, etc.

On-Going Recordkeeping

Records should be set up for practical use during a year (i.e., knowing positions easily) and for periodic special purpose use such as filing income tax returns, completing main summary schedules and financial profiles, and various other analyses.

The on-going records should be "closed out" at the end of each year to the Permanent Storage System—some records in the ongoing system should be partially closed out during the year (such as budgeting sheets on a monthly basis). New on-going records should be set up at the beginning of each year. Be careful not to mix business and personal recordkeeping if you are a business owner. Business records should be handled differently than personal records.

Files or a binder system should be divided into sections similar to the following:

- Current Implementation Summary and Financial Calendar.
- Cash Flow   Worksheets for balancing statements from banks and other financial institutions; current budgeting sheets; sheets for tracing savings to a money market fund (or other control account) for later payment of taxes, expenses, or investing.
- Income Tax   Projections; income tax payments; income tax payment or filing forms; income (losses), adjustments to gross income, itemized deductions, exemptions and tax credits for the current year; tax records such as W-2s, 1099s, etc.
- Investments   Checklist for current investment objectives; summary sheet for new investments or new investment repositionings; separate sheet for each investment media; sheet for keeping track of investment media of interest.
- Records of Economic Variables and Movements.
- Current Business Records Pertaining to Personal Matters.

As receipts or statements are received, temporarily hold them in a safe place (such as "incoming box").

Set an optimal time each month to pay bills. Make sure that it is good for personal reasons and that it will allow payment due dates to be met. As income is received monthly and expenses are paid, record inflows and outflows on the budgeting sheets. If an income receipt or expense has an income tax or investment ramification, note it on the appropriate sheet. After recording transactions, file the statements or notices.

Storing Receipts, Statements, Cancelled Checks, and Other Materials Held For Precautionary Purposes

Set up two files for each calendar year—one to store items that are needed for proof in the event tax returns are audited and the other for items which do not affect taxes.

If the on-going record system is properly maintained, tax return filing will not require gathering and searching through receipts. Upon closing the files at year end, store them in a safe but convenient spot.

COMPUTERIZED FINANCIAL PLANNING

Many possibilities exist for using computers in personal financial planning. Recordkeeping, financial scheduling and profiling, analyzation, action steps timing, and other financial management functions can be computerized for increased efficiency. However, you must be adept at using computers and have access to a computer with reasonable capabilities.

Programs can be purchased to project income taxes, prepare and track budgets, access investment information, and for doing other important planning functions. "Shop" computer hardware and software products very carefully because there is a wide array of quality and cost combinations.

Electronic spread sheets, graphics, and other computer function add-ons can be very useful depending upon the level of sophistication desired for computer use.

We do not, though, consider computer use a prerequisite to high quality financial planning; we view it as an aid to planning. With or without computer use, decisions must be made by individuals. We have yet to see a good computerized financial planning program or system which makes recommendations or determines appropriate choices. The "human" element is still very much needed in the planning process because of all the various factors, financial and nonfinancial, which must be blended to make optimal decisions.

COMMON SIGNS OF FINANCIAL SECURITY

- Comfortable in making financial decisions and choices.
- Established relationships with financial advisors and financial service organizations.
- Concentration on use of funds rather than on adequacy of inflow sources.
- Infrequent banking trips or check cashing for cash needs.
- Common family financial goals, which are easily discussed.
- Able to regularly take advantage of sales and other discounts in timing purchases of basic goods.
- Quick access to accurate personal financial data and information.
- A feeling that family members will have sufficient financial resources in the event of death of a family income earner.
- Income taxes do not seem excessively burdensome.
- Debt payments are easily managed.

- Investments are well diversified and risks within chosen comfort zones.
- Travel and other luxury items are participated in on a reasonable basis.
- Finances contribute to, rather than detract from, other important success areas such as career or family.
- Deterioration in programs such as Social Security will not cause hardship.
- "Shopping" for goods, services, and financial products is a regular practice.
- Thinking of family financial matters is enjoyable.
- Frequently looking for new investment opportunities.
- The time value of money is factored into many financial decisions.
- Major future expenditures such as college costs or retirement are currently being planned and funded.
- Awareness of taxation, investment markets, and other financial matters is continually increasing.
- Emergency/opportunity funds are readily available.
- Net worth is increasing year-to-year both through annual savings and investment growth.
- A feeling that adverse economic times can be comfortably survived.
- New financial ideas are interpreted with possible personal applications.
- General economics are personalized for planning opportunities.

PUBLICATIONS

Below find listings for some publications we like. We cannot guarantee the accuracy of the publications, nor do we endorse them. However, we do believe that you will find these helpful in managing your money and improving your knowledge of finances.

Executive Wealth Advisory, published by The Research Institute of America, Inc., 589 Fifth Avenue, New York, New York, 10017

Financial and Estate Planning, published by Commerce Clearing House, Inc., 4025 W. Preston Avenue, Chicago, Illinois 60646

The Hulbert Financial Digest, published by The Hulbert Financial Digest, Inc., 409 First Street, SE., Washington, D.C. 20003

The Handbook For No-Load Fund Investors, published by the No-

Load Fund Investor, Inc., Post Office Box 283, Hastings-on-Hudson, New York 10706

** *NoLoad Fund *X,* published by DAL Investment Co., 235 Montgomery Street, San Francisco, California 94104

Stock Market Logic by Norman G. Fosback, published by The Institute for Econometric Research, 3471 North Federal Highway, Fort Lauderdale, Florida 33306

Index

A

Accountants, 281
Accounts, investing, 222–223
Adjustments to gross income
    components of, 155–156
    see also Income tax
Alternative minimum tax, 149
Annuities, 2
    see also Investments
Assets
    recording of, 46
    recording of miscellaneous, 40–41
    subject to estate taxes, 242–243
Attorneys, 281
    estate documents, 250

B

Balance, 59–60
    analysis of, 213
    guidelines, 214
    sample portfolio, 219
    see also Investment principles and Investments
Banks
    fees, 101
    services, 102
    use of bankers, 281
Beneficiaries, 255, 274

Benefits
    employee, 278–279, 286–287
    flexible programs, 180
Bonds
    economic upturn, 79
    recording of, 28, 30
    zero-coupon, 224
    see also Investments and Mutual funds
Brokerage services
    discount, 102
    switching from, 222–223
    use of brokers, 281–282
Budget worksheets, 92–98
Budgeting
    principles, 91, 99
    steps, 90–91, 99–100
Business
    forms, 174
    ownership in estate, 271–272
    principles, 4
    recording of interest, 38
    ventures, 79
    see also Investments
Buy/sell agreements, 271–272

C

Capital gain (loss)
    defined, 151–152
    postponement of taxation, 153–154, 181

Capital gain (loss) *(cont.)*
  short-term/long-term, 151, 154
  see also Investments
Cash accounts
  use of, 100–102
  see also Investments
Cash and equivalents
  economic upturn, 79
  recording of, 24–25
  see also Investments
Cash flow
  analysis of, 20–21
  control of, 99–100
  inflow/outflow application, 120
  management defined, 12
  management questions, 120–122
  recording of, 50–51
Charitable contributions
  see Deductions, Estate, and Gifting
Checking accounts, 101
  see also Budgeting
Commodities
  economic upturn, 79
  see also Investments
Common law, 241
Community property, 241
Computers, 305
Corporations—*see* Business
Cost basis
  defined, 154–155
  step-up in, 253–254, 266, 272

D

Death estate
  analysis of, 20
  determination of, 49
  see also Estate, etc.
Debt
  payment calculation, 112–114
  use of, 102–105
  see also Liabilities
Decisions
  investments, 226–228

Decisions *(cont.)*
  making and implementing, 8
Deductions
  income taxation, 157–159
  net after tax cost, 158
  see also Income tax
Deferred compensation, 175, 218
Deflation, 77
Disability
  definitions, 134
  funding of, 67–70
  Social Security, 132–133
  see also Trusts
Disability insurance
  agents, 281
  coverage, 132–136
  sample rates, 136
  taxation of, 133–134
Disinflation, 76–77
Diversification, 59–60
  analysis of, 213
  guidelines, 214
  sample portfolio, 219
  see also Investment principles and Investments
Dividends
  annual exclusion, 180
  corporate exclusion, 180–181
  utility, 180
Documents, 17–18
  see also Estate documents and Recordkeeping

E

Economic upturn
  impact on investments, 79
  variable movement, 78
Economic variables
  lead/lag, 75–76
  using, 77–79
Economy, 74–75
Education
  sample funding, 109–111

Education *(cont.)*
  see also Disability funding and Estate funding
Emergency funds, 102
Employee stock ownership plans, 175
Equipment leasing
  economic upturn, 79
  see also Investments
Estate
  administration costs, 243, 245
  charitable bequests, 245
  funding of, 63–67
  general planning, 272–274, 276
  marital deduction, 245
  planning defined, 12
  planning of, 240, 250–252
  reduction of, 268
Estate documents
  provisions of, 258–261, 263, 264
  revision of, 273
  selection of, 255–256, 258
  storage of, 272
  suggested use, 258
  tax savings from, 259
Estate taxation
  estimating, 243–245, 247–248
  federal and state, 240–241
  federal rates, 246
  state tax credit, 247
  unified tax credit, 248
Executors, 269, 271
Exemptions
  federal income tax, 160
  see also Income tax
Expenses
  financing questions, 107–110
  pre-tax vs after-tax, 180
  reduction of, 106–107

F

Filing—*see* Recordkeeping
Filing status, 148–149

Financial management
  heirs, 261
  in event of death, 251
  self-directed, 282
  see also Money managers and Trusts
Financial planners, 2
  use of, 282–283
Financial planning
  benefits of, 5
  general tips, 283–284
  guidelines, 6
  process, 6–8
  rules, 9
Financial planning changes, 279–280
Financial products, 2, 3
Financial ratios
  average tax rate, 57
  current savings rate, 57
  growth/no-growth investments, 59
  guidelines, 55
  indebtedness, 54–56
  investment accumulation, 58–59
  liquidity, 56
Financial security, 11
  common signs, 305–306
Financial services
  supermarkets, 3, 283

G

Gifting
  appreciated property, 181–182
  between spouses, 267
  limitations, 178
  outright, 254
  present vs future interest, 252–253
  taxes on, 253
  tax rates on, 246
  trusts, 254
  UGMA, 178–179
Goals
  application, 13
  defined, 10
  financial objectives, 15–16

Goals *(cont.)*
  surveying, 6
  targeting, 14
Gross taxable income, 151
  see also Income tax
Growth factors, 230–234
Guardians, 271

H–J

Heirs
  assets to, 251–252, 257, 261
Implementation
  impacts of, 279–280
  planning summary, 279, 288–289
  sources of, 280–283
Income
  capital gain, 151
  directing sources, 99, 117–118
  loss, 151
  ordinary, 151
  retirement, 118–120
Income averaging, 149
Income shifting, 178–179
Income tax
  amended returns, 166
  analysis of, 21
  audits 166–167
  federal payment of, 161–163, 166
  general considerations, 182–184
  impact on decisions, 168
  loss, 154–155
  planning considerations, 167
  planning defined, 12
  projections, 164–165
  rates, 144–148
  records, 166
  state and local, 150–151
  summary of, 52–53
  understanding, 143
Indexing, 146, 147, 178
Inflation, 76
Information
  background, 18

Information *(cont.)*
  gathering personal, 7
  personal summary, 22–23
  publications, 306–307
  review of, 19
Inheritance taxes, 240–241, 247
Installment sale, 181
Insurance
  automobile, 137–138
  coordinating purchases, 140–141
  coverages, 127–128
  homeowners/renters, 138–139
  medical, 136–137
  myths, 126–127
  planning defined, 12
  purchasing of, 128–129
  records, 141
  representatives, 281
  self-insuring, 81–83
  see also Disability insurance, Liability insurance, and Life insurance
Interest
  after-tax rates on debt, 105
  see also Deductions and Income
Investment principles
  explained, 198–200
  see also Investments comparison of alternatives
Investments
  as related to other planning areas, 191–192
  comparison of alternatives, 193–197
  composition of, 20, 48
  decision specifications, 290
  general thoughts for, 207–210
  income favorableness, 177
  miscellaneous recording, 36
  misconceptions of, 206–207
  new investment appropriateness, 291–292
  planning defined, 12
  questions to ask, 194, 198
  returns, 229–230, 236
  sample portfolio, 215–218
  theories, 200
  types of, 214

IRAs
  decision tree for, 228
  limitations, 156
  trustees, 157
  withdrawals, 156–157
  see also Retirement plans

K–L

Keogh
  limitations, 176
  see also Retirement plans
Liabilities
  in taxable estate, 242–243
  recording of, 42–43, 47
Liability insurance
  automobile, 137
  homeowners, 138
  umbrella, 140
Life expectancies, 72–73
Life insurance
  agents, 281
  analysis of summary, 19
  coverage, 129–132
  estate taxation, 242–243
  irrevocable trusts, 268–269
  recording of, 44–45
  sample rates
Limited partnerships
  described, 204–205
  recording of, 34–35
  see also Business and Investments
Liquidity, 56
  analysis of, 212–213
  guidelines, 214
  sample portfolio, 219
  see also Investment principles and Investments
Loans
  interest-free, 179
  see also Liabilities

M

Marginal tax (bracket) rate, 145

Money managers
  affiliations, 282
  use of, 79, 201, 218, 220
Money market
  account vs fund, 101
  as control, 102
  summary recording, 123
  see also Investments and Mutual funds
Monitoring
  Investments, 227, 229
  planning areas, 297–300
  reviewing, 8
  summary of steps, 294–297
Mutual funds
  control summary, 237–238
  family funds, 222
  no-load vs load, 203
  objectives, 202
  recording of, 24, 27, 28, 31
  returns, 229
  sample portfolio, 220–221
  timing purchase, 220
  types, 202–203
  see also Investments

N–O

Net worth
  analysis of, 19–20
  summary of, 46–47
Objectives
  defined, 10
  financial, 12
  goals, 15–16
  surveying, 6
Observations, 7
Oil and gas
  economic upturn, 79
  see also Investments

P–Q

Partnerships—*see* Business, Investments, and Tax shelters

Pension and profit sharing plans
    limitations, 175
    see also Retirement plans
Pooled investments
    types of, 202–206
    see also Investments
Present value factors, 71, 188
Qualified terminable interest, 260–261

R

Real estate
    economic upturn, 79
    recording of, 32–33, 34, 38
    sample portfolio, 221
    see also Investments
Recapture, 155, 173, 181
Recordkeeping
    general, 300–301
    on-going, 303–304
    permanent storage, 301–303
    receipts, etc., 304–305
Residence
    exclusion from tax on sale, 154
    recording of, 38
    rent vs buy, 110
Retirement funding, 60–63
Retirement plans
    estate taxation of, 243
    multiple use, 157, 176
    recording of, 38–39
    use of, 173–174
Risk
    comfort with, 85, 87–88
    insurable exposure, 125
    management of, 81–83
    reduction of investment, 201
    tolerance, 82, 84, 85, 86

S

Safe deposit box, 302
Safety—*see* Investment principles

Savings
    accumulations review, 112
    allocation to goals, 111
    education, 109–111
    flow to investments, 99, 102
    retirement, 118–119
    techniques of, 89–90, 114–117
    see also Cash flow
Securities—*see* Investments
Securities dealers—*see* Brokerage services
Social Security
    reduction of tax, 150
    see also Disability funding, Estate funding,
        and Retirement funding
Stock options
    employee described, 177–178
    investment in, 224–225
    see also Investments
Stocks
    economic upturn, 79
    employer, 223
    for high return, 225
    recording of, 26
    see also Investments and Mutual funds
Strategies, 8
    for investment, 192–193

T

Tangible investments
    recording of, 36
    see also Investments
Tax credits
    federal income tax, 160–161
    see also Income tax
Tax shelters
    analysis of, 173
    at risk rules, 170–171
    calculation of returns, 184, 186–187, 189
    comparison of, 171
    description of, 170–173
    fees on, 172–173
    registration, 170

Tax shelters *(cont.)*
  use of, 142
  see also Investments
Taxes
  progressive, 144
  regressive, 150
  underpayment of, 143
  see also Estate taxation and Income tax
Ten year forward averaging, 149–150
  as to IRAs, 156
Titling
  between spouses, 266
  investment accounts, 222
  joint in estate, 255
  separate/joint, 241
Trade-offs (opportunity cost), 11, 76
Trust officers, 282
Trustees, 261, 263
Trusts
  charitable lead, 182
  Clifford, 178, 254
  irrevocable, 256, 258, 268–269, 271, 275
  marital, 260
  residuary, 260
  revocable, 256, 264, 268, 270, 271, 275
  spousal remainder, 178
  testamentary, 255–256
  2503(c), 179, 254

U

Unified tax credit, 245, 248
Unit trusts
  described, 203–204
  recording of, 28, 30
  sample portfolio, 221
  see also Investments
Updating—*see* Monitoring

W–Z

Wealth accumulation, 211–212

Wills
  flow of, 262, 265, 267, 270, 273, 275
  specifics of, 273–274
  types, 256
Zero bracket amount—*see* Income tax